Bonhoeffer
as Martyr

Bonhoeffer
as Martyr

*Social Responsibility
and Modern Christian Commitment*

Craig J. Slane

Brazos Press
A Division of Baker Book House Co
Grand Rapids, Michigan 49516

Published by Brazos Press
a division of Baker Book House Company
P.O. Box 6287, Grand Rapids, MI 49516-6287
www.brazospress.com

Printed in the United States of America

Library of Congress Cataloging-in-Publication Data
Slane, Craig J., 1960–
    Bonhoeffer as martyr : social responsibility and modern Christian commitment
/ Craig J. Slane.
        p.   cm.
    Includes bibliographical references.
    ISBN 1-58743-074-6 (pbk.)
    1. Martyrdom—Christianity. 2. Bonhoeffer, Dietrich, 1906–1945. I. title.
BR1601.3.S58 2004
272—dc22   2003021323

Scripture is taken from the New Revised Standard Version of the Bible, copyright 1989 by the Division of Christian Education of the National Council of the Churches of Christ in the USA. Used by permission.

To my wife, Sandra,
who has borne my trials.

The past is filled with a host of parentless actors and actions, but of all history's orphans possibly the martyr is the most lonely and isolated, appearing to us, like both the hero and the traitor, as a two-dimensional stereotype. We find it jarring to imagine the pusillanimous hero, the specious martyr, or the open-hearted traitor. By definition the hero is cleft-chinned and stalwart, the martyr serene-faced and compassionate, and the traitor evil-eyed and conniving. But place martyrs within an historical sequence, relate them to their close cousins the fool and the traitor, assign them siblings and descendants, and ask what personal and cultural interests motivated their sacrifices, and they become complex personalities subject to analysis and criticism. For if a single truism can be claimed for martyrdom, it is that their lot is not an easy one.

Lacey Baldwin Smith, *Fools, Martyrs, Traitors*

Contents

Preface

Dietrich Bonhoeffer's story is like that tune we catch off the radio and can't get out of our head. Hardly a day passes without a Bonhoefferian phrase or two crossing my mind. I often think about life's problems with him in mind.

To be honest, though, there are times when I wish I could forget the tune. It can be as haunting as it is rapturous. Over the years, I have discerned a pattern in my life with the Bonhoeffer story. Precisely at those times when I am most alone with my self and thoughts, at my most solitary points, the story often feels the most depressing and heavy. Living with the sober realities of death, martyrdom, and the Holocaust, as one must to write a book such as this, can be a nearly suffocating experience. On many occasions I have found myself at the edge of an abyss, uncertain how to respond in the face of such massive evil. Of Western civilization's many scars, the Holocaust remains the ugliest. No amount of human doctoring can cover it. It will remain forever a unique manifestation of evil. At the same time, as long as human existence is caught in the compulsions of sin, we know we cannot consider ourselves immune to the *impulses* that brought about the singular horror of the Holocaust. Whatever hell is, we know we cannot confine it to some underworld.

Conversely, when I have the opportunity to share Bonhoeffer's story with others I experience tangibly the promise of God's goodness and grace. Since 1996 I have been telling Bonhoeffer's story regularly in my Faith and Culture class at Simpson College. As I argue for "Bonhoeffer as martyr," my students occasionally find the proposition hard to digest. Without fail, however, they are drawn by his passion and understand him as a Christian who helps them navigate the issues of their lives. After three weeks or so, when we emerge exhausted from the emotional weight and theological complexity of the story, we find that Bonhoeffer has quietly transformed our class into a community, has given us a sense of social responsibility and a language to speak about it.

We need Bonhoeffer. He can give us the courage to tell the more macabre truths of the last century to the next generation without bringing it to despair. In the disturbing "exhibition hall" of the twentieth century, lined with genocide, abuse of power, forces of cultural disintegration, and sheer hatred for humanity, Bonhoeffer is a witness to God's love, to justice, and to hope. In community, we can open our eyes to the world's evil and still be hopeful for the human race and the world we create and inhabit.

Singer-composer Ken Medema expresses my hope in his provocative song "Dance in the Dragon's Jaws." For according to the Christian way of looking at things, at the center of history, perhaps at the center of reality itself, stands a hellish episode of redemption in which God established life in the jaws of death. Even at the edge of an abyss, perhaps especially there, we can dance.

As for Paul and Silas, dancing in spirit while their feet were bound by stocks in the inner recesses of a Philippi prison, external dangers do not easily douse the flame that burns inside the martyr. On the continuum of human emotion it is often, surprisingly, extreme joy that accompanies the final phase of the martyr's ordeal. This is because martyrs manage to reach a kind of rapprochement between life and death. Having found the true significance of their lives, they seem all the more willing to sacrifice them, though never on a whim.

From my childhood I can recall fantastic stories of missionaries who had "given all" for Christ. I remember praying for relatives of missionaries who had been recently martyred, people known to my parents. At these times I had the inchoate sense that I was somehow traveling to the most real region of the universe itself. As an undergraduate student, I lived in a dormitory complex named in honor of Nathaniel Saint and James Elliot, martyrs at the hands of the Aucas of Ecuador on 8 January 1956. Though we were separated from Saint and Elliot by more than two decades, their story hovered above all of us who slept and studied there.

At that time Bonhoeffer was to me only a regular footnote in sermons or class lectures. I could not have imagined then that these "footnotes" would eventually grab my attention and come to dominate the horizon of my adult life. The Bonhoeffer I knew from sermons and lectures was a soft, contemplative, devotional man who bequeathed to the church gems of spirituality like *The Cost of Discipleship* and *Life Together.* I knew nothing of political plots, conspiracies, treason, and murder. Of course, I also knew little about the extraordinary complexities of ethical decision-making. And I had only the faintest appreciation for the fact that some of the most powerful and profound impulses of Christianity were world-affirming ones.

When I first encountered the "real" Bonhoeffer, I was smitten, provoked, and held captive by the riddle: is it possible for someone who planned treasonous and murderous acts to be honored as a martyr? Over time, it became evident that I was opening a staggering set of issues that would require of me historical competence, interpretive imagination, and nuanced theological reflection. To be blunt, if Bonhoeffer is a martyr, he is not an easy one! Bonhoeffer—with his colleagues in the resistance movement—did not succeed in bringing down Hitler's rule by violent means. But he *tried*. Had he succeeded, we would likely know him as an "assassin." It offends the conscience of many to try to legitimate Bonhoeffer's activities on a Christian basis, let alone praise them with the accolade "martyr." The Bible certainly provides no clear grounds for tyrannicide, although later prominent Christian voices have justified it. Sometimes, under carefully prescribed circumstances, it has even been considered an offering to God (for example, by Philipp Melanchthon). If God establishes the ruling authorities for the public good, and if those authorities then turn tyrannical against their subjects, the subjects have the right to remove them. For the tyrant has abdicated responsibility both to humanity and to God. So runs the argument.

Most of us would not be unhappy to learn that someone *else* had taken on such responsibilities in a time of grave injustice, even if that someone gave her life for the cause. We abhor violence, but when an unpleasant thing needs doing, someone has to do it. Cultures generally honor those who make the supreme sacrifice of their lives for just causes. Citizens operating from overt Christian convictions may show public restraint, inquiring to see whether every option for a more peaceful solution had been deployed. Nevertheless, of all people, Christians understand acts of conscience. Even those bound in conscience by their pacifist convictions find sympathies for Bonhoeffer and his course, whether or not they can endorse it. The problem comes when we try to *name* him a martyr. Why?

Perhaps because we have been marinating our theologies of martyrdom exclusively in "religion." Among its many consequences, secularization in Western culture has opened a rift between public and private life. Usually politics belongs to the public sphere while religion belongs in the private sphere of "the circle of Christian community," or even "one's own heart." I find it helpful to think spatially here. When one acts in the public sphere out of Christian conviction, this amounts, culturally speaking, to a *departure* from one reality in order to *arrive* at another. We have difficulty seeing both the religious dimensions of political action and the political dimensions of Christian existence. Assuming martyrs' actions must be *either* religious *or* political, we wonder about their "true motives." Often we find ourselves at an impasse, imprisoned in our own categories.

The categories exist for a reason, no doubt. We cannot obliterate the distinction between politics and religion. We can learn, however, to see them both against the comprehensive reality of God's created order. Martyrs do exactly that. Understanding the totality of God's claim on human life, they perform their religious commitments openly.

As part of the audience, I find myself enamored by their moral courage and earnestness. In an age of asymmetry in belief and behavior, they spawn hope that I might yet weave my own life into a unity of word and deed. I am finding that the esoteric eddies of my personal intrigue yearn for release into a mightier stream where great currents of historical development are flowing. Indeed, if martyrdom is a river, I imagine it to be cutting its channel deeper into the earth. That is, martyrdom is a phenomenon whose connections to the created order—political, social, and ethical—are being illumined as never before. For many recent martyrs, their "giving all" for Christ became also their fullest expression of love for the neighbor, and in the neighbor, God's creation. At the surface, these newer martyrs of the church seem to die for reasons only loosely connected to the Christian faith. But what faith is it that can love God and not tend to the least in God's family (Matt. 25: 40)? The lives and deaths of these newer martyrs call for a much more nuanced and sophisticated understanding of martyrdom and its relation to social responsibility and Christian commitment. This insight is relatively new. However, amid the swirl of postmodern reflection, a consensus is growing that someday will likely yield a full-scale revision in our understanding of martyrdom. My work, I hope, is a contribution toward that end.

As in any study, personal experiences and commitments figure prominently in this exploration. Yet I have tried not to permit my experiential and theological idiosyncrasies to set the terms for my work. I choose to understand theology as a response to the living, active God, and I am confident that my experiences are therefore part of the matrix of human response to something prior and greater. For God himself has established life amidst death in the work of Jesus Christ, and it is he who acts both in and through the lives of both Christian martyrs and those who wonder about them. As such, Christian martyrdom is a *theological* phenomenon in the most direct sense imaginable.

Chapters 1–6 of this book represent my attempt to solve the Bonhoeffer riddle. I examine Bonhoeffer's life and death in the context of the early Christian martyr tradition, taking into consideration also some key evolutionary developments in the idea of martyrdom itself. Chapters 7–8 investigate the inherent interpretive powers of martyrdom to sum up Christian existence. In them I propose martyrdom as a hermeneutic key for interpreting Bonhoeffer's life and thought. Chapters 9–12 contain my interpretation of Bonhoeffer's life and theology from the perspective of martyrdom. Though theological interpretations of Bonhoeffer abound, to my knowledge none has moved the theological datum of martyrdom itself to the fore. As a result, the term *martyr* has, in Bonhoeffer's case at least, functioned more as a kind of moral epitaph on a theologian's life than as a theological epitaph on a life lived toward death. I aspire to make Bonhoeffer's martyr epitaph a *theological* one. In so doing I hope his life might open to us in fresh ways. Perhaps that alone constitutes the uniqueness of this book. For the Bonhoeffer materials have been diligently quarried and hewn by two generations of scholars before me.

As near as I can now discern, my earlier engagement with the thought of Alfred North Whitehead and Wolfhart Pannenberg created the structural possibility for the dawning of the idea of a martyrological interpretation of Bonhoeffer. Granted, neither of these figures has written pointedly of martyrdom. But I found Pannenberg's term *prolepsis* to unpack a cornucopia of possibilities, especially in regard to the configuration of temporality along theological-biblical lines. Whitehead's concept of "concrescence," which Donald Sherburne aptly described as "the *growing together* of a many into the unity of the one," is similar in its capacity to evoke wonder concerning God's guidance in the creation. This may have contributed to my teleological reading of Bonhoeffer's works in the final chapters, where I test the hermeneutic of martyrdom in its power to illumine the deathward curvature of Bonhoeffer's life by closely examining his Christology and ethics and the so-called Finkenwalde experiment. As ideas gradually become one's own, it is increasingly difficult to sort out origins with precision. But I am confident that these two ideas lie at or near the roots of my thesis.

Abbreviations

ATTF	*A Testament to Freedom* (revised edition)
DB	*Dietrich Bonhoeffer: A Biography* (revised edition)
DBW	*Dietrich Bonhoeffer Works* (German)
DBWE	*Dietrich Bonhoeffer Works* (English)
GS	*Gesammelte Schriften*
IKDB	*I Knew Dietrich Bonhoeffer*
LPP	*Letters and Papers from Prison*

Part One

Is Bonhoeffer Really a Martyr?

1

Diary of a Bourgeois Priest

Christ kept himself from suffering till his hour had come, but when it did come he met it as a free man, seized it, and mastered it.

Dietrich Bonhoeffer

In Georges Bernanos's *The Diary of a Country Priest,* an obscure young priest has tried without success to implement a more radical form of Christianity in his small parish in northern France. Guided by Jesus' path of powerlessness and poverty, he explores the complex topography of his interior life by means of his diary. His parish is "like all the rest." The parishioners are "bored stiff." They won't come to Mass. They suspect their priest is an alcoholic consumed by greed. In truth, the priest suffers secretly from stomach cancer. He consumes wine to alleviate the pain. Steadily he grows weak and frail. The humble curé battles all odds, traveling from home to home to carry out his seemingly unimportant ministry. As the end draws near, he writes:

> And I know now that youth is a gift of God, and like all His gifts, carries no regret. They alone shall be young, really young, whom He has chosen never to survive their youth. I belong to such a race of men. I used to wonder: what shall I be doing at fifty, at sixty? And of course I couldn't find an answer. I couldn't even make one up. There was no old man in me. This awareness is sweet.[1]

1. Georges Bernanos, *The Diary of a Country Priest,* 2d ed. (New York: Carroll & Graf, 2002), 291.

In his short life, the priest has found inwardly a prayerful trust in God despite the clumsiness of his youth and the swarm of misunderstanding that marks his parish. He reaches the end alert to the realities of his own death and God's grace. No longer embarrassed by his youth, the priest makes his peace with the old man that never was and experiences "the deep peace of evening." He continues:

> Before I realized my fate, I often feared I should not know how to die when the time came, as there is no doubt I am too impressionable. I remember a saying of dear old Dr. Delbende, which I believe was recorded in this diary, about monks and priests not always being the best at dying. . . . But I have no more qualms about that now. I can see how a man, sure of himself and his courage, might wish to make of his death a perfect end. As that isn't in my line, my death shall be what it can be, and nothing more. . . .
>
> I would like to add that to a true lover, the halting confession of his beloved is more dear than the most beautiful poem.[2]

Bernanos's readers are never quite certain whether the priest is a pathetic figure absorbed in his self-reflection or a kind of saint in the making. In his own eyes, he is nothing but a common priest in a common parish struggling to keep a precarious faith alive. In God's eyes, perhaps he has become a saint. In the priest's last words, uttered faintly but distinctly, Bernanos seems to blur the line between the holy and the banal. "Grace," says the dying Curé de Campagne, "is everywhere."

Bernanos was one of the earliest literary influences on Bonhoeffer. Bernanos's writings captivated him. During his days as director of the Finkenwalde Seminary, he recommended *Diary of a Country Priest* to his young seminarians. Earlier he had taken an interest in Bernanos's novels *Sous le soleil de Satan* (Under Satan's Sun) and *Der Abtrünnige* (The Apostate) when they appeared in German translations during the late 1920s.[3] Eberhard Bethge noted that Bonhoeffer found these novels "disturbing" because they dealt with the most intimate problems of his own life—"the priest and saint as the chosen target of the tempter, the man barely able to resist the alternative assaults of desperation and pride."[4] Like Bernanos's priest, Bonhoeffer had an interest in a radical form of Christianity that put him at odds with many of his contemporaries. He suffered inwardly. He died in the relative obscurity of a concentration camp, yet inwardly reconciled both to God and to his fate. Many would contend that he gave only a "halting confession" of faith.

2. Ibid., 293–94.

3. In English, see Georges Bernanos, *Under Satan's Sun,* trans. J. C. Whitehouse (Lincoln: University of Nebraska Press, 2001).

4. Eberhard Bethge, *Dietrich Bonhoeffer: A Biography,* rev. ed. (Minneapolis: Fortress, 2000), 139–40.

In his own eyes, he was not a saint. For him the religious and secular realms could not easily keep their borders. And, most certainly, there was no old man in him.

Bonhoeffer's bourgeois heritage and keen intellect could easily overpower others. Measured by almost any index he was a rich man. His father was an esteemed professor at Berlin University. The child Dietrich lived in the luxurious Grunewald district of Berlin, attended by a cadre of household employees: a tutor, a nanny, a housemaid, a cook, a receptionist for his father, and a chauffeur. His family had contacts at the highest levels of German society. But he was perceptive enough to know that earthly riches make one less secure, not more. He suspected God is nearer to those who have need. And so his heritage became a kind of burden to be overcome. If he were to live a life devoted to Christ, pride and power would have to be monitored on a continuing basis.

Like Bernanos's priest, Bonhoeffer came to believe God needs those who "break down" and can come to him with empty hands. Bonhoeffer wanted to become such a poor and radical "priest." But he also enjoyed the privileges of his heritage and the many advantages it brought him. Thus he was caught in a most difficult tension. Wherever he went, opportunities opened before him as a matter of course. Those opportunities, or to be more precise, what they *represented*, often stood in conflict with his vision of the Christian reality. He frequently found himself paying for books, meals, and trips for his friends. Though these actions, and many others like them, may have been undertaken on the overt basis of friendship and Christian charity, they also became, in part, a means of releasing some of the power tied to his social status. He may have been bourgeois by birth, but Christian commitment required a choice.

Perhaps the inner conflict between bourgeois security and radical Christianity reached its most acute point in the summer of 1939. Faced with the imminent prospect of his draft into Hitler's army, Bonhoeffer accepted the invitation of Reinhold Niebuhr and Paul Lehmann to embark on a lecture tour in the United States. This was an opportunity to live in safety, to write and publish freely, and perhaps to find a respite for his conscience as war clouds thickened over Europe. Earlier Niebuhr had successfully rescued Paul Tillich from his political dilemma in Germany. And now another of Germany's brightest theological minds was arriving in the port of New York.

The opportunities afforded by bourgeois society were surfacing once again, but this time Bonhoeffer could not find a salve for his troubled conscience. Arriving shortly before 13 June, he sensed he had made a bad decision. He managed to stay only a little less than a month.

He made this entry in his diary on 15 June:

Since yesterday evening I haven't been able to stop thinking of Germany. I would not have thought it possible that at my age, after so many years abroad, one could get so dreadfully homesick. What was in itself a wonderful motor expedition this morning to a female acquaintance in the country . . . became almost unbearable. We sat for an hour and chattered, not in a silly way, true, but about many things which left me completely cold—whether it is possible to get a good musical education in New York, about the education of children etc., etc. . . . The whole burden of self-reproach because of a wrong decision comes back again and almost overwhelms me.[5]

By 20 June, after Niebuhr and Lehmann tried to persuade him to stay, his "wrong decision" has clearly been reversed, and his conscience begins to ease:

The decision has been made. I have refused. They were clearly disappointed, and rather upset. It probably means more for me than I can see at the moment. God alone knows what. . . .

How much anxiety there is in today's decision, however brave it may seem. The reasons one gives for an action to others and to one's self are certainly inadequate. One can give a reason for everything. In the last resort one acts from a level which remains hidden from us. So one can only ask God to judge us and to forgive us.[6]

Until the decision taken on this day, there might have been an old man in Bonhoeffer. But his resolve to return quickly to the turmoil in his own land could now only mean that he was prepared to immerse himself in the dangers of illegal activities and accept fully whatever the outcome might be.

In diary entries made in the days following, Bonhoeffer continues to process "the decision" and reaches for an interpretation of his soul's ordeal. He imagines that he has learned more in this brief visit than during the whole of his prolonged stay in 1930.[7] He says he has acquired "an important insight for all future decisions."[8] Yet a precise justification for the decision is nowhere to be found. Instead there are a plurality of concerns: his desire to be in contact with friends in the Confessing Church in Germany, the need to share in the suffering of his people, possibilities for participation in the reconstruction of German life after the war, the joy of "working at home," and finally "the other, that I am

5. *ATTF,* 469.

6. *ATTF,* 472.

7. In September 1930, Bonhoeffer went to New York to study as a Sloane Fellow at Union Theological Seminary and remained for the entire academic year.

8. *ATTF,* 477.

trying to suppress," a cryptic allusion that seems to reveal already his intent to enter the resistance. Bonhoeffer can name "reasons" easily enough if asked, but these seem inadequate to him. He seems unable to summon forth the deepest reason and assign it a name.

Perhaps that is because it is a decision of faith, or a decision of the heart, emanating more from character than from rational calculation. Inwardly, in a storm of soul, Bonhoeffer had become aware that his current path was not the path of discipleship as he had come to understand it. At least at this moment, the path of discipleship was heading away from a land of academic opportunities. To a large extent it ran away from his heritage, too, although it remained true that only a person with Bonhoeffer's connections could have assimilated himself into the German resistance movement even after his university license was revoked and he was known to have illegally directed a seminary of the Confessing Church. In one sense Bonhoeffer could not possibly break away from his past. If he were a pastor it would be a "bourgeois pastor." If he were a monk it would be a "bourgeois monk." Indeed, upon his arrest in 1943 he even became a "bourgeois prisoner," procuring certain privileges inaccessible to most of his fellow prisoners!

The point here is not that Bonhoeffer had to break away from his heritage in a final sense but that his key decisions are best understood as a kind of resolution of the complex inner tension that defined his personhood. Occasionally one hears the suggestion that Bonhoeffer's key decisions were motivated primarily by issues pertaining to his family heritage. The suggestion is helpful, but only to the extent that it illumines one pole of the dialectic. The full motivation for his decisions is understood only when the tension *(Spannung)* itself is appreciated and explored for those competing impulses between his heritage and Christ's call to discipleship.

It is not difficult to imagine how Bonhoeffer found the literary works of a figure like Bernanos helpful, even if "disturbing," as he tried to explore this central tension of his life. He was in a similar way attracted to Kierkegaard, Simone Weil, Fyodor Dostoyevsky, Nicolay Berdyayev, and a particular piece by George Santayana titled *The Last Puritan.* These literary interests are important and often overlooked as guides to understanding the decisions that carried him along the martyr's way. Indirectly they contain an answer to the problem of his bourgeois heritage and help us to understand his quite deliberate movement toward powerlessness and solidarity with powerless others. In his death by hanging at Flossenbürg, naked and with hands tied, he epitomizes the poor and helpless man whose need has brought him nearer to God and neighbor.

Person and Myth

During one of her lecture tours in the United States, Renate Bethge was asked when she had discovered her uncle Dietrich to be something special. She replied, "Never!"[9] Bonhoeffer devotees may wish to dismiss this response as family chatter, but there is a coded message here for those outside the family. Dietrich Bonhoeffer was a person.

One might wish for a more flamboyant observation at the beginning of a book about Bonhoeffer. However, as I write I sit in the living room of the Bonhoeffer House at 43 Marienberger Allee in Berlin (Charlottenburg), where the Bonhoeffer family lived from 1935 to 1951. A gallery of photographic panels decks the walls on all sides, showing at a glance the amazing diversity of his friendships and associations. The kitchen just across the hall is used daily by volunteer staff and visitors. Burckhard Scheffler, a prison pastor, lives with his family on the second level. Bonhoeffer's personal study sits on the upper level of the house. In it Bonhoeffer's writing desk—at which part of the *Ethics* was constructed—has been returned to its place, arranged as it was the day the Gestapo arrived to arrest him on 5 April 1943. The house is a splendid memorial. It forces visitors to honor the fixed witness of a life without permitting them to abstract that life from reality. Here there is no Bonhoeffer myth. The mundane sights, sounds, and smells call to mind the daily chores that mark human life around the globe. Life builds upon life.

A person such as Bonhoeffer, endowed with both pedigree and abundant natural gifts, is easy to use and misuse. We can make of him a moral exemplar, a model of piety, a model of impiety, an intellectual juggernaut, and more. Perhaps he was all these. But even more he was a person who lived from the heart with a Kierkegaardian sense of inwardness. He felt remorse, laughed, grieved at loss, suffered from confusion and depression, yearned for relationships with others, and loved. These things we know, for we are persons ourselves. But since we scholars tend to fix our gaze on literary artifacts, as finally we must, and since these artifacts are—especially in Bonhoeffer's case—so interesting in themselves, the danger is that we might over time drift toward a one-sided presentation of him. When combined with constant pressure to make new and interesting contributions to an area of scholarship, our quest for angles and interpretive keys to better understand his message and the world that might benefit from it, in short our desire to *do* something with Bonhoeffer, it is not surprising that we should easily lose sight of

9. Uwe Schulz, *Dietrich Bonhoeffer: Ein abgebrochenes Leben* (Lahr, Germany: Verlag der St. Johannes Druckerei, 1995), 100.

the person. Pastors are no less susceptible to this danger. The Bonhoeffer literature is rife with pithy turns of phrase which may serve to rouse congregations from social slumber, to invoke deeper communal life, to observe carefully the contemporary situation, or to press forward along the many winding paths of Christian discipleship.

Yet there is a person besides Bonhoeffer whom we must keep before us. Some lines from poet Diana Exon could without harm become a manifesto for everyone interested in Bonhoeffer.

> I have been called Bonhoeffer's disciple.
> Woe is me, for I am not his disciple,
> but Christ my God's.
> People look at me and say,
> "There she is, always preaching Bonhoeffer
> this and Bonhoeffer that,"
> And all I want to say is,
> "He shows the way to Christ,
> listen to what he says,
> Open your ears, your eyes, your minds,
> your hearts!"
> How easy it would be for me to become
> a Bonhoeffer Freak,
> So easy for those in authority
> to wipe me off as "Nutty!",
> And in years to come, when I am
> scattered ash upon a hill,
> Some will perhaps remember in a haze
> of blurry thoughts:
> "Yes she was trying to tell us something . . .
> to save our souls, she said . . . I think . . .
> I wonder what it was?
> But then she had this chap Bonhoeffer
> buzzing in her bonnet . . .
> Poor thing!"
>
> If I am remembered so in days to come,
> I will have failed my calling
> To build up His Church through
> love and suffering,
> which is the "fear" of God.[10]

It seems to me that Bonhoeffer is often used to show the way to lots of things other than Christ. I am making no particular judgments here.

10. Diana Exon, "Be What You Are" in *Catching Diamonds* (Braddon, Australia: Trendsetting, 1990), 34–35. Used by permission of the author.

Certainly it is not wrong to use Bonhoeffer. Better for our race that he be used poorly than ignored altogether. Yet there remains a difference, I think, between use and misuse. When he is pressed into a particular thematic so as to suggest that *this* is what Bonhoeffer was about, or when he is made cheerleader for a cause, however good, we ought at least to ask ourselves who or what we are promoting.

In the Berlin lectures of 1933, fighting against many of his contemporaries to find a transcendent foundation for Christology, Bonhoeffer insisted that so long as it is really the *person* of Christ the theologian wants to encounter, "Who?" is the proper question. For him this meant that the work of Christ is knowable only as we move outward from a consideration of his person. This was a theological commitment to be sure, but precisely because it was theological it was for him also intensely personal. Theology was not intellectual play but an engagement with reality, with truth, with God. And he knew the danger of reversing this sequence: the theologian might never encounter Christ as the final authority over his or her life, and thus might evade the all-important question of obeying him. By his own life Bonhoeffer answered affirmatively the question of Christ's authority.

As a method of reflection, theology implies a kind of control, even mastery, over its subject matter. Although a theologian, Bonhoeffer retained a skepticism about theology, at least skepticism regarding its use. "The Devil might have been the first theologian," he said. Theologians ought always to be wary about their own deepest motivations. For theology may easily become a protection against Christ's authority, a mechanism whereby God can be handled. Bonhoeffer understood this maneuver as a matter of personal experience. One can and should be a good theologian, but not overdependent on theology. It is inconceivable that in a work on Bonhoeffer we could allow Christ's authority to remain at arm's length and still aspire to be "faithful to Bonhoeffer."

Let us be clear, then, that Bonhoeffer is not the way. In the words of the poem, he "shows the way" and we are compelled to "listen to what he says." The Christ who lived in and through Dietrich Bonhoeffer is far more captivating than Bonhoeffer himself. If it is otherwise in our eyes, then we have become idolaters.

Yet strangely, as I hope to show, martyrs are special witnesses whose lives and deaths are deeply submerged in the life and death of Christ. To the degree that they are transparent to Christ, their authority is quite linked to Christ's own. By their sacrifice they acquire an authority, the authority of the truthful witness who, as a point of fact, insists relentlessly upon the authority of Another. As such, they lay a claim upon us. It is my intent, then, that this should be as much a book about Christ and martyrdom as about Bonhoeffer.

In his *Of the Difference between a Genius and an Apostle,* Kierkegaard made a bold distinction between two kinds of authority. On the one hand there is the authority of the genius, whose work develops importance and gains appreciation by its own content and weight. On the other hand there is the divine authority of the apostle, who has been arrested by God and has inherited a mission. Kierkegaard lamented the well-meant attempts of his contemporaries to make a genius of St. Paul. "They talk," he said, "in exalted terms of St. Paul's brilliance and profundity, of his beautiful similes and so on." But these attributions of "genius" are no compliment to a man like Paul, whose life of learning was suddenly undone and called to question in a quite spectacular encounter with God. The authority of the apostle is transcendent, "teleologically situated" in respect to the remainder of the human race. The apostle's "calling is a paradoxical factor, which from first to last in his life stands paradoxically outside his personal identity with himself as the definite person he is."[11]

Whether Bonhoeffer should be considered an apostle in Kierkegaard's terms is not the point. The significance of Kierkegaard's distinction lies in the perspective it lends to the task of interpretation. Wherever and whenever the transcendent horizon beyond an individual life exerts its pressure, however great the theological miracles and maneuvers, in short the genius, that might be attributed fairly to such a clever man as Dietrich Bonhoeffer, we must take notice of that horizon itself. We must do so as a matter of faithfulness to Bonhoeffer.

11. Søren Kierkegaard, *The Present Age* and *Of the Difference between a Genius and an Apostle,* trans. Alexander Dru (New York: Harper and Row, 1962), 89–108.

2

From Flossenbürg
to Westminster Abbey

"It is vanity to desire to live long, and not care to live well."

Thomas à Kempis, *The Imitation of Christ*

On the morning of that day between five and six o'clock the prisoners, among them Admiral Canaris, General Oster, General Thomas and *Reich-gerichtsrat* Sack were taken from their cells, and the verdicts of the court martial read out to them. Through the half-open door in one room of the huts I saw pastor Bonhoeffer, before taking off his prison garb, kneeling on the floor praying fervently to God. I was deeply moved by the way this lovable man prayed, so devout and so certain that God heard his prayer. At the place of execution, he again said a short prayer and then climbed the steps to the gallows, brave and composed. His death ensued after a few seconds. In the almost fifty years that I worked as a doctor, I have hardly ever seen a man die so entirely submissive to the will of God.

So reads the only putative eyewitness report of Bonhoeffer's death on 9 April 1945 at the Flossenbürg concentration camp. These words have nestled themselves in the collective consciousness of several generations and will be, I imagine, difficult to dislodge. They are unabashedly pious, portraying Bonhoeffer in a way we would like to see him, perhaps even expect to see him, at the hour of death: courageous and at prayer. The report, received by Wolf-Dieter Zimmermann, was written 4 April 1955 by H. Fischer-Hüllstrung, a medical doctor who ostensibly had attended to the prisoners on that morning. But it may be as bogus as the trial that preceded the execution.

J. L. F. Mogensen, a Danish survivor of the Flossenbürg camp, has taken the doctor's account to task at several points. First, he notes that on that morning the hangings were taking an unusually long period of time, from about six o'clock until close to noon. He conjectures that the reason for the length had to do with a torture technique sometimes used by the Nazis: to hang the victim with the tips of the toes touching the ground so as to prolong the death. When death drew near, the victim might be revived and the process repeated. Mogensen believes this practice would help to explain the prolonged nature of the killings. Second, he notes that the door to the execution area was always closed during killings. Even if it were left open by chance, there were no barrack buildings with a view of the place of execution. Third, he doubts whether the executioner would have allowed Bonhoeffer the uncommon privilege of kneeling and praying. This would have been outside normal procedures.[1]

The camp doctor may have known what happened to Bonhoeffer and decided to create an alternative account in order to wash his hands of these deaths. Or he may not have been an eyewitness at all. It also remains possible that he is telling the truth and that Mogensen has misinterpreted his own experience in some way. At the very least, Fischer-Hüllstrung had to have signed Bonhoeffer's death certificate. Even so, the doctor's report is losing its credibility among Bonhoeffer scholars and interpreters. The physical details of Bonhoeffer's death may have been much more difficult than we earlier had imagined. But aside from some kind of recantation, which is practically unthinkable, it is hard to imagine how the harrowing details of his final minutes or hours could make a real theological difference, though they might shape our psychological identification with him.

No one knows where Bonhoeffer's remains are. Perhaps they are intermingled with the ashes of others that form a high mound outside the Flossenbürg crematory. Perhaps they are in the mass grave that the Allied forces prepared to dispose of the rotting corpses they found when they liberated the camp.

---

1. The German original of Fischer-Hüllstrung's letter is reproduced in Wolf-Dieter Zimmermann, *Wir Nannten Ihn Bruder Bonhoeffer* (Berlin: Wichern-Verlag, 1995). The English translation can be found in Edwin Robertson, *The Shame and the Sacrifice* (New York: Macmillan, 1988), 277. Mogensen's discussion appears in Rainer Mayer and Peter Zimmerling, eds. *Dietrich Bonhoeffer Heute*, vol. 2, *Dietrich Bonhoeffer—Mensch hinter Mauern: Theologie und Spiritualität in den Gefängnisjahren* (Giessen: Brunnen Verlag, 1993), pp. 106–109.

Like all the camps, Flossenbürg took away the dignity of its victims, smearing individual faces into a collective, faceless death. When I visited Flossenbürg, I had wanted to follow the last steps of Bonhoeffer, to get into his frame of mind and his thoughts to the best of my ability. Unexpectedly, I found myself completely unable to focus on Bonhoeffer in that barbaric place. As if by some metaphysical law, the fraternity of suffering itself would not allow the visitor to single out any one face from the others. This experience has become for me a metaphor of Bonhoeffer's solidarity with those who suffer. It was obvious to me that he had identified with those who suffer in his life, but I had not yet considered the kind of solidarity implied by his death.

The Problem of Bonhoeffer as Martyr

And yet, posterity has singled out Bonhoeffer from the others. A quick glance at the Bonhoeffer literature quickly reveals that the term *martyr* is in high currency. The term is such a commonplace that one is tempted to consider the investigation of its legitimacy unwarranted, perhaps even an insult to the man behind the label. It would seem that the crown of martyrdom is forged mostly in the furnace of popular sentiment and thus is difficult to remove.[2] In the broader context of this study, I am considering the question of Bonhoeffer's martyrdom not to remove the honorific title but to secure it on a theological basis.

Despite popular sentiments, the relation between Bonhoeffer's confession of faith and his eventual death does not easily fit the pattern of Christian martyrdom in its classic expression. Upon his return from New York in the summer of 1939, Bonhoeffer involved himself in various acts of subterfuge against the German government, and as an active member of the Abwehr[3] he participated in tyrannicide by plotting to assassinate Adolf Hitler. It was for his participation in this treasonous conspiracy that he was ordered hanged by the Gestapo. The Gestapo saw only his "high treason."[4] On the surface at least, Bonhoeffer's Christian convictions in the matter seem to have been an irrelevant factor in the immediate circumstances of his death. Hence this final and highly

---

2. In the Roman Catholic tradition, even sainthood, that most auspicious honoring of the dead, begins with the practice of local communities' bringing persons before the church for consideration.

3. The counterintelligence agency of the armed forces in Germany, headed by Admiral Wilhelm Canaris during the Nazi period. The agency was an epicenter of resistance activities against the Nazi government.

4. Not until 6 August 1996 did a Berlin court exonerate Bonhoeffer and rehabilitate his reputation by ruling that he was innocent of high treason.

politicized period of his life (1939–1945) renders ambiguous the relationship between his Christian confession and his death and thus calls into question the authenticity of his martyrdom when weighed against the traditional Christian understanding.

The ambiguity was immediately recognized by his own church of Berlin-Brandenburg when, after the war, it refused to embrace him as a martyr once the facts of his conspiratorial activities were known.[5] On the first anniversary of the plot's failure, Paul Schneider (Lutheran pastor at Dickenshied who refused to comply with the Nazi order not to preach and, after several years of torture in the Buchenwald camp, was given a lethal injection of Strophantine on 18 July 1939) was presented to the churches as "a martyr in the full sense of the word" while Bonhoeffer's name was not even mentioned. The refusal to name Bonhoeffer was neither a personal rejection of Bonhoeffer nor a repudiation of his conspiratorial activities per se. Rather, it was a theological statement about martyrdom and its limits. For similar reasons, Lutheran bishop Hans Meiser ostentatiously stayed away from the 1953 memorial celebrations for Bonhoeffer at Flossenbürg.[6]

Interestingly, the reticence of Bonhoeffer's own church was met by a certain enthusiasm in the ecumenical community. Even while the dust of war was settling, Reinhold Niebuhr was hailing Bonhoeffer as a martyr whose story belonged amongst "the modern Acts of the Apostles."[7] Bishop George Bell of Chichester, Bonhoeffer's chief contact in the ecumenical movement, echoed Niebuhr's sentiments as he recounted the background of the Hitler plot.[8] On the occasion of his visit to Canterbury Cathedral in 1982, Pope John Paul II presided over the lighting of candles in the "Chapel of Saints and Martyrs of Our Own Time" to honor Dietrich Bonhoeffer along with others. The others honored included Maximilian Kolbe, Janani Luwum, Maria Skobtsova, Martin Luther King, Oscar Romero, and "those unknown."

It was highly significant that Pope John Paul II should honor Bonhoeffer in this way. Yet the honor accorded on this occasion should not

---

5. Eberhard Bethge, *Dietrich Bonhoeffer: A Biography* (hereafter cited as *DB*), rev. ed., ed. and rev. Victoria Barnett (Minneapolis: Fortress, 2000), 931–32. See also Eberhard Bethge, "The Challenge of Dietrich Bonhoeffer's Life and Theology," *Chicago Theological Seminary Register* 51, no. 2 (February 1961): 2.

6. Renate Wind, *Dietrich Bonhoeffer: A Spoke in the Wheel*, trans. John Bowden (Grand Rapids: Eerdmans, 1992), 146.

7. Reinhold Niebuhr, "The Death of a Martyr," *Christianity and Crisis* 5, no. 11 (25 June 1945): 6–7.

8. [Bishop George Bell], "Chichesters Darstellungen 1945 und 1957," in *Gesammelte Schriften*, vol. 1, ed. Eberhard Bethge (Munich: Christian Kaiser Verlag München, 1958), 390–98; this volume is hereafter cited as *GS*.

be taken as an official Roman Catholic pronouncement on Bonhoeffer's martyrdom. The Catholic Church has shown restraint, even reluctance, to ascribe titles to those outside its communion. During the 1960s, encouraged by the Vatican II declaration that there would be "real but imperfect" communion between Rome and its "separated brethren," a small delegation of Lutherans urged the Catholic Church to consider the canonization of Bonhoeffer as a dramatic ecumenical act. The Vatican responded that it was up to the German Lutheran Church to define its own saints and martyrs. In the eighteenth century Pope Benedict XIV had established the Catholic guidelines for determining martyr status that have remained in effect to the present day: that those responsible for the victim's execution operate *in odium fidei* ("in hatred of the faith").[9]

In any case, since 1945 it has become fashionable in various religious contexts to esteem Bonhoeffer with the title martyr. The enthusiasm continues. On 9 July 1998 Dietrich Bonhoeffer was memorialized along with nine other martyrs of the twentieth century at Westminster Abbey. Statues of the ten were unveiled and now stand in the abbey's west portal. Those included with Bonhoeffer are the Grand Duchess Elizabeth of Russia, Manche Masemola of South Africa, Licuinan Tapeidi of Papua New Guinea, Maximillian Kolbe of Poland, Esther John of Pakistan, Martin Luther King Jr. of the United States, Wang Zhiming of China, Janani Luwum of Uganda, and Oscar Romero of El Salvador.[10]

Gradually Bonhoeffer's own church tradition has inched closer to the prevailing sentiment.[11] But there are still dissenters. Detlev Daedlow,

---

9. Gordon S. Wakefield, "Martyrdom, Martyrs," in *The Westminster Dictionary of Christian Spirituality*, ed. Gordon S. Wakefield (Philadelphia: Westminster, 1983), 260–61. Details on the Roman Catholic position and process can be found in Kenneth L. Woodward, *Making Saints: How the Catholic Church Determines Who Becomes a Saint and Why* (New York: Simon & Schuster, 1990), 400–403.

10. This information was originally obtained from the newsletter of the International Bonhoeffer Society (no. 66, February 1998). Essays on the ten martyrs have since been published in Andrew Chandler, ed., *The Terrible Alternative: Christian Martyrdom in the Twentieth Century* (London: Cassell, 1998). The spirit of Chandler's volume is aptly contained in its epitaph, culled from John of Salisbury (c. 1115–1180): "Whoever he be that is willing to suffer for his faith, whether he be a little lad or a man grown, Jew or Gentile, Christian or Infidel, man or woman, it matters not at all: who dies for justice dies a martyr, a defender of the cause of Jesus Christ."

11. Philip H. Pfatteicher, in *Festivals and Commemorations: Handbook to the Calendar in Lutheran Book of Worship* (Minneapolis: Augsburg Fortress, 1980), 151–54, commemorates Bonhoeffer on 9 April under the heading "Theologian, Martyr." In the brief biographical description that follows, one reads, "From the first days of the Nazi accession to power, 1933, Bonhoeffer was involved in protests against the regime, especially its anti-Semitism . . ." The account continues, "On the new Lutheran calendar for North America he is not accounted a martyr since he was killed not for his adherence to the Christian faith but for his political activities against the German government. The distinction cannot be pressed, however, for

for example, stipulates that while Bonhoeffer may be a political-secular martyr he is not an ecclesiastical one—a distinction dating at least to the time of the Reformation,[12] and a provocative one coming from someone who was himself a member of the Confessing Church.[13] Lacey Baldwin Smith, a historian of martyrdom, casts his vote similarly:

> Dietrich Bonhoeffer was a political martyr, a nomenclature that has bedeviled martyrdom from the start. The moment society began to classify and define its martyrs, the dilemma emerged: how to differentiate within a Christian context between religion and politics, faith and social justice. Becket, More, Charles I, John Brown, and Bonhoeffer were all convinced in their various ways that they were defending their faith against the Antichrist, but the moment the devil dressed himself in secular garb and began playing politics, the trouble began. All five men died as a consequence of their "treason." In each case faith was the motivating force, but when doing battle with the Antichrist, that faith quickly became synonymous with their private definitions of what constituted the true structure of God's kingdom on earth.[14]

Smith regards Bonhoeffer's motives as suitably religious but considers the risks of blunting the distinction between politics and faith too high. Daedlow represents the uneasiness of many who simply find it too difficult to establish biblical justification for Bonhoeffer's political action, a sentiment shared by a significant portion of my own students over the years. Granted, there is no easy biblical justification for such activities. When the *Saturday Evening Post* ran a two-part profile of Bonhoeffer in

---

his resistance was surely rooted in his Christian commitment. The German Evangelical Calendar of Names lists his as 'Martyr in the Church Struggle,' and there is in Bonhoeffer's life a remarkable unity of faith, prayer, writing, and action." Prayers suggested are "for a deepened discipleship," "for courage to resist tyranny in all its forms," "for strength to pay the price of following Christ into places where we are beyond familiar rules," and "for those whose names we do not remember who with Bonhoeffer resisted tyranny" (151–54). Interestingly, the *Lutheran Book of Worship* does not itself call Bonhoeffer a martyr. In a personal conversation with Pfatteicher, I learned that the absence of the title *martyr* in the *Lutheran Book of Worship* does not suggest a polemic against Bonhoeffer, much less an official position of the church. Instead it reflects a two-decades-old conciliatory decision in view of some Lutherans who had difficulty with the title.

12. Wakefield, "Martyrdom, Martyrs," 260–261. The sixteenth century saw martyrs on both sides, but while Roman Catholic martyrs were said to be killed primarily for political reasons, Protestant deaths were considered religious.

13. Georg Huntemann, *The Other Bonhoeffer: An Evangelical Reassessment of Dietrich Bonhoeffer*, trans. Todd Huizinga (Grand Rapids: Baker, 1993), 269–70.

14. Lacey Baldwin Smith, *Fools, Martyrs, and Traitors: The Story of Martyrdom in the Western World* (New York: Knopf, 1997), 336.

1997, it conveniently avoided religious controversy by referring to him as "Hitler's would-be assassin."

There seems to be at least as much reservation about Bonhoeffer's case from the Jewish side, although it has nothing to do with his martyrdom. Early in 1998 Stephen A. Wise, a Connecticut lawyer, launched a public crusade in support of Bonhoeffer's recognition as one of the "Righteous among the Nations" *(Hassidei Umot Haolam)*. Since 1953 Yad Vashem, functioning at the behest of Israel's parliament, has aimed to highlight the role of individual non-Jews who tried to save Jews from the Nazi Holocaust. At present there are over sixteen thousand names on the official list, but Bonhoeffer's case has been rejected on principle. Mordecai Paldiel, director of Yad Vashem's Department for Righteous among the Nations, explains:

> The issue is not whether Bonhoeffer deserves our admiration for his courageous anti-Nazi stand, which eventually doomed him—he is a martyr in the struggle against Nazism. Our Program of "Righteous Among the Nations," however, is geared to persons who specifically helped Jews, and this aspect has not been established in regard to Dietrich Bonhoeffer.

Paldiel then expands the point, saying that Bonhoeffer's arrest and execution were for "matters dealing with church-state policies and his involvement in the anti-Hitler plot of July 1944, and not, to the best of our knowledge and the known record, to any personal aid rendered to Jews."[15]

Motives are always a slippery matter and naturally given to subjectivity, but in Bonhoeffer's case probing them is critical to ascertaining the legitimacy of his martyrdom. Decades ago John Godsey raised the troublesome question for Bonhoeffer's interpreters:

> My real question is this: Did he do what he did because of Christian convictions or because of the inbred and inculcated qualities derived from his unusual family? In the final analysis, what distinguishes him from his brother Klaus and his two brothers-in-law, all of whom also entered into the resistance and paid with their lives?[16]

15. Many Bonhoeffer scholars, myself included, disagree with this assessment on the grounds that Bonhoeffer's arrest was directly linked to his participation in so-called "Operation 7," by which fourteen Jews were smuggled to Switzerland. See Marilyn Henry, "Who, exactly, is a 'Righteous Gentile?" *Jerusalem Post*, 22 April 1998, 12f.

16. John Godsey, "Theologian, Christian, Contemporary," *Interpretation* 25, no. 2 (April 1971): 211.

These varied responses and concerns call for a careful examination of martyrdom in the Christian tradition to see whether and to what extent Bonhoeffer can be fitted into the category. This is no easy task, for the category itself has an evolutionary history. In the course of the examination it will become obvious that the Christian understanding of martyrdom is a matter of historical development of and elaboration upon the relation between the life and death of Jesus and the lives and deaths of his followers. Insofar as martyrdom is tied to church-historical development, it will be necessary to ask whether and what new dimensions of martyrdom may be surfacing in our own historical epoch, and whether Bonhoeffer himself may be a factor in the illumination of such dimensions. For the martyrs themselves are surely active agents in the evolution of the concept and therefore must be permitted to contribute to the church's understanding.

3

Martyrdom in Early Christianity

Imitatio Christi

The true Christian is one who becomes a sacrifice in order to call attention to the truth that Christ is the only true sacrifice.

Søren Kierkegaard

Before I make a case for Bonhoeffer as a Christian martyr, we must consider the tradition of Christian martyrdom. In this chapter I examine the historical development of the idea of martyrdom from the New Testament period through the second century, when something approximating the contemporary understanding can be said to have emerged.[1] In chapter 4 I then propose several theses to help amplify the various theological dimensions of martyrdom in the Christian tradition. All the while, Bonhoeffer's life and death looms on the horizon. Nevertheless I hereby put my readers on notice that a formal consideration of Bonhoeffer's death and its significance begins only in chapter 5.

---

1. As an example of the modern sentiment on martyrdom, I cite the definition from the glossary of David B. Barrett, George T. Kurian, and Todd M. Johnson, eds., *World Christian Encyclopedia: A Comparative Study of Churches and Religions in the Modern World,* 2d ed., 2 vols. (New York: Oxford University Press, 2001), 1:29, as follows: "A Christian martyr is a believer in Christ who loses his or her life, prematurely, in a situation of *witness,* as a result of human hostility."

Problems of Interpretation

In the hagiography of early Christian martyrdom, martyrs experience miraculous visions and are usually spared the physical pain of fire, sword, and the like. Their deaths appear to be part of a drama wherein supernatural powers demonstrate supremacy over natural powers. Martyrs were the charismatic Christians of the early centuries. As such, they were depicted as persons with direct links to divine authority and power. We should not be surprised, then, that the extant accounts have been worked over by posterity so as to maximize such power and authority. Since these prized accounts became the possession of a church tradition that all but worshiped martyrs, they were almost certainly ornamented and embellished, which makes it difficult to distinguish fact from fiction.

But this difficulty easily is overcome. Much of the embellishment seems to have been aimed at clinching in the minds of readers, sometimes indirectly, the martyr's identification with Christ. For example, as the body of Polycarp of Smyrna is burning, it gives off the odor not of burning flesh but of bread in the oven. After he succumbs to the flames, someone plunges a dagger into his body, at which point a dove emerges together with a great quantity of blood. In subtle and not so subtle ways, these images direct readers' attention from the martyr to the eucharistic sacrifice of Christ and reveal a more or less coordinated understanding of the martyrs' role in relation to their Lord.

Despite the sometimes fantastic descriptions of the physical aspects, the eventual outcome of the martyr's struggle remains indistinguishable from the myriad other deaths that humans die. Whether she is tortured in some extended manner to maximize pain like the Lyons martyrs, killed quickly and mercifully by a skilled executioner, or somehow relieved of pain completely, death eventually comes. True, deeper sympathies may accompany a painful and prolonged death, but the title martyr seems not to have been won in proportion to mere pain and suffering.

It seems clear, therefore, that a theology of martyrdom does not rest solely on the accidentals of physiological extinction. At the same time, we should not rule out entirely the factor of physical suffering for a theology of martyrdom. Indeed, one of the concrete aspects of human death is the prospect of physical suffering that may accompany it. In some cases this rightfully factors into theological considerations of the martyr's death, as when, for example, extreme pain and suffering are used in a threatening manner so as to incite the martyr to withdraw her confession. Within the ranks of the martyrs we find the suggestion that intensity of suffering translates to degrees of glory. In the martyrdom of Marian and James, for example, we read, "Those whose victory is slower and with greater difficulty, these receive the more glorious crown."[2] Nevertheless, in the Christian tradition, the concept of martyrdom has evolved in a way that transcends and relativizes the accidentals of physical expiration. We might say that the concept of martyrdom has evolved as an *interpretation of death itself.*

To modern readers this proposition causes little stir. In the Christian tradition, the interdependence of the terms *martyrdom* and *death* has been long assumed and widely held. In truth, the proposition would have met no more opposition in the third century than in our own. From the time Origen writes his *Exhortation to Martyrdom* at the latest, and probably well before, this interdependence was already established.

This makes all the more interesting the consensus of contemporary scholarship: the connection of martyrdom with death is *not* a feature of the New Testament documents. Instead, these documents emphasize the giving of one's witness in life. How does one account for the move-ment away from the earliest viewpoint? The matter has become a com-plex puzzle whose solution demands, seemingly, a variety of sublime, labyrinthine arguments. On one side are those like H. A. Fischel[3] and W. H. C. Frend,[4] who stress an inner continuity between Christian and Jewish views of martyrdom. Here the development of the Christian idea can be explained along the lines of Christian appropriation of Jewish sources, from the suffering, rejection, and death of Israel's prophets to the deaths of the Maccabean martyrs. On the other side are those like H. Strathmann,[5] H. Delahaye,[6] H. von Campenhausen,[7] and more recently G. W. Bowersock,[8] who stress the originality of the Christian view. In this camp the development of the Christian idea is explained, with a variety of shadings and emphases, as a result of the intersection of Christian impulses and the social matrix of Greco-Roman culture. These writers contend it was the brute fact of martyrological engagement in Roman

2. See Herbert Musurillo, *The Acts of the Christian Martyrs* (Oxford: Clarendon, 1972), 207.

3. H. A. Fischel, "Prophet and Martyr," *Jewish Quarterly Review* 37 (1946–1947): 265–80, 363–86.

4. W. H. C. Frend, *Martyrdom and Persecution in the Early Church: A Study of Conflict from the Maccabees to Donatus* (Oxford: Blackwell, 1965).

5. H. Strathmann, "μάρτυς, μαρτυρία," in *Theological Dictionary of the New Testament,* 10 vols., ed. Gerhard Kittel (Grand Rapids: Eerdmans, 1967), 4:474–508.

6. H. Delehaye, "Martyr et confesseur," *Analecta Bollandiana* 39 (1921): 20–49.

7. H. von Campenhausen, *Die Idee des Martyriums in der alten Kirche* (Göttingen, Germany: Vandenhoeck & Ruprecht, 1936).

8. G. W. Bowersock, *Martyrdom and Rome* (Cambridge: Cambridge University Press, 1995).

society that forged within the church's consciousness an inevitable and irrevocable union of life-witness and death.

Naturally, the set of assumptions the historian brings to the task of tracing out the development of Christian martyrdom largely determines the nature of the martyr profile that gets drawn. The various criteria by which a candidate for martyrdom might be evaluated, consciously or not, rest on these assumptions. For example, in Bowersock's work one finds this statement: "Without the glorification of suicide in the Roman tradition, the development of martyrdom in the second and third centuries would have been unthinkable."[9] Add to this Rome's love of spectacle and public entertainment, and to Bowersock the conclusion seems unavoidable that "Christianity owed its martyrs to the *mores* and structure of the Roman empire."[10]

One cannot dispute that the broader matrix of culture is surely a critical factor in the development of any theological idea and must be allowed a contribution to the interpretation of martyrdom. Nor can one gainsay the de facto and perhaps indelible impressions Roman society left upon the Christian idea of martyrdom. However, one must exercise a bit of caution here, for an interpretation of this kind explains the development chiefly as a function of external causes. One might then receive the impression that as the idea of martyrdom evolved, an alien element was at work that obscured the earlier and simpler understanding of martyrdom as "witness." In this case, the martyr as "one who dies for the faith" could be construed as a historical accident or an aberration of the original idea. This may be an arguable thesis.

Still there remains the question whether a theology of martyrdom might be better approached from some internal impulse that can be traced out genetically. From this angle one could argue that the church's martyrological engagement with Roman history did not *introduce* the idea of death into martyrdom but rather created a situation in which the nature of Christian witness in a pagan world could be clarified from within.

In this vein I will argue that the development from life-witness to death is best understood along the axis of the *imitatio Christi* (imitation of Christ). The trajectory of Jesus' own career, in its movement from life-witness to death, provides the essential pattern for Christian martyrdom. Insofar as Jesus himself may be fitted into an extant Jewish martyr tradition, it will enrich our investigation to situate the Christian development against the Jewish background. The inclusion of the Jewish element, though perhaps not logically necessary to the task, seems

9. Ibid., 72.
10. Ibid., 28.

more than appropriate in view of my goal of determining the legitimacy of Bonhoeffer as martyr, especially since one of the truly remarkable features of Bonhoeffer's life is his growing sensitivity to and solidarity with the Jews of the Holocaust. We must allow for the possibility that the essential link between Christ and the Jews that he achieved in his own thinking may have influenced his behavior in quite specific ways. In any case, our course eventually will provide ample space for the sort of profile that best helps to decide Bonhoeffer's case.

It may have an immediate payoff, too, for if Jesus' own career lies at the heart of Christian martyrdom, then the historical development from life-witness to death is not so dramatic as it first appears. Indeed, to say that the Christian understanding of martyrdom evolved as an interpretation of death can be somewhat misleading if we overlook the fact that death, however important as the final episode of an individual life, represents precisely the completion of a life. What is really at issue for us is the *life* whose end evokes the appellation "martyr." This theme will be taken up in earnest in the next chapter, but even here it will be helpful to stay pegged to the subtle dialectic of death and life which martyrdom brings to view, for the martyr's death interprets his life and his life interprets his death. The life means what it means in connection with this particular end; the end means what it means only as an end to this particular life.

Aside from historiographical issues, interpreters are beset with problems such as the authenticity of the early Acts of the Martyrs, the possibility that Montanist influence in Asia Minor may have contributed disproportionately to the development as a whole,[11] and a host of thorny problems pertaining to the interpretation of Jesus' own death. These matters will be treated only as they directly pertain to the narrative flow. They will not be entertained for their own sake. In keeping with these and other concerns, the following profile of martyrdom in the Christian tradition will adhere to what is most clearly a development of the Christian self-understanding.

New Testament Era

Analysis shows that the thread of continuity running throughout the New Testament understanding of martyrdom is the idea of a *witness* to the truth of the gospel founded in Christ. In combination, the Lukan, Pauline, and Johannine materials evince the center of Christ the crucified

11. Ibid., 17–18.

as the pattern for the Christian martyr, a theme the church elaborated through its earliest centuries. This development can be traced linguistically in the word group *martys, martyria, martyrein*, in which meanings overlap and can be treated as a whole.[12] Etymologically, *martys* was probably "one who remembers, who has knowledge of something by recollection, and who can thus tell about it." The verb form *martyrein*, typical of Greek verbs formed with -*eō*, denotes a state of habitual activity and can mean *being* a witness as well as "to come forward as a witness" or "to bear witness to something."[13]

This bare notion of bearing witness, whether once or repeatedly, is constitutive of the earliest layer of Christian tradition, in which the martyr bears witness to certain "facts." For example, Timothy makes his "good confession" (1 Tim. 6:12) in the presence of many witnesses *(pollōn martyrōn)*. In New Testament literature, *martys* may indicate one who witnesses to legal facts outside the purview of the gospel, evidenced in such cases as 1 Timothy 5:19 where multiple witnesses are required in order to verify charges brought against an elder, or *martys* may signify a specifically evangelical witness, as in the case of Luke 24: 48, where the resurrected Jesus calls *martyres* those who can testify to the facts of the Messiah's death and resurrection. Thus the *martys* is a witness both to general facts and to evangelical facts, t
he two aspects standing side by side with no apparent tension.

However, in the Lukan narratives the evangelical form of witness opens upon a new dimension, that is, witness to *truth*. This development is tied to the unique nature of Paul's apostleship.[14] As Paul defends his ministry before governmental authorities, Luke has him rehearsing the words Ananias spoke to him when he was relieved of his temporary blindness: "The God of our ancestors has chosen you to know his will, to see the Righteous One and to hear his own voice; for you will be his *martys* to all the world of what you have seen and heard" (Acts 22:14–15). Unlike that of older apostles, Paul's witness does not depend so much on direct witness to historical facts, however much their factual authenticity is implied, for he cannot appeal to firsthand knowledge of the Christ-event. Paul's witness is more to *truth* than to historical facts, with the result that "when the term *martys* is applied to Paul the second aspect begins to predominate over the first, whereas the reverse is true when the term is used of the older apostles."[15] It is Luke's account of Paul's situation

---

12. George Dragas, "Martyrdom and Orthodoxy in the New Testament Era: The Theme of Μαρτυρία as Witness to the Truth," *Greek Orthodox Theological Review* 30, no. 3 (1985): 287–96.

13. Strathmann, "μάρτυς, μαρτυρία," 475.

14. Ibid., 493.

15. Ibid., 494.

that first opens the way to the critical link from a witness to facts *(Tatsachenzeuge)* to a witness that confesses faith *(Bekennenzeuge)*.

This transition reveals something about the witness himself, whose standpoint now transcends mere remembrance of facts and their declaration, though he still includes this in his testimony as an essential part of what has been received and must be passed on. The witness now assumes a personal stance vis-à-vis those facts and their relevance for others. To be lacking in firsthand knowledge of Jesus' life and death, and yet to witness to them as "truth," entails a certain commitment to them as a revelation of God. Strathmann hints at this when he calls Paul "a witness to the truth who seeks to propagate the Christian faith by confession." The activity of witnessing is now intensified by the activity of confessing the truth.

This is not the place to open a discussion of the nature of confession, yet it must be observed here that "confessing" eventually became an integral component of Christian martyrdom. In fact, the label "Confessor" acquired a technical precision in the church, being applied to persons who suffered for the name of Christ but for various reasons did not die for their confession, or to those who were on their way to martyrdom but had not yet been sealed in it.[16] If confession discloses the identity of self,[17] we might consider Christian confession to be the disclosure of one's self in proximity to Christ. Confessors progress to martyrdom when, in refusing to be dissuaded from open confession amidst dangerous forces, they meet the consequences. Nowhere in the New Testament is one called *martys* because she suffers unto death for her confession of Christ. This is clearly a later development. Yet if confession entails a coming out with one's own identity in respect to Christ, then the emergent interdependence of *martyria* and death is contained in the embryo of the *imitatio Christi*. Just as Christ bore witness to the truth of God and died, so too his followers.

Perhaps it is in Luke's rendering of Stephen's death that the most important developmental step forward is taken. Stephen is not called a martyr because he dies but rather dies because he is a witness *(martys)* to Christ.[18] Stephen's speech opens to a historical horizon against which

16. Eusebius, *Ecclesiastical History* 5.2.2–5. Those awaiting death, and those returning from encounters with the beasts with various wounds and scars, refused to be called martyrs. Reciting from the *acta*, Eusebius says that "they gladly conceded the title of martyrdom to Christ, the faithful and true martyr. . . . They are already martyrs, whom Christ vouchsafed to be taken up at their confession, and sealed their witness by their departure, but we are lowly and humble confessors."

17. An excellent discussion of confession as public disclosure of identity can be found in Tom F. Driver, *The Magic of Ritual: Our Need for Liberating Rites That Transform Our Lives and Our Communities* (New York: HarperCollins, 1991), 114–20.

18. Strathmann, "μάρτυς, μαρτυρία," 494.

the suffering of God's faithful ones forms a precise lineage dating from Israel's prophets forward to Jesus and then by implication forward to Stephen himself. In death, Stephen imitates Christ by being dragged out of the city, by praying the words "Receive my spirit," and by asking God to "not hold this sin against them" (Acts 7:58-60). Revealed is Luke's commitment to a certain christological axis that unifies the sufferings of Israel's prophets, the death of Jesus, and the death of a follower like Stephen. More than an echo of Jesus' suffering and death is heard in Stephen, who is considered by Luke to be both prophet and martyr.[19] As a point of fact, the christological pattern of Stephen's death became constitutive in the subsequent literature, where early historians Sozomen and Eusebius call him a "proto-martyr"[20] and "perfect martyr" on the rationale of his proximity to Christ.[21]

It is not without significance for a theology of martyrdom that Paul[22] justified his apostleship by the same kind of identification with Christ. "We are afflicted in every way . . . persecuted . . . struck down . . . always carrying in the body the death of Jesus, so that the life of Jesus may also be made visible in our bodies." About these things Paul wishes not to boast, yet he cannot evade the conclusion that more floggings, more imprisonments, and more sufferings in general mark the "true apostle" (2 Cor. 4:8–10; 11:7–12:12). Paul may not have gone so far as to see the suffering and death of believers as redemptive, but such affliction he clearly traced to Christ. To the Colossians he asserted, "In my flesh I am completing what is lacking in Christ's afflictions for the sake of his body, that is, the church" (Col. 1:24; also Eph. 3:13). What applies to Paul applies also to his readers at Rome, who are reminded that their very baptisms were a plunge into the structure of Christ's life and death. Already marked by death, they are urged to offer their own bodies as living sacrifices to God (Rom. 6:1–4; 12:1–2). To Paul, "suf-

19. Frend, *Martyrdom and Persecution*, 79–99. Frend sees in the Gospel stories of Jesus' death strong parallels to both late Jewish and early Christian traditions. Like the accused in 2 and 4 Maccabees standing before Antiochus, Jesus is silent before Pilate. Later on, the circumstances of Jesus' trial—Pilate's raised tribunal, the bringing of seditious and conflicting charges, the "legal precision" of Caiaphas's pinning down the charge of blasphemy—fit the Roman framework remarkably well.

20. Sozomen, *Ecclesiastical History* 8.24.

21. Eusebius, *Ecclesiastical History* 5.2.5.

22. In consideration of the ongoing scholarly debates concerning Paul's authorship of Ephesians and Colossians, by "Paul" the reader may understand Paul the apostle, someone writing under his name, or a deutero-Pauline source. However, for a recent work that supports apostolic authorship of both books, see Markus Barth and Helmut Blanke, *Colossians: A New Translation with Introduction and Commentary*, trans. Astrid B. Deck, *Anchor Bible* 34B, ed. William Foxwell Albright and David Noel Freedman (New York: Doubleday, 1994), esp. 125–26.

fering for the faith and the task of witnessing to it were equally urgent and inextricably interwoven."[23]

In the Johannine literature the relationship between the witness of Jesus and that of his followers comes into even sharper focus, especially in the Apocalypse. In the Gospel, *martyria* is given by the Baptist, by Jesus, by God through the works of Jesus, and by the Evangelist whose writing itself is called a *martyria*. Of particular interest is the way John deciphers his own witness to Jesus' death in 19:35, which implies "not the historical attestation of a remarkable event but the witness to an event which intimates the saving efficacy of the death of Jesus."[24] In Revelation, repeated use of the striking phrase *hē martyria Iēsou* points to that witness that Jesus himself gave, which can now be used as a circumlocution for the Word of God and Christian revelation in general. Those who bear witness to Jesus do so in service to the *martyria Iēsou*. Further, because *hē martyria Iēsou* contains for John a reminiscence of Jesus' passion, witnesses must bear consequences similar to those of Jesus. John deduces that he himself was banished to Patmos "because of the word of God and the testimony of Jesus" (1:9), and the martyrs must fight against the dragon and be put to death because of the testimony of Jesus (12:17). After the dragon's defeat the connection is made more lucid:

> For the accuser of our comrades has been thrown down,
>   who accuses them day and night before our God.
> But they have conquered him by the blood of the Lamb
>   and by the word of their testimony,
> for they did not cling to life even in the face of death.
>
> Rev. 12:11

Granted, this text portrays death as the final seal placed upon oral testimony, not a form of the witness itself. What applied in Stephen's case still applies here: the deceased are called "martyrs" because of the faithfulness of their oral testimony and not because of their deaths. Yet this text deals with a testimony that results in the sacrifice of life.[25] In this way it anticipates the connection between Christ, the first martyr, and those who bear his witness. This identification is apparent in a rare stained-glass window in a Shropshire church, which depicts Jesus Christ as the "King of Martyrs."[26]

23. Frend, *Martyrdom and Persecution,* 86.
24. Strathmann, "μάρτυς, μαρτυρία," 500.
25. Ibid., 502.
26. See Wakefield, "Martyrdom, Martyrs," in *The Westminster Dictionary of Christian Spirituality,* ed. Gordon S. Wakefield (Philadelphia: Westminster, 1983): 260–61.

To sum up, the New Testament sources reveal that the earliest "martyr" is simply a witness, first to facts and then to truth. Further, it is clear that any direct terminological association of *martys* and death must be an interpolation from later generations and not a feature of the New Testament itself. Even so, on the strength of Luke's testimony concerning Stephen's death, Paul's understanding of his suffering as related to Christ's own, and John's conviction that the Christian martyr is a participant in the deathward witness of Jesus *(martyria Iēsou)*, it must be said that the New Testament is pregnant with the idea that one's witness may include suffering and death. The territory traversed by the church of the second and third centuries is thus anticipated by that of the first in the conscious recognition that the trajectory of Christian life cannot be disconnected from the Christ of the cross. To speak in terms of the "genetic" metaphor, the impression of the crucified Christ was encoded in Christian faith from the start, before the larger doses of vicious if sporadic persecutions meted out by Roman magistrates and populace. Without question, the events of the second and third centuries were a catalyst to what appears at times to have been an exaggerated form of the *imitatio Christi*, but the merging of death and witness appears to derive from an impulse belonging to the basic structure of the faith founded upon Christ.

Second-Century Developments

Development of the idea of martyrdom in the second century was far from uniform, some locales having reached a highly technical understanding by midcentury and others not at all. The older use of the term continues in writers like Hegesippus and Hippolytus, each of whom calls *martyres* those who confess at risk to their lives but without suffering death.[27] In a figure like Ignatius of Antioch, clearly resonant with the idea of martyrdom as an imitation of Christ's death, there is as yet no evidence of technical usage.[28] The term "technical usage" is here intended to convey the emergence of a new aspect in the idea of *martyria:* the older idea of witness surely survives but in a way increasingly focused

27. Strathmann, "μάρτυς, μαρτυρία," 506.
28. It is nothing short of remarkable that Ignatius's letters are completely lacking in technical usage. This fact provides extrabiblical evidence that the idea of martyrdom was deeply embedded in Christian consciousness in advance of what I have termed its technical usage. Ignatius, martyred A.D. 107 in Rome, describes himself as one who strives to imitate *(mimētēs)* Jesus and as a student *(mathētēs)* of Jesus, terms that recur frequently in the later *Acta.* See Bowersock, *Martyrdom and Rome,* 77–81, and Strathmann, "μάρτυς, μαρτυρία," 506.

upon death, such that a true martyr is the one who *suffers and dies* for the sake of witness. That is, one qualifies as a martyr not simply by bearing faithful witness, as in the New Testament literature, but by bearing that witness in a situation hostile to the gospel and thereby incurring the penalty of death.

When this use was established in the broader church is difficult to say, but by the time of Polycarp's death it was present at least in Smyrna and probably in the entire region of Asia Minor, where, with the approval of the masses, Christians were subjected to great persecutions from A.D. 161 to 178.[29]

An Interpretation of Polycarp's Martyrdom

In the *Martyrdom of Polycarp* several important elements come to light, two of them in the opening paragraph of the text:

> We are sending you, brethren, a written account of the martyrs and, in particular, of blessed Polycarp, whose witness to the faith as it were sealed the persecution and put an end to it. By almost every step that led up to it the Lord intended to exhibit to us anew the type of martyrdom narrated in the Gospel. For instance, just as the Lord had done, he waited to be betrayed, that we, too, might follow his example, not with an eye to ourselves alone, but also to our neighbors. It is certainly a mark of true and steadfast love, not only to desire one's own salvation, but that of all the brethren as well.[30]

In this opening portion of the account of Polycarp's death, written from his church at Smyrna to the church at Philomelium, two interesting features come into view. First, the writer of this account draws a clear

29. Strathmann, "μάρτυς, μαρτυρία," 505–6 (cf. Frend, *Martyrdom and Persecution,* 268; also Eusebius, *Ecclesiastical History* 4.15.1). Asia Minor, particularly the region of Anatolia, was the geographical setting for a disproportionate number of early martyrological writings. Moreover, many of the accounts originating outside this region can be connected to it in some way. One explanation is that this region was strongly influenced by Montanus, who had allegedly received the injunction from the Holy Spirit, "Seek not to die on bridal beds, nor in miscarriages, nor in soft fevers, but to *die the martyr's death,* that He may be glorified who has suffered for you" (emphasis added). Another explanation lies in what was, even by Roman standards, a peculiar fascination with public contests and games and a thirst for blood sport in the province. These, combined with the official status of Christianity as *illicita religio* (unregistered religion), left Christians there exposed to higher than normal levels of risk. The putative injunction received by Montanus can be found in Tertullian, *De fuga in persecutione,* 9.

30. *The Martyrdom of Polycarp,* trans. James A. Kleist, in *Ancient Christian Writers,* vol. 6, ed. Johannes Quasten and Joseph C. Plumpe (New York: Paulist, 1948), 90.

connection between the specific events surrounding Polycarp's death and his "witness to the faith." Witness and death are here forged together such that one can speak justly of Polycarp's "witness in death" or perhaps the "witness of his dying." Second, this kind of witness is linked to the figure of Christ. In the providence of God, Polycarp's martyrdom is said to be a revelation of "the type of martyrdom narrated in the Gospel." The preparer of this account obviously is concerned to highlight the similarities between Polycarp's death and that of Jesus. Like Jesus, "he waited to be betrayed." Elsewhere in the account, knowing his arrest was imminent, "Polycarp withdrew to a farm not far from the city," where "day and night he did nothing but pray for all the Churches throughout the world, as was his custom." Other details only intensify the point: the chief of police in the city "providentially bore the same name as Herod," and when arrested Polycarp was seated "upon an ass." He was arrested on a Friday "about supper time" and led into the city "on the Sabbath." When the flames of the fire did not consume him, there "was ordered an executioner to approach him and run a dagger into him," whereupon blood (in some manuscripts a dove, though Eusebius omits it) issues forth.

Why was Polycarp martyred? The chronicle is somewhat imprecise concerning the reason(s). Apparently a certain Germanicus, during the episode of his own martyrdom, had enraged the assembled crowd. As the proconsul attempted to persuade him to curse Christ out of respect for his young age, Germanicus, eager to be done with the depravity of his persecutors, dragged a wild beast (to whose torment he had been condemned) toward him, ostensibly hastening his death and putting an abrupt end to the contest. The crowd appears to have detected some insolence in Germanicus's action, at which point, "astonished at the heroism of the God-loving and God-fearing race of the Christians," they shouted, "Away with the atheists! Let Polycarp be searched for!"[31]

In the arena, after Polycarp repeatedly refuses to offer incense and say "Lord Caesar," a herald is sent to the center to announce three times that Polycarp has confessed to being a Christian. At that moment the mob exclaims, "This is the teacher of Asia, the father of the Christians, the destroyer of our gods!" Polycarp's extraordinary profile, which derived from his stalwart reputation as the longstanding bishop of Smyrna, made him a logical target of the mob's anger at Christians in general, many of whom, it can be presumed, traced their spiritual ancestry directly to him.

---

31. Here we encounter the typical Roman accusation that Christians were "atheists." This should not be interpreted in a literal sense, of course, but as an indication of the popular belief that Christians had defected from the Roman gods. See ibid., 91–92.

To the author, the commendable nature of Polycarp's martyrdom before the Christians at Philomelium and "all the communities of the holy and Catholic Church" lay in its power to exemplify the death of Christ, especially its character as a *death for others*—"not to ourselves alone, but also to our neighbors," as the text reads. From the Christian point of view, death for others is a constitutive element of Christ's passion, which inspires the writer to illumine this feature of Polycarp's ordeal. The writer labels Polycarp an "outstanding martyr" because his martyrdom "was in accord with the gospel of Christ."[32] The vicarious aspect of Polycarp's death surfaces in the author's judgment that he "sealed the persecution and put an end to it." We may assume that the death of this high-profile Christian gave the crowd a way to vent its anger, making his martyrdom an instrument by which a measure of peace came to the churches of Asia Minor.

The Lyons Martyrs

In the summer of 177, under the reign of Marcus Aurelius, a series of grisly persecutions broke out in the region of Gaul.[33] The events transpired in the two capital cities of Vienne and Lyons, each of which lay on the banks of the Rhone. Eusebius, the only source for the text, had access to a "document about the martyrs," ostensibly written by an anonymous survivor, which the "distinguished churches of this country" sent on to Asia and Phrygia as an encyclical, and he preserved a summary of it in his *Ecclesiastical History*.

Introducing the account, Eusebius attributes the Gallic persecutions to "popular violence" against Christians in the cities rather than to any state-instigated pogroms against Christianity. The official mood during the reign of Aurelius seems to have been not much different from the mood under Trajan some eighty years earlier.[34] In the case of Gaul, any

32. Ibid., 99.

33. In this section, my quotations from the acts of the Lyons martyrs are taken from Musurillo, *Acts of the Christian Martyrs*, 63–85. Pertinent historical details are culled from the scholarly treatment of Frend, *Martyrdom and Persecution*, 1–30.

34. Trajan replied to a letter from Gaius Pliny, the governor of Asia Minor, in which Pliny had requested clarification on the state policy toward Christians. Trajan's reply: "It was impossible to lay down a general rule to a fixed formula. These people must not be hunted out; if they are brought before you and the charge against them is proved, they must be punished, but in the case of anyone who denies that he is a Christian, and makes it clear that he is not by offering prayers to our gods, he is to be pardoned as a result of his repentance however suspect his conduct may be." Translation taken from Robert L. Wilken, *The Christians As the Romans Saw Them* (New Haven, Conn.: Yale University Press, 1984), 28. For the similarity between Trajan's and Aurelius's policies, see Frend, *Martyrdom and Persecution*, 8.

Christian who was a Roman citizen and came to the attention of authorities was to be beheaded; all others were subjected to various forms
of torture both in prison and in the amphitheater, including beatings,
strangulations, repeated bouts with beasts, roastings on a gridiron,
stretching on blocks, and serving as stand-ins for gladiators.[35] In this
document such themes as the struggling athlete of Christ caught in the
apocalyptic conflict between God and Satan, the unique presence of
Christ amid the martyr's suffering, the notion of the martyr's death as
sacrifice to God, and the martyr's death as an alternative to idolatry all
appear vividly before us. But my special interest at the moment is to
trace out the development of the church's understanding of martyrdom
to a point where it roughly approximates our contemporary viewpoint.
In this vein we can ascertain several important developments.

First, the strong undercurrent of the *imitatio Christi* is no less a feature
in the deaths of the Lyons martyrs than in Polycarp's death. Early in this
extraordinary litany of events, Vettius Epagathus, "a man of position . . .
having much zeal toward God and being fervent in spirit," volunteered
himself as a defender of Christians who were being incarcerated and subjected to the typical charges of atheism and immorality. During his defense
the governor asked whether Vettius himself was a Christian, whereupon
he "confessed in clear tones" and was escorted to the company of the others. Vettius is described as the "Christians' Advocate" who lays down his
life for the brethren, which makes him "a true disciple of Christ, and he
follows the Lamb wheresoever he goes." Trying to capture the main theme
of Vettius's life, the author of the Lyons *acta* notes that he had gained a
reputation for being "untiring in his service of his neighbor." "Being of
such a nature," he became indignant when some of those neighbors were
targeted for public cruelty and humiliation. But when he came forward to
speak in their defense, he was forced by the angry crowd to declare that
he too was a Christian and then was thrown into the ranks to suffer their
common fate. The author of the account sees in this action a vivification
of Christ's selfless devotion to those whom he loved,[36] a feature of the
imitatio that rises to prominence among modern martyrs.

Later on, the "Blessed Pothinus," bishop of Lyons and predecessor to
Irenaeus, was "dragged before the judgement seat" accompanied by the
authorities and "all the populace," and bore the humiliation of "all kinds
of howls . . . as though he was Christ himself." When Blandina, in one

35. Frend finds a high demand for inexpensive combatants in the ritual games, especially in the Gallic provinces. In response to financial pressure, a *senatus consultum* of A.D.
177–178 had legalized the procurement of common criminals to alleviate the high cost of
hiring a gladiator fifth class. See Frend, *Martyrdom and Persecution*, 5.

36. See Musurillo, *Acts of the Christian Martyrs*, 65.

of her several contests, was put on a stake to entice beasts as they were let into the arena, she "seemed to be hanging in the shape of a cross."

Second, amongst the Lyons martyrs, the connection between confession and death is unmistakable and is put forth with unique clarity. Confession of the name (publicly admitting to being a "Christian") was the only evidence necessary to earn a death sentence, and thus confession became the immediate precipitating cause of one's death. As if to stress the point, one Attalus, "ever a witness for truth among us," was "led around the amphitheatre and a placard was carried before him on which it was written in Latin 'This is Attalus, the Christian.'"[37] And Sanctus, a deacon from Vienne, would disclose nothing of his identity to the authorities—not his race, home, name, nor whether he was slave or free—but repeated the same answer in Latin to every question: "I am a Christian."[38] So important is the connection between confession of the name and death that the writer expresses concern that being weakened in the ordeal one woman may not have been able to make confession, and there exists a grave concern about the future of about ten others whose confession was "uncertain."

It is noteworthy that though numerous persons die in prison from maltreatment, the spotlight falls repeatedly on those whose struggle carries them into a fully public contest where the either/or character of their identity can be displayed for all to see. Even after their deaths, the bodies of the deceased are left exposed in public for six days and watched over by a military guard. Some of the angry mob continue to vent their disgust by hurling insults, while others laugh and jeer. From the writer's point of view, the authorities are by such action aiming to show the preposterous nature of the Christian belief in a bodily resurrection, "as though they would make some great gain, that the bodies should not obtain burial." The worldly powers are attempting to refute the martyrs' confession by accentuating the apparent failure of their belief in a resurrection from the dead. Presumably, they want onlookers to see the "preposterousness" of all that is intended by Christian confession. Here we see a dispute over the interpretation of death in relation to confession. Christians say death secures confession; the Roman powerholders say death discredits confession. What is not in dispute, apparently, is the importance of the connection between confession and death, which is here confirmed (backhandedly) even by the actions of worldly powers.

37. Ibid., 75.

38. Ibid., 69. Elsewhere in the literature, in one of the most convincing accounts of martyrdom, the trial of the Scillitan martyrs in A.D. 180, Vigellius Saturninus hears the same response from one of the accused. Here again, the declaration "I am a Christian" *(Christianus sum)* is enough to justify condemnation. See Gerald Bonner, "Martyrdom: Its Place in the Church," *Sobornost* 5, no. 2 (1983).

Third, there emerges among the Lyons martyrs a distinction most important in the subsequent literature—between martyrs and confessors—which throws the accent on martyrdom as "witness unto death" in a way heretofore absent.

> And they carried so far their zeal and imitation of Christ, "who being in the form of God, thought it not robbery to be equal with God," that for all their glory, and though they had testified not once or twice but many times, and had been taken back from the beasts and were covered with burns and scars and wounds, they neither proclaimed themselves as martyrs, nor allowed us to address them by this title. But if ever any one of us called them martyrs (*martyras*) either in a letter or in speech they rebuked him sharply. For they gladly conceded the title of martyrdom (*martyrias*) to Christ, the faithful and true martyr (*alēthinō martyri*) and first-born from the dead and author of the life of God. And they reminded us of the martyrs who had already passed away, and said "they are already martyrs, whom Christ has vouchsafed to be taken up at their confession, and sealed their witness by their departure, but we are humble and lowly confessors" (*homologoi*).[39]

In this portrait, death is depicted as the seal of confession. Until death ensues, one should not be called, properly speaking, a martyr but should be content with the lesser title "confessor." It is true that the account of the Lyons martyrs is strewn with the older understanding of the martyr as witness, but this should not be dismissed as mere inconsistency and left to obscure what is a genuinely new development. Here the terminological interchangeableness may mean only that, at the linguistic level, usage lags behind the genetic growth of the idea in the church's actual experience of martyrdom. It is clear, however, that a certain *group* preferring to be called "confessors" has distinguished itself from another group for whom they have reserved the term *martyrs*, and that the latter have attained something which the former have not.

Here martyrs are in the process of being more narrowly defined by the Christian community, which marks the beginning of the technical use of the term.[40] Bearing witness before the authorities and contending with various tortures apparently was not enough. Their "perfection" was still hanging in the balance as long as defection remained a possibility. Death alone could render the final judgment on their faithfulness, as it had already with Stephen, the "perfect martyr," and that "faithful and true martyr," Christ himself. By implication, taking to one's self the title martyr involves a presumption that the living simply cannot make.

---

39. Eusebius, *Ecclesiastical History*, 5.2.1–3.
40. Strathmann, "μάρτυς, μαρτυρία," 505.

4

An Alphabet of Martyrdom

The easiest thing of all is to die; the difficult thing is to live.

Søren Kierkegaard

To this point I have been tracing out the emergence of the classical idea of martyrdom. I chronicled its development from a bare witness to historical facts about Christ, to confession of the truth of Christ, to a growing consensus that in death the martyr bears a unique and complete witness to the deathward movement of Christ's own life, an end that "confessors" do not reach. Finally, I reached the conviction that martyrdom involves voluntary acceptance of the consequences of open confession. The task of giving theological nuance and amplification remains.

In the theses that follow, I want to enter some letters into the alphabet of Christian martyrdom. Though incomplete, my alphabet enables me to begin to pronounce the syllables necessary for larger structures of meaning.

Martyrdom Is a Dialectical Witness of Life and Death

There are circumstances under which it may be more difficult to live for Christ than to die for him. Perhaps this could be said of Cyprian of Carthage, who under the Decian persecutions considered himself more valuable as an encouragement to his flock than as a dead man, and therefore went into hiding. Perhaps it could also be said of Origen, who, though longing to emulate his father by entering the eternal company of the martyrs, devoted himself to a life of austerity and sacrifice.

If death were the essential element in martyrdom, then any Christian at death's door might qualify as a martyr. In that case *martyrdom* would be nothing more than a synonym for something like a Christian rather than pagan death. Again, if death were the essential element, anyone who nurses a death wish and therefore sets upon a fatal course may qualify. In that case, *martyrdom* would be only a synonym for some form of suicide.

Under stresses related to its engagement with Roman power, the church forged a union of utmost importance between the martyrs' death and their confession of the name of Christ. This union means that, however important death may be in an emerging theology of martyrdom, *death as such does not make the martyr*. As Augustine put it when he contended against those who had died heroically for the Donatist cause, "men are made martyrs not by the amount of their suffering, but by the cause in which they suffer."[1]

Causes make martyrs. To discern them, however, one must glance away from death and observe life. Confession, after all, is an activity of the living. As far as the martyr is concerned, willingness to live for Christ is at least as important as willingness to die for him, perhaps more so. In A.D. 250, it may have been easier for Cyprian to surrender to authorities and personally relinquish his hold on life,[2] yet his flock needed the direction, support, and encouragement his letters could bring.[3] The confessor's commitment to life, then, especially in difficult circumstances, forms a basis for distinguishing between martyrdom and spiritualized forms of suicide. In Cyprian's case, we see also a salient dimension of ethical life: the interests of others rise above self-interest. Most important, however, the choice for life reinforces the all-important causal connection between confessing and dying, albeit in a subtle way. The more directly death can be connected to the particular confessing of Christ performed in one's life—as opposed to death's being a benign state toward which one is favorably disposed or reconciled—the more convincing the martyr becomes. It would seem that to proceed too willingly diverts the attention of the onlooker from the outward confession of Christ and leads her instead to examine the inner psyche of the

---

1. Augustine, *Letters*, 89.2. Luther would later use the same argument against the Anabaptists.

2. Personal courage does not seem lacking in Cyprian. Eight years later he was martyred by beheading during one of the persecutions of Valerian.

3. Compare with Paul, who tells the Philippian church (Phil. 1:21–26) that he is hard pressed to decide between life or death. Death is "far better," yet "to remain in the flesh is more *necessary* for you."

martyr. The connection between the confession and death is crucial at various levels.

Just how closely must one draw the connection? No doubt there are important differences between the martyrdoms of a Bonhoeffer and a Polycarp that deserve careful consideration. Not least among these differences is Polycarp's reply to the insistence of proconsul that he swear by the Fortune of Caesar: "If you flatter yourself that I shall swear by the Fortune of Caesar, as you suggest, and if you pretend not to know me, let me frankly tell you: I am a Christian!"[4] In Polycarp's situation, death immediately follows upon confession, leaving little work for the interpreter. In Bonhoeffer's case, much interpretive work needs doing. The similarities are obvious: each is put to death by political powers without seeking it directly, and each bore confession to Christ. The fact that one can speak nevertheless of important differences underscores the point that at issue in martyrdom is neither Christian confession as such, which earns only the accolade "confessor," and even then only in dangerous times, nor Christian death as such, which is distinguishable only as a more general "death in Christ." Really at issue in martyrdom is the nature of the relationship between confessing Christ—either in the positive sense of bearing witness to him or in the mere refusal to deny him—and being put to death. How does one begin to assess this relationship?

Clearly it presents a challenge to anyone interested in classification. For example, in their research on the biographies of twentieth-century martyrs, James and Marti Hefley admit to their readers the difficulty of knowing whom to include. In the end they argue for inclusiveness on the grounds that it is an "oversimplification . . . that Christian martyrs always die strictly for their testimony of Christ. This idea persists because accounts of martyrdom often do not include sufficient backgrounding of the events. When all the details are known, it is apparent that most Christian martyrs die in circumstances *related* to their witness for Christ."[5]

No doubt background investigations bring important things to light. Ultimately, however, the relation between confession and death remains vague unless we develop criteria by which to understand it. How obvi-

---

4. *The Martyrdom of Polycarp*, trans. James A. Kleist, in *Ancient Christian Writers*, vol. 6, ed. Johannes Quasten and Joseph C. Plumpe (New York: Paulist, 1948), 95.

5. See James Hefley and Marti Hefley, *By Their Blood: Christian Martyrs of the Twentieth Century* (Milford, Mich.: Mott Media, 1979), vii (preface). Similarly, when he wrote the foreword to Diana Dewar, *All for Christ: Some Twentieth Century Martyrs* (Oxford: Oxford University Press, 1980), Bishop Leslie Brown of Uganda confessed, "It is rare nowadays for a Christian to be condemned on the ground of his faith. Some alleged crime, political or otherwise, is almost always the ostensible reason for his death."

ous must the relationship between confession and death be? Are we to prefer the more obvious to the less obvious? Who has the authority to make these judgments?

As the questions pile up, perhaps the time has come to offer a preliminary definition: A Christian martyr is a person whose death, in the consensual opinion of members of the Christian community who survive him, is ascertainably connected to and precipitated by Christian confession. Much remains unsaid in this definition. For example, what counts as "confession"? Do actions count as much as words? What do we affirm as the content of Christian confession? Is it the bare historicity of Christ? Does it include specific theological dimensions or angles? In Bonhoeffer's case, both the form and the content of confessing will prove critical. Despite these questions, what is clear in this preliminary definition is that the term *martyr* supposes a careful probe of the reciprocal relationship between confession and death, and that martyrs are products of at least some ecclesiastical reflection on the part of the communities to which they belonged. Thus calling someone a martyr carries the force of a favorable judgment or resolution on the nature of her life. The life of the martyr is inseparable from the identity bestowed in death. At one level, this dialectic is a matter of common sense. We imply it every time we use the term *martyr.* There could scarcely be any official recognition of martyrs without it. Yet at another level it is surprising how feebly this dialectic influences those interested in ascertaining the essence of martyrdom.[6]

Martyrdom Is an Act of Freedom

While martyrs do not seek death, neither do they easily run away from it. The voluntary acceptance of death as the consequence of bearing witness is critical to an understanding of martyrdom, because it reveals the sense in which death might be an offering or sacrifice, and

---

6. Against the stream, one finds Gerald Bonner and the Russian priest Alexander Menn. Bonner, a writer about martyrdom, distills it to the willingness *to live* for Christ (see Gerald Bonner, "Martyrdom: Its Place in the Church," *Sobornost* 5, no. 2 [1983]: 6–21). Menn, himself a martyr, on the evening before being struck from behind by an ax, stressed the lives of martyrs over against their deaths when he said in a Moscow lecture, "No living creature, except for a man, is able to take a risk, and even the risk of death, for the sake of truth. Thousands of martyrs *who have lived* are a unique phenomenon in the history of all our solar system" (emphasis added). This quotation taken from Larry Woiwode, "Aleksandr Menn" in Susan Bergman, "Twentieth-Century Martyrs," in *Martyrs: Contemporary Writers on Modern Lives of Faith*, ed. Susan Bergman (San Francisco: HarperSanFrancisco, 1996), 28.

moreover a participation with Christ. Christian life may bring with it the natural corollary of suffering, but such suffering is always much more than an imposition by force.[7]

Jesus invites his followers to take up their own cross, to dedicate themselves to a life of this kind. Jesus himself pioneered the freedom of voluntary acceptance when under weight of death in Gethsemane he prayed, "If it is possible, let this cup pass from me; yet not what I want but what you want" (Matt. 26:39).[8] The prospect that death may yet be averted by some kind of escape plan, or that perhaps a heroic political venture might yet be undertaken, characterizes this moment as one of profound choice. John has Jesus say, speaking of his own life under the metaphor of shepherding, "No one takes it from me, but I lay it down of my own accord" (John 10:18). Hebrews makes Jesus' self-sacrifice as priest—he "offered himself" (Heb. 7:27)—an integral piece of its theology of atonement.

The pattern continues in the early Christian martyrs. When the mounted police are closing in on Polycarp, the account reads, "Even there escape to another place of hiding was still possible; but he decided against it, saying: *'God's will be done!'*"[9] According to Eusebius's testimony, in the crucible of conflict some of the Lyons Christians proved ready by their acceptance of death and became martyrs, while others failed in strength and training.[10] Origen urges Ambrose on to martyrdom, for as a valiant athlete accepts the tribulation of training, so he should accept his impending tribulation.[11] In the extended narrative of Pionius's martyrdom, the accused defends himself against a crowd that ridicules his faith in a man who died as a criminal. Pionius retorts, "What these people forget is that this criminal departed from life *at his own choice.*"[12]

The educated classes of Roman society usually found the voluntary aspect of Christian martyrdom repulsive. One governor in Asia Minor, after witnessing eagerness for death on the part of all the Christians in the province, exclaimed in exasperation, "You wretches, if you want to die,

---

7. See Acts 15.26, where Paul and Barnabas are described as those "who have risked their lives for the sake of our Lord Jesus Christ."

8. For an interpretation that incorporates martyrdom into Jesus' self-understanding, see Markus Bockmuehl, *This Jesus: Martyr, Lord, Messiah* (Downers Grove, Ill.: InterVarsity Press, 1994), 77–102.

9. *Martyrdom of Polycarp,* 7.20–21.

10. Eusebius, *Ecclesiastical History,* 5.1.11

11. Origen, *Exhortation to Martyrdom,* 1.1.

12. Herbert Musurillo, *The Acts of the Christian Martyrs* (Oxford: Clarendon, 1972), 153. Emphasis added.

you have cliffs to leap from and ropes to hang by."[13] Celsus thought the deliberate rush to death was ample evidence of Christians' insanity.

Yet opposition to the voluntary aspect came from within the church as well as without. Origen, Clement of Alexandria, Cyprian, and Lactantius all spoke against such enthusiasm by attempting to draw tighter boundaries around the ranks of the martyrs, reserving the title only for those who endured suffering and death in the face of persecution.[14] The distress (perhaps embarrassment) of certain Christians over the behavior of others who had not adequately appropriated the passion of Christ appears to have motivated this corrective move. It met with only sporadic success. The same Cyprian who had condemned by word and deed the foolhardy rush to martyrdom was followed by a crowd from his own flock that apparently wanted to share death with him.[15] Yet though the message did not always get through, one notices concern to curtail the "rush to death." Even the at-times-overzealous Tertullian of Carthage could show a measure of restraint: on the one hand, "we do not feel constrained to rush forth to the combat" as if to prove that we were without fear, and on the other hand we "will neither stoop to flee from persecution nor buy it off." With Christ in mind, what matters most is "the willing spirit" by which Jesus entered his passion even when, humanly speaking, flight may have been preferred. The request for the cup to pass can be made, but one should not take to one's self the responsibility for its passing.[16] Later Socrates would set Jesus at the font of the tradition, accentuating his freedom to forestall death before finally accepting it.[17] Thus in the passing of time, a shot of temperance

---

13. Tertullian, *Ad Scapulam*, 5. This translation given by G. W. Bowersock, *Martyrdom and Rome* (Cambridge: Cambridge University Press, 1995), 1.

14. Bowersock, *Martyrdom and Rome*, 4.

15. Pontius, *The Life and Passion of Cyprian*, 16. According to the account, ". . . a numberless army hung upon his company, as if they had come as an assembled troop to assault death." After Cyprian's death, "that which the general wish desired could not occur, viz., that the entire congregation should suffer at once in the fellowship of a like glory. . . ."

16. Tertullian, *Ad Scapulam*, 5 (cf. *De fuga in persecutione*, 8–14).

17. Socrates, *Ecclesiastical History*, 3.8. Trying to justify the several flights of Athanasius, Socrates gave this interpretation of Jesus: "When he had raised Lazarus from the dead, and they had become still more intent on destroying him, [we are told that] Jesus walked no more openly among the Jews, but retired into a region on the borders of the desert. Again when the Saviour said, 'Before Abraham was, I am;' and the Jews took up stones to cast at him; Jesus concealed himself, and going through the midst of them out of the Temple, went away thence, and so escaped. . . . Finally, when John had suffered martyrdom, and his disciples had buried his body, Jesus having heard what was done, departed thence by ship into a desert place. . . . The cause for retreat and flight under such circumstances as these is reasonable and valid, of which the evangelists have afforded us precedents in

derived from Jesus' own life met up with the earlier zeal. Even so, the voluntary aspect of martyrdom remained constitutive.

Modern martyrs exhibit the same sense of acceptance. Bishop Kallistos of Diokleia tells the story of Iulia de Beausobre, who, engulfed in hopelessness, was preparing yet another meal for her jailed husband. "To what end?" she was asking herself, when suddenly she felt a blow on the back of her neck and heard what she described as "the unspoken words of Another":

> Of course it's no earthly use to any one of you. It can only cripple your bodies and twist your souls. But I will share in every last one of your burdens as they cripple and twist you. In the blending heat of compassion I will know the full horror of your deliberate destruction by men of your own race. I will know the weight of your load by carrying it alongside of you, but with an understanding greater than yours can be. I want to carry it. I need to know it. Because of my Incarnation and your Baptism there is no other way—*if you agree.*[18]

Bishop Kallistos follows the story with this comment: "For innocent suffering does not by itself make someone into a martyr. It is also required that we on our side should *accept* that suffering, even though we may not have originally chosen it." In a similar way, Archbishop Oscar Romero, conscious of his precarious situation, said:

> If they should go so far as to carry out their threats, I want you to know that I now offer my blood to God for justice and the resurrection of El Salvador.

> Martyrdom is a grace of God that I do not feel worthy of. But if God accepts the sacrifice of my life, my hope is that my blood will be like a seed of liberty . . .[19]

---

the conduct of our Saviour himself: from which it may be inferred that the saints have always been justly influenced by the same principle, since whatever is recorded of him as man, is applicable to mankind in general. . . . [Jesus] neither permitted himself to be apprehended before the time came; nor when the time was come did he conceal himself, but voluntarily gave himself up to those who had conspired against him."

18. Bishop Kallistos of Diokleia, "What Is a Martyr?" *Sobornost* 5, no.1 (1983): 8. In this article numerous martyrdoms are recalled, several in the twentieth century, which conform to the pattern of voluntary acceptance. When external persecution is not a factor, the author argues, monasticism preserves in its initiation rituals the free acceptance of a form of "martyrdom."

19. Plácido Erdozaín, *Archbishop Romero: Martyr of Salvador,* trans. John McFadden and Ruth Warner (Maryknoll, N.Y.: Orbis, 1981), 75–76.

Martyrdom Is a Response to Evil and the Demonic

It is impossible to miss the predominance of militaristic metaphors in the *acta*. Victims of persecution tend to see themselves as participants in an apocalyptic struggle between the forces of God and the devil. Where apocalyptic overtones are minimized, the focus of the battle may be restricted to a personal struggle for holiness in the face of sin's destructive power. In either case, the prospective martyr is like an athlete who strives to endure the enemy and win the victory. No theological analysis of martyrdom could be complete without attention to so dominant a theme. Within the theme of martyrdom as resistance against evil, at least two avenues await exploration: the demand that the martyr preserve some measure of "innocence" so that his death may prove potent against evil, and the necessary engagement of the martyr in the dense thicket of politics, where, according to the testimony of some, evil was institutionally supported.

Insofar as Christian martyrdom grows genetically out of the complex relationship of life and death manifested in the career of Jesus the Christ, we would expect the innocence of Christ to play at least a subsidiary role in distinguishing martyrs from nonmartyrs. We would also expect the political dimension of martyrdom to find its origin in Christ's own death at the hands of Rome for what were ostensibly political reasons.

The Value of Innocence

In *The City of God* Augustine takes up a discussion of death as the penalty for Adam's sin, in the course of which a question arises: if death is a penalty for sin, and if by the grace of regeneration sin is overcome in the lives of the righteous, then why must the righteous suffer death? Augustine answers that God in his creativity leaves the consequences of sin in place so that he might achieve in them a good purpose.[20] By this argument, death for the regenerate functions as the "instrument by which life is reached."

Augustine's argument may or may not be convincing, but, interestingly, he employs the martyrs as exemplars of God's using evil for good and thereby lends his powerful voice to our theme. He observes that the martyrs' persecutors proposed the alternative "apostasy or death." He then reaches his conclusion: whereas in the beginning (in Adam's case) death came as the result of sin, now (in the martyr's case) *death comes by not sinning*. By the mercy of God, "the very punishment of

---

20. Augustine, *City of God*, 13.4.

wickedness has become the armor of virtue." Here the martyr is one who dies in order to keep from sinning, her death having the character of a protection against sin.

When Tertullian claimed that the blood of the martyrs was "seed," he pronounced a dictum full of the evangelical impetus. Yet to a great degree, the dictum's truth hangs upon the martyr's actual fidelity to the pattern of Christ's death, characterized at most points more by political submission than by resistance. Augustine would not have condoned forceful resistance in the context of tyrannical or despotic rule but would have pointed instead to one's own death as a powerful weapon. For whoever reconciles himself with his own death and comes to see it in the brightness of God's grace, a freedom emerges wherein one might actually employ death against one's persecutors. Such a death, though it appears to play into the hands of tyrannical rulers, may assist in exposing to the broader public their real intentions and cruelties in ways that are otherwise impossible, and in ways that bring counterpressures to bear through public resentment and outrage. "To be killed rather than kill confounds the killer"[21] and brings into bold relief the contrast between persecutor and persecuted. More than a millennium after Augustine, Martin Luther would echo his sentiments. It was, he thought, one of God's miracles that he does not accomplish things by force but rather by the suffering and death of his saints.[22]

Ironically, in the moment of execution the victim may become stronger than her executioners. Again Tertullian: with the Spirit "you gain power, when you are before the eyes of men."[23] The ironic shift of power from persecutor to persecuted happens largely because the victim is proportionally more innocent. The resulting contrast can elicit faith. According to the Markan tradition, just as death overcame Jesus the Roman centurion facing him expressed his conviction: "Truly this man was God's Son!" (Mark 15:39). One could attribute the evangelical success of Jesus' martyrdom to his innocence, his body "the canvas on which the portrait of their sins can be most clearly drawn," and "the more innocent the victim, the clearer the focus."[24]

More often than not the portrait is rejected, though in this case God may still use it as a means of judgment. However, the dominant interest

---

21. Winston A. Van Horne, "St Augustine: Death and Political Resistance," *Journal of Religious Thought* 38 (fall-winter 1981–1982): 34–50.

22. Martin Brecht, *Martin Luther*, 3 vols., trans. James L. Schaaf (Minneapolis: Fortress, 1990), 2:349.

23. Tertullian, *De fuga in persecutione*, 9.

24. Marilyn McCord Adams, "Redemptive Suffering," in *Rationality, Religious Belief, and Moral Commitment: New Essays in the Philosophy of Religion*, ed. Robert Audi and William J. Wainwright (Ithaca, N.Y.: Cornell University Press, 1986), 258.

of the tradition is the redemptive *possibility* such portraits offer to the onlooker. This possibility lies in the background of Origen's treatment of martyrdom, where the martyrs' fruit is identified with the spiritual progeny they may leave behind. Attempting to provide encouragement and solace for his great friend who had been put in prison during the persecution of Maximinus sometime near A.D. 235, Origen says that should Ambrose weather this "winter's storm," God will recognize his seed even as he has the seed of Abraham. Those who endure to the end produce spiritual children. As "the baptism of martyrdom, as received by our Savior, atones for the world; so too, when we receive it, it serves to atone for many."[25]

Kierkegaard provided some insight on this matter as well in one of his riveting journal entries:

> The first form of rulers in the world were the "tyrants," the last will be the "martyrs". . . . Between a tyrant and a martyr there is of course an enormous difference, although they both have one thing in common: the power to compel. The tyrant, himself ambitious to dominate, compels people through his power; the martyr, himself unconditionally obedient to God, compels others through his suffering. The tyrant dies and his rule is over; the martyr dies and his rule begins. The tyrant was egoistically the individual who inhumanely made the others into "the masses," and ruled over the masses; the martyr is the suffering individual who educates others through his Christian love of mankind, translating the masses into individuals—and there is joy in heaven over every individual whom he thus saves out of the masses.[26]

Seizing upon the early Christian *acta*, Anabaptist theologies of martyrdom made innocence a prerequisite for the redemptive impact of the martyr's death. As the spotless Lamb went to his sacrifice without defense or provocation, his disciples too, like sheep among wolves, must follow him wherever he goes.[27]

It seems a stretch, however, to make innocence the central aspect of martyrdom, or even, in the vein of Tertullian's dictum, to connect it too tightly to the further growth of the church. For one thing, among Christ's

---

25. Origen, *Exhortation to Martyrdom*, 4.30–39. A good bit of autobiography lies behind this statement, for Origen sees himself as a spiritual child of his father Leonidas's martyrdom in A.D. 202 under the reign of Septimius Severus. Origen was seventeen years old at the time.

26. Søren Kierkegaard, *The Journals of Kierkegaard*, ed. Alexander Dru (New York: Harper and Row, 1958), 151.

27. A representative treatment of the Anabaptist view can be found in Ethelbert Stauffer, "The Anabaptist Theology of Martyrdom," *Mennonite Quarterly Review* 19, no. 3 (1945): 179–214.

followers "innocence" can be found only among the guilty, and only in degrees, partly because of the at times ambiguous nature of moral life in general and partly because a Christian life is intelligible only in the dialectics of sin and grace. Further, it is doubtful whether "innocence" can illumine the more subtle and complex aspects of Jesus' death.

Still, one must make room for certain gradations in the deaths of those martyrs who in greater and lesser proportion bring forward their witness in either transparency or opaqueness to Christ. As if to boost the impact upon readers, the redactor of Polycarp's martyrdom slipped right into the middle of the fiery narrative the comment that Polycarp "had always been honored for holiness of life."[28] Conversely, the absence of a credible reputation could apparently precipitate a review of the deceased's status. On at least one occasion, the holiness of a martyr was opened to reinvestigation and the title revoked because in the popular view of the community some basic element of innocence was lacking.[29] Even when the life of the martyr was not exemplary, her martyrdom might achieve the forgiveness of sin, as, for example, in the well-publicized doctrine that martyrdom constituted a baptism of blood. Martyrdom itself was a grace that accomplished both justification and sanctification.

Therefore, the best way to characterize the kind of innocence one must exhibit to qualify for the title martyr is not the high standard of Jesus' sinlessness, nor some lofty standard of general holiness, but rather the innocence of nonprovocation in the events directly related to the death itself. That is, in the temporal stream of occasions that mark the movement from confession to suffering and death, one may neither instigate any phase in the process nor surrender to any violent or retaliatory impulses that might be construed by one's persecutors as attacking, taunting, or ridiculing. Naturally, one must not abandon one's confession.

One striking feature of the *acta* is the belief that the final struggle is not really between the martyr and her persecutors at all. Instead it is a struggle before God for the preservation of one's confession and, as the accounts testify almost unanimously, the struggle against the devil.

---

28. *Martyrdom of Polycarp*, 13.

29. A monk loyal to Cyril of Alexandria named Ammonius, offended by the "pagan idolatry" of one of the provincial governors, threw a stone and wounded him. He was apprehended, tortured, and killed. Afterward his body was deposited in a church, and Cyril "ordered him to be enrolled among the martyrs," eulogizing him as "one who had fallen in a conflict in defence of piety." However, the account continues, "the more sober-minded, although Christians, did not accept Cyril's prejudiced estimate of him; for they well knew that he had suffered the punishment due to his rashness, and that he had not lost his life under the torture because he would not deny Christ." See Socrates, *Ecclesiastical History*, 7.14.

Consequently, prayers to God and renunciations of the devil who stands behind the actions of the persecutors are common. In such circumstances, the martyr is obliged to demonstrate love and compassion for her persecutors and even to pray for their forgiveness as Jesus himself did. This "innocence" holds sufficient capacity to join the martyr's ordeal together with Christ. Most early Christian martyrdoms were extended temporally in a volley of threats, tortures, requests for recantation, and the like. Thus a sufficient amount of time elapsed wherein there might be created in the minds of the persecutors and onlookers a relationship of trust between the martyr's ordeal and the content of her confession. Onlookers detect the martyr's courage (though it could also be seen as foolishness), but that does not dominate the horizon of the *acta*. What comes across most clearly is the intentional self-identification of the martyr with Christ. In the best of scenarios, the martyr becomes transparent to Christ, lifting the gaze of those assembled to the goodness God has shown.[30] Accomplishing this does not require absolute innocence on the part of the martyr. It takes only enough innocence to deflect the cynicism of persecutors and onlookers, that is, only enough to prevent the explaining away of the martyr's actions in terms of religious heroism, triumphalism, or some more veiled form of self-interest.

The Political Dimension of Martyrdom

Speaking of Justin Martyr, as well as all those who were inspired by the likes of him, Elaine Pagels writes that the Christian tradition has often missed the fact that he was not simply following his religious convictions but offering a public challenge. As far as Justin was concerned, the Roman gods sanctioned by the state were more than benign fictions. They were euphemisms used by sophisticated pagans to refer to the spiritual elements of the universe. Justin believed in those cosmic forces no less than the Roman emperors, but his interpretation of them was that they were demonic and hence responsible for the whole spectrum of social injustices visited upon Christians like him. Enlightened people like Socrates and Jesus had perceived the truth about the demonic, and each brought it out into the open in ways that cost him his life.[31]

The Rome of Justin's day would accede to his challenge no more than Athens to that of Socrates. In the face of what must have seemed, at least to the majority of the populace, the petty obligation of sacrificing to the gods, Christians were at best ridiculously obstinate and noncompliant and at worst subversive to the social order. Yet from the perspective of

---

30. Adams, "Redemptive Suffering," 259.
31. Elaine Pagels, *Adam, Eve and the Serpent* (New York: Random House, 1988), 43.

those who had learned to see the true forces at work behind the imperial demands, there was more at stake than political submission. Christ, to whom God had given the ultimate authority in the cosmos, would be betrayed. In order for Justin to offer a faithful witness in such a context, entanglement in the political sphere was a moral necessity.

Perhaps one might even say that it was an ontological necessity. St. Paul, plumbing the depths of the mystery of Christ crucified, had come to the conclusion that the unseen forces of the universe were exposed, and consequently disarmed, precisely because Jesus made a public example of them on the cross (Col. 2:15). The terrible predicament of Justin, who would himself follow the lead of the crucified Christ, was that he, like most martyrs, did not despise the Roman authorities themselves. Instead he urged Christians to pay taxes and pray for emperors and sovereigns.[32] The authorities were not demons, but merely the tools of demons.[33] This helps to explain how Christians could express concern for the Roman rulers, pray for them, and appeal to them for understanding even while they were so recalcitrant toward Christians' demands. Similarly, St. Paul could speak of Jesus' public confrontation with the powers and at the same time urge honor and respect for the governing authorities. The faithful martyr does not so much witness against the politicians as against the powers that drive them.

Writing about Jesus' dealings with the powers, John Howard Yoder concludes that Jesus broke their sovereignty, because his

> life brought him, as any genuinely human existence will bring anyone, to the cross. In his death the Powers—in this case the most worthy, weighty representatives of Jewish religion and Roman politics—acted in collusion. Like everyone, he too was subject (but in his case quite willingly) to these powers. He accepted his own status of submission. But morally he broke their rules by refusing to support them in their self-glorification; and that is why they killed him. . . .
>
> His very obedience unto death is in itself not only the sign but also the firstfruits of an authentic restored humanity. Here we have for the first time to do with a man who is not the slave of any power, of any law or custom, community or institution, value or theory. Not even to save his own life will he let himself be made a slave of these Powers. This authentic humanity included his free acceptance of death at their hands.[34]

32. Hugo Rahner, *Church and State in Early Christianity,* trans. Leo Donald Davis (San Francisco: Ignatius, 1992), 23.

33. Pagels, *Adam, Eve,* 47.

34. John Howard Yoder, *The Politics of Jesus,* 2d ed. (Grand Rapids: Eerdmans, 1994), 145.

When followers of Jesus are willing to share his fate, they "despoil with him the principalities and powers and triumph with him."[35] With a tinge of irony, one could argue that the public and political dimension of the martyr's death discloses the deeply secular quality of Christ's lordship. In precisely those places where Christ is presumed not to rule, martyrs participate with Christ to make known the truth that, despite appearances, the powers of this age are not ultimate.[36]

Of course, the demonic may threaten from within the church as easily as from without. Among the purposes martyrdom served was that of distinguishing orthodox Christians from heretics. Gnostics, Docetists, and any others who denied the crucifixion of God in the flesh had either played down the necessity of martyrdom or dismissed it altogether.[37] Tertullian, writing amid persecution, likens the devil to a scorpion that, through the heretical views of the Valentinians, repeatedly stings the church. While orthodox Christians had locked themselves in battle, hemmed in and pursued from all sides and subjected to cruel instruments of torture, heretics were roaming about freely. Not only that, but preying upon the natural fear of suffering, they were teaching that martyrdom is unnecessary. Thus they roused the ire of a stalwart like Tertullian. The opponents of martyrdom, he retorted, prefer "this wretched life to that most blessed one," turning "sweet to bitter" and "light to dark." More important, by tempting the weak away from martyrdom they are encouraging idolatry. Idolatry is the devil's "sting." Martyrdom is Christ's cure. Just as the Israelites chased after the idols of Baal and Astarte and were therefore given up to their enemies, so it will be with those who imagine they can release a pinch of incense to Caesar and still remain in good standing with God. Martyrdom is God's weapon of choice against idolatry.[38]

Similarly, in his *Letter to the Smyrnaeans,* Ignatius emphasized repeatedly against the Docetists the physical reality of Christ's passion, resurrection, and postresurrection appearances. The Docetists keep themselves away from the Eucharist, he points out, because they cannot accept it as the flesh of Christ.[39] Neither are they concerned with

35. Origen, *Exhortation to Martyrdom*, 42.

36. Even while working in his so-called pacifist period Bonhoeffer saw the inevitably political nature of Christian life. He called the church a *polis* by God's design and admitted that it would necessarily impinge upon public life. See *DBWE* 4, 261.

37. I wish to express my gratitude to David F. Wright, ["The Testimony of Blood: The Charisma of Martyrdom" *Bibliotheca Sacra* (October–December, 2003)] for alerting me to the importance of Ignatius and Tertullian for this theme.

38. Tertullian *Scorpiace*.

39. Johannes Quasten and Joseph C. Plumpe, gen. eds., *Ancient Christian Writers* (New York, N.Y./Ramsey, N.J.: Newman Press, 1946–present), vol. 1: *The Epistles of St. Clement of Rome and St. Ignatius of Antioch*, trans. James A. Kleist, 92.

"works of charity, nor widows, nor orphans, nor the distressed, nor those in prison or out of it, nor the hungry or thirsty."[40] If Ignatius can attain to a death like his Lord's, he will become a witness against the heretics. As a man on the way to martyrdom, Ignatius considers the suffering and sacrifice of his own body useless if Christ had only a "make-believe" body. Like Peter and those who actually saw and touched Christ's flesh and then proceeded to die as martyrs, it will be not a ghostly but a solid and fleshy Jesus who will enable him to overcome death.

In the final analysis, the enemy lurking behind the politicians is identical to the enemy that chips away within the ranks of the Christians. In either case, martyrdom serves to expose the enemy as an opponent of the truth.

40. Ibid.

5

New Letters in an Old Alphabet

In many ways, declares Jesus, the attitude of the world and its authorities will help to determine his true followers.

Desmond Tutu

In *Ohnmacht und Mündigkeit* (Powerlessness and Coming of Age), Eberhard Bethge explores modern martyrdom as a common problem for Protestants and Catholics. While doing so, he dredges up a gem from the German theological tradition when he quotes from Michael Baumgarten (1812–1889), professor of Old Testament in Rostock:

> There are times in which speeches and writings no longer suffice to make clear the essential truth. In such times, the deeds and sufferings of the saints must create a *new alphabet* in order to reveal afresh the secret of truth.[1]

Bethge was the first to attempt any interpretation of Bonhoeffer along the lines of a "new alphabet." He suggested some characteristics of martyrs based on a mixture of early and modern materials: (1) freely chosen suffering, (2) rejection of self-sought martyrdom, (3) solidarity of guilt, (4) authentic Christian character, and (5) the authority of death.

I did not discover Bethge's seminal work until my thinking about martyrdom had advanced to a significant degree. Upon finding a clear

---

1. Michael Baumgarten, quoted in Eberhard Bethge, *Ohnmacht und Mündigkeit: Beitrage zur Zeitgeschichte und Theologie nach Dietrich Bonhoeffer* (München: Chr. Kaiser Verlag, 1969), 135. Translation and emphasis mine.

correspondence between his insights and my own, however, I had a renewed confidence that my direction was similar to that of Bonhoeffer's
faithful friend and leading interpreter. As I see it now, in many ways this
book represents a logical development of Bethge's insights.

Bonhoeffer himself seemed quite aware that a new world situation
was bound to transform our understanding of martyrdom. Preaching
at the Kaiser-Wilhelm Memorial Church in Berlin on 19 June 1932,
he speculated that a time was approaching when the blood of martyrs
would flow again in his own church, only it would not be as guiltless and
gleaming as that of the first witnesses.[2] Blood stained with guilt—this
would be a feature of modern martyrs. In 1938, in view of the coming
war, seminary student Hans-Werner Jensen observed something about
Bonhoeffer's views on martyrdom that astounded his fellow students for
its sheer novelty. Their teacher apparently believed it was worthwhile
for a Christian to die for the sake of worldly freedom, thus challeng-
ing the older notion that a martyr had to die exclusively for the sake
of Christ. As a result of Bonhoeffer's thinking on this matter, it was
no longer easy for the students to distinguish between religious and
political grounds for their activities.[3]

In this chapter I aim for three interrelated goals. First, I demonstrate
how modern martyrdom expands our understanding of the *imitatio
Christi*. Second, using a template of the "classic form" of martyrdom, I
trace significant external correspondences between Bonhoeffer's journey
toward death and the progression that typifies the narratives of the early
acta. Third, I explore Bonhoeffer's own disposition toward death and
martyrdom, showing its fidelity to the *imitatio Christi* theme.

Modern Martyrdom: New Letters in the Alphabet

Previously, I examined the evolution of the term *martyr* from its
New Testament meaning of life-witness to its classical expression
in the second century. I argued that the deaths of Christian martyrs
in the Roman Empire were logically included in Christ's death. The
conscious appropriation of the *imitatio Christi* motif in the early *acta*
suggested to early followers of Christ that they must neither prefer

2. *GS* 4:71.
3. Wolf-Dieter Zimmermann, *Bruder Bonhoeffer: Einblicke in ein hoffnungsvolles Leben*
(Berlin: Wichern Verlag, 1995): p. 93. Zimmermann recounts discussions that took place
during 1938–1939 in Gross-Schlönwitz, where Bonhoeffer was still training seminarians
after the closure of the Finkenwalde Seminary. During this time, Bonhoeffer had dictated
the text of *Life Together* to Jensen.

nor evade the rejection and persecution he endured. My argument assumed that the evolutionary course of the word *martyr* is best understood within the framework of Christianity and its Founder, with the peculiarity of the Roman sociopolitical matrix functioning as an external catalyst for development.

What cannot be explained so easily from within, however, is the swift temporal movement from the act of confession to death so characteristic in these *acta*. The public taunts, torture, and predilection for clear verbal confessions of faith with which the authorities besieged Christians in the early centuries constituted a phenomenon more or less unique to the Roman Empire. Not accidentally, writes Bowersock, "the early martyrdoms provide a checklist of the most prosperous and important cities of the eastern Roman empire," because "spectacle was an important element in martyrdom in the early church." It is quite clear that the gruesome deaths of Christians were a form of public entertainment, which explains why "no early martyr was taken aside discreetly and executed out of sight, just as no interrogations were conducted in small towns." Assigning the contests to urban centers and orchestrating them on major holidays, the Roman governors gave them the greatest public profile.[4] Of course with large crowds attending these events, often in the city amphitheater, Christians too capitalized on their visibility, using their public profile to give the strongest possible public witness for their faith. A great part of the crowd's excitement lay in the unpredictability of the outcome. Thus the taunts and tortures were designed specifically to heighten the contest and move the Christian toward either a confession of faith or a recantation.

Modern-day oppressors do not regularly give their victims the opportunity to confess faith under these conditions. Granted, one may still find among modern martyrs cases where the choice between apostasy and death is very clear and thus directly analogous to early Christianity. More often than not, however, the patent connection between confession and death disappears, leaving us to deal with a more ambiguous temporal correlation. Commenting on this difficulty in our time, Susan Bergman observes:

> A martyr's determination has been complicated by political or racial difference layered over the issue of direct spiritual opposition, making a martyr's choice whether to continue to follow a spiritual call and remain in known danger or to cease, whether to stay in the path of jeopardy or whether to find another place to serve.[5]

4. See G. W. Bowersock, *Martyrdom and Rome* (Cambridge: Cambridge University Press, 1995), 41–57.

5. Susan Bergman, "Twentieth-Century Martyrs," in *Martyrs: Contemporary Writers on Modern Lives of Faith*, ed. Susan Bergman (San Francisco: HarperSanFrancisco, 1996), 4.

Other writers on the subject relate similar concerns, suggesting that the strict requirement of dying directly for one's testimony of faith amounts to an "oversimplification" and that when sufficient background work is provided, martyrs more often than not die in circumstances *related to* their witness.[6] A set of questions arises: Do modern martyrs require a more nuanced theological treatment? Can one justify moving away from the classical understanding? Can we elaborate or broaden the classical understanding without cheapening the achievements of the early martyrs?

It seems to me that one can find a foothold for answering these questions within the early martyrdoms themselves. On the one hand, early Christian martyrs died because they were sensitive to the reality of the crucified Christ and because, in deference to him, they preferred confessing and dying to flight or denial. Yet unlike suicide, martyrdom requires oppressors and executioners. Someone *else* must decide for the martyr's death. Though at times popular uprisings—not politically motivated—against Christians did and still do occur, the vast majority of Christianity's martyrs have come into conflict with the political machinery of their day. In early Christianity, for example, the stark alternative put to believers was none other than "God or Caesar." In the eyes of Christians, lighting incense to a deified Roman emperor was as reprehensible as worshiping the Roman deities assimilated from the Greeks. A yes to Caesar meant the "religious" transgression of idolatry and political protection; a no to Caesar meant religious fidelity and political subversion. The question was not so much *whether* a crime was going to be committed as *against whom*.

This political connection is not accidental. Since Christian faith possesses some propensity not merely toward confession but toward a confession that leads to concrete earthly actions in pursuit of love, justice, peace, and so on—that is, since Christian faith involves ethics—it impinges necessarily upon the *polis*. Of course, martyrdom's political dimension in and of itself does not make a case for a broadened theological treatment. But variations in political structure and the application of power from one situation to the next do provide an entrance point into the complexities of confession and death.

Karl Rahner anchored his plea for a broadening of the classical concept of martyrdom in the distinction between "free, tolerant acceptance of death for the sake of the faith" and "death suffered in the active struggle for the Christian faith." Typically, the latter category has been the basis for excluding those like soldiers from the ranks of the martyrs.

---

6. James Hefley and Marti Hefley, *By Their Blood: Christian Martyrs of the Twentieth Century* (Milford, Mich.: Mott Media, 1979), vii (preface).

Not everyone who struggles actively for Christian faith deserves to be a martyr, says Rahner, because secular motives are too pervasive and it is difficult to tell whether a genuine acceptance of death is present. But when evidence of free acceptance accompanies active struggle, as in the case of Catholic Archbishop Oscar Romero (one of Rahner's chief interests), "who died while fighting for justice in society, a struggle waged out of the depths of his conviction as a Christian," Rahner finds just cause for further deliberation.

Jesus himself brings together these two kinds of death:

> First of all, the death Jesus "passively endured" was the consequence of the struggle he waged against those in his day who wielded religious and political power. He died because he fought: his death must not be seen in isolation from his life. Putting this argument the other way around, someone who dies while fighting actively for the demands of his or her Christian convictions . . . can also be said patiently to endure his or her death. It is not death directly sought for itself. It includes a passive element, just as the death of a martyr in the usual sense includes an active element, since by his or her active witness and life this kind of martyr has conjured up the situation in which he or she can only escape death by denying his or her faith.[7]

A host of late-twentieth-century scholarly publications support Rahner's viewpoint and seem to render problematic the conventional portrait of Jesus as a passive recipient of death. Among these publications, I cite as examples Richard Horsley's *Jesus and the Spiral of Violence* and the posthumous G. B. Caird's *New Testament Theology*, each of which gives voice to an emerging consensus.

Horsley shows that passive portraits of Jesus have depended chiefly either on the Zealots as a foil for Jesus' position or on an interpretation of Jesus' command to "love your enemies" that emphasizes the universal aspect. When these two pillars are chipped away, a new portrait emerges. If Jesus' many pronouncements of forgiveness, exorcism, and opening of the kingdom of God to the poor are investigated in their imperial context, it becomes clear to Horsley that "Jesus aggressively intervened to mitigate or undo the effects of institutionalized violence." Just as surely as Jesus understood the political repercussions of his own actions, he surely left his disciples with no illusions about their future. As evidenced in the saying about taking up one's cross (Mark 8:34 and parallels), he understood they were as likely as he to be executed as rebels. From the standpoint of worldly rulers, then, "the crucifixion of Jesus was not a

---

7. Karl Rahner, "Dimensions of Martyrdom," in *Martyrdom Today*, ed. Johannes-Baptist Metz and Edward Schillebeeckx (New York: Seabury, 1983), 9–11.

mistake. . . . The charges brought against him, however apologetically handled by the gospel writers, were in effect true. . . . He had definitely been stirring up the people."[8]

Caird put his conclusion concerning Jesus' death even more tersely:

> If he found himself at the end embroiled in a political crisis which resulted in his execution on the order of a Roman governor, it was not because he avoided politics. *It was because for him politics and theology were inseparable.*[9]

Since it would have been impossible to draw a hard and fast distinction between politics and theology in first-century Palestinian life, and since Jesus the Jew would have understood God's aims for Israel as inherently *national*, Jesus could not have avoided politics. His important decision to go to Jerusalem rather than remain in the Galilean countryside reveals that, for him, any strict apartheid between politics and religion was impossible. Though crusted over by centuries of piety, the "inexorable fact" about the Gospels, says Caird, is that Jesus' teaching, and therewith his death, has a strong political element.

Naturally, politics isn't the only explanation for Jesus' death. From the perspective of institutional religion, it appears to be the price of blasphemy and contempt for the law. One might also see it simply as fulfillment of Jewish prophecy, or perhaps pious subjection to the will of God. However, while the political angle may be only one of several, recent studies show that it simply cannot be overlooked.

Aside from recent scholarship, martyrs of the twentieth century themselves have helped bring this political element to our attention. Rahner is particularly interested in the case of Salvadoran archbishop Oscar Romero,[10] but other instances come to mind: the 156 South Africans,

8. Richard Horsley, *Jesus and the Spiral of Violence* (San Francisco: Harper and Row, 1987), 318–26.

9. G. B. Caird, *New Testament Theology*, completed and ed. L. D. Hurst (Oxford: Clarendon, 1994), 345–69. The above quotation is found on p. 357.

10. In the Louvain address given less than two months before his death, Romero explained the political dimension of his own work: "I am going to speak to you simply as a pastor, as one who, together with his people, has been learning the beautiful but harsh truth that the Christian faith does not cut us off from the world but immerses us in it, that the church is not a fortress set apart from the city. The church follows Jesus who lived, worked, battled and died in the midst of a city, the polis." For Romero's address, see Archbishop Oscar Romero, "The Church's Mission amid the National Crisis," *Voice of the Voiceless: The Four Pastoral Letters and Other Statements* (Maryknoll, N.Y.: Orbis, 1985), 138. For a comparison of Bonhoeffer and Romero see Geffrey B. Kelly, "Bonhoeffer and Romero," *Theology and the Practice of Responsibility*, ed. Wayne Whitson Floyd Jr. and Charles Marsh (Valley Forge, Penn.: Trinity Press International, 1994), 85–105.

black and white, who were charged with treason and executed in 1956 for their campaign of defiance against apartheid; the three Mirabel sisters, who were pushed off a steep mountain road in the Dominican Republic for their participation in a plot against the dictator Leonidas Trujillo; Ugandan bishop Janani Luwum, who protested injustice and called Idi Amin to account for abusing his God-given authority; Martin Luther King Jr., preacher and lover of the church, murdered for trying correct the church's social neglect. Political entanglements are a salient feature in each of these cases, and scores of others. None of these persons came into the political sphere because they derived a political program from their faith which they subsequently tried to implement. Rather they were impelled by the variable circumstances of their world to engage themselves politically as an extension of their extant confession of faith. They could do nothing else:

> To stand apart from the complex and often morally corrupt world of political involvement and responsibility in the name of Jesus Christ is to dishonour that name—the name of one who was hauled before the authorities precisely because his "saving work" was perceived to be (and really was!) political.[11]

In the broadest possible sense, martyrdom has always been political. Polycarp, the Lyons martyrs, and a host of others were objects of political oppression no less than their twentieth-century counterparts. Yet there is a difference. Whereas in the early period the Christian identity of martyrs as such was sufficient to render them objects of political oppression, today's martyrs become objects of political oppression because they are first *subjects* who engage themselves politically in the interest of human justice. Though harder to recognize in the case of the contemporary martyr, Christian identity is fundamental to both.

So long as Jesus remains constitutive for a theology of martyrdom, yet another dimension of his death comes into consideration here: its vicarious and sacrificial nature. Jesus is depicted as the Suffering Servant who in dying receives the sins of the whole world. According to the Christian story, Jesus' death represents others, includes others, and redeems others. Under the *imitatio Christi* the Christian may also be required to reach toward the outer limit of love and "lay down one's life for one's friends" (John 15:13).[12] Is it not clear that for persons like Bonhoeffer, Kolbe, Romero, and King, speaking and acting on behalf

11. Douglas John Hall, *Confessing the Faith: Christian Theology in a North American Context* (Minneapolis: Fortress, 1996), 378.
12. John 15:13 NRSV.

of others was a constituent feature of their life and death? Anyone who comes to terms with the social nature of the body of Christ can avoid the sufferings of others only at the peril of his own soul. "God has so arranged the body, giving the greater honor to the inferior member," wrote Paul, such that "if one member suffers, all suffer together with it" (1 Cor. 12:24–26).

We might, then, consider the merit of a twofold claim. *First, because by virtue of Christ a believer's life is inextricably bound up with other lives, he may, under certain oppressive conditions, and with reasoned Christian convictions, enter freely into the political arena under the calculation that while he may be gravely endangering his own future, the futures of others might be improved. Should that person suffer death in the process, he becomes a martyr, for he has imitated Christ by laying down his life for his friends.* In the twentieth century, the confession "I am a Christian" has not normally been a sufficient cause for propelling persons into the web of politics; instead it has been the concrete commitment of one's life and labor to the neighbor which grows out of deep convictions concerning the social nature of Christian faith.[13] The form such commitment takes may be described as identification, solidarity, or participation with those who suffer.[14] At the critical point, where solidarity turns to a defense of those who suffer, political stands are inevitable.

Granted, it is difficult to measure when and where conditions for such political stands are ripe. Even more difficult is the task of isolating one's highest and purest motivation from the broader nexus of personal concerns. Further, there are the existential difficulties of decision-making, of calculating and weighing in advance the larger consequences of political action. Is it reasonable to assume that a particular word or deed will alleviate the sufferings of others, or will it perhaps place them in direr straits? What are the chances of success? Yet despite numerous a priori and a posteriori difficulties attending this elaborated understanding,

13. Leonardo Boff has taken up this theme, using Thomas Aquinas as an ally. According to Aquinas, "Human good can become divine good if it is referred to God; therefore, any human good can be a cause of martyrdom, in so far as it is referred to God." It would follow, then, that Christians who incur death for the sake of their brothers and sisters are no less martyrs than those of old who confessed *"Christianus sum"* and then accepted their fate. Boff also points out that Aquinas objected to the claim that "only faith in Christ gives those who suffer the glory of martyrdom" by stipulating that those who are of Christ also perform actions in the spirit of Christ. See Leonardo Boff, "Martyrdom: An Attempt at Systematic Reflection," in *Martyrdom Today*, ed. Johannes-Baptist Metz and Edward Schillebeeckx (New York: Seabury, 1983), 12–17.

14. Reflecting on a sample set of three twentieth-century martyrs—Maria Skobtsova, Jon Daniels, and Waldo Williams—A. M. Allchin finds two consistent features: "the value attached to voluntary acceptance, and the insistence upon participation, solidarity, identification." See A. M. Allchin, "Martyrdom," *Sobornost* 6, no. 1 (1984): 19–29.

difficulties visited upon martyrs and their communities alike, the fact remains that many persons have sacrificed themselves in the effort to achieve justice for others precisely on a Christian basis. If we elaborate classical martyrdom in this way, we shall have to be more cautious and more deliberate with our ascriptions, but in so doing we will be bringing to fuller expression some essential features of Jesus' life and death. An elaborated understanding of martyrdom and an elaborated understanding of Christ are correlative.

At the risk of attenuating the first part of the above claim, I propose a second. *Since political intervention on behalf of groups cannot be assumed to be action exclusively on behalf of Christians, but in a great number of cases extends to "humanity," and since the intervention is nonetheless undertaken for Christian reasons, martyrs (in the above sense) may be said to have pushed their ultimate horizons to the kingdom of God.* In this they share remarkably the essential concerns of Jesus. Of all the advances in twentieth-century biblical scholarship, perhaps none has been more influential than the rediscovery of the kingdom as the primary horizon for Jesus' life and teaching. What reasons could be given to safeguard a theology of martyrdom from such an important development? The time has come to see to it that the repercussions of this important advance work their way into some of the more remote channels of theological reflection.

Most (but not all) pioneers—and there are not many—in this direction have come from the adherents of liberation theology. John Sobrino writes of a kenotic love that must involve itself in politics and that leads, "almost *ex opere operato*," to persecution and death. "Politics is necessary for holiness" because it is the way the poor may receive the good news of the kingdom and the way the church may recover the foundation of its kingdom mission.[15] Sobrino calls those who die in defending others "Jesus Martyrs." The political powers kill them not so much from hatred of faith *(odium fidei)* as from hatred of justice *(odium iustitiae).* Their martyrdom is not because of Christ but because they are like Christ, looking after others as the Good Shepherd looks after the sheep.[16]

Enda McDonagh, writing in the Irish context, finds that the kingdom aptly joins the martyr's cause with Jesus' cause:

> Despite the obvious connection between the Church community and kingdom of God, Christian martyrs do not die solely or even primarily

---

15. Jon Sobrino, "Political Holiness: A Profile," in *Martyrdom Today,* ed. Johannes-Baptist Metz and Edward Schillebeeckx (New York: Seabury, 1983), 18–23.

16. Jon Sobrino, "Our World: Cruelty and Compassion," in *Rethinking Martyrdom,* ed. Teresa Okure, Jon Sobrino, and Felix Wilfred (London: SCM, 2003), 19.

for the sake of the Church community but for the kingdom which may be seeking expression and demanding recognition within the bounds of the historical Church, in causes not explicitly religious. So much the central-ity of love of neighbor to the appearance and practice of the kingdom should always tell us.[17]

While in Bonhoeffer's case I do not find this horizon absolutely nec-essary, it provides a spaciousness wherein his concern for Jews, replete with political manifestations and repercussions, can be traversed within the theme.

Bonhoeffer's Death in Light of the "Formal Pattern" of Jewish-Christian Martyrdom

In his monumental study "Martyr and Prophet,"[18] H. A. Fischel, after closely examining both Jewish and Christian *acta*, located what he called an "almost stereotyped scheme" of martyrdom. "The uniformity of these *martyria*," he suggested, makes a compelling case for "identification of the prophet with the martyr," a connection I noted earlier in Stephen. Here I am not interested in Fischel's theological rationale for the prophet-martyr identification. Instead I am interested in the overarching narra-tive pattern—that "stereotyped scheme"—by which Fischel united the numerous details of the Jewish and Christian *acta*. If Bonhoeffer's own death can be fitted reasonably into this scheme, then the case for the legitimacy of his martyrdom will have been strengthened.

According to Fischel, the following table comprises in chronological order the characteristic progression of events that mark the martyr's trail:

1. The martyr receives foreknowledge of his death.
2. He refuses to flee.
3. The great publicity of the trial.

---

17. Enda McDonagh, "An Irish Perspective on Martyrdom," in *Martyrdom Today*, ed. Johannes-Baptist Metz and Edward Schillebeeckx (New York: Seabury, 1983), 34.

18. Fischel belongs to a school of scholars who ascribe deep continuity to the Jewish and Christian literary patterns. This premise is not, of course, unanimously shared. The typical objection is that either Christian martyrdom is unique or it is not "Christian" at all. Once again, in view of the growing respect for Jewish categories of thought that Bon-hoeffer displayed in the course of his life, and especially his continued nourishment at the reservoir of Jesus' Jewishness, it seems more appropriate to accept what truth there is in the premise than to divert the discussion into this *aporia*. H. A. Fischel, "Martyr and Prophet," *Jewish Quarterly Review* 37 (1946–1947): 265–80, 363–86.

4. The significance of the special day (Sabbath, Passover, Day of Atonement, etc.).
5. The witnesses (often false ones) accuse the martyr.
6. The prosecutor ridicules or threatens the martyr.
7. The martyr refuses to retract.
8. He increases the offense by repetition, etc.
9. He ridicules or threatens the prosecutor (divine retribution).
10. He glorifies his cause.
11. He remains victorious in the last debate.
12. He comforts his disciples (adherents or relatives).
13. He pronounces his fate as just and/or forgives his torturers.
14. The tortures.
15. The miracle(s) counteracting them.
16. The martyr's strength of soul, even gladness.
17. The admiration of the executioner, prosecutor or onlookers.
18. The vision of the martyr.
19. His last words.
20. His angelic appearance.
21. Pronouncement of his immortality.
22. Miraculous signs in nature.
23. The saving of his corpse for burial.
24. The death of the tyrant.[19]

It will be obvious at once that not every feature of Fischel's scheme applies in Bonhoeffer's case. Strict adherence cannot be expected even among the individual *acta* of the early centuries. The scheme is proposed as a *pattern*, a composite sketch. I have already noted ancient Rome's love of sport and public taunt, which lent to the early *acta* certain peculiarities that did not follow in later historical periods, like 1940s Germany. Moreover, there is the matter of incomplete data in Bonhoeffer's case. In the final period of his life he was beset with writing restrictions and limited contact with the public, which effectively obscured many of the final details from public view (particularly the proceedings of the trial, so frequent in the early *acta*). So we should not be surprised that Bonhoeffer does not fit the pattern exactly.

Nonetheless, on the strength of both primary and secondary literature it remains possible to draw out some striking parallels. I will not parlay these narrative parallels into a formal argument. My aim is more modest: to illumine *plausible* connections between Fischel's version of the classic pattern of martyrdom and Bonhoeffer's trail to death. Hence,

19. Ibid., 384–385.

by means of narrative, I will underscore those features that do coincide with Fischel's pattern and ignore aberrant ones.

The Martyr Receives Foreknowledge of His Death

On numerous occasions, from his childhood to those final months following the failure of the 20 July 1944 plot, Bonhoeffer gives indication that his life will end in what might be described as a "heroic" death, though in his mature years the idea of heroism fades from view. Walter, the second of the Bonhoeffer children, was wounded in World War I and died five days later in a field hospital. The event sent shock waves through the Bonhoeffer family, creating a very tense and difficult situation especially for the parents. Dietrich's childhood reflections upon death began in this period, possibly as way to work through his parents' reactions to Walter's death:

> He liked thinking about death. Even in his boyhood he had liked to imagine himself on his death-bed, surrounded by all those who loved him, speaking his last words to them. Secretly he had often thought about what he would say at that moment. To him death was neither grievous nor alien. He would have liked to die young, to die a fine, devout death. He would have liked them all to see and understand that to a believer in God dying was not hard, but was a glorious thing.[20]

Bethge finds in this fragment "evidence of his life-long preoccupation with whether and how he would face up to death."[21] Kenneth Morris argues that the family tremors surrounding Walter's death are partly responsible for Dietrich's decision that same year to become a theologian, and even frame the essential context for the welding together of death and discipleship in his thought.

Sabine Leibholz-Bonhoeffer recalls an incident in 1937 at their parents' home. Dietrich was in bed from the flu. Gerhard Leibholz was bedside having a conversation with Dietrich, when suddenly Dietrich said to him, "You and I will not live long lives."[22]

In prison, much of Bonhoeffer's inner wrestling with death expressed itself in artistic form. In the opening scene of his drama fragment, which

---

20. An autobiographical reflection from Bonhoeffer's own hand, ostensibly dating from the year 1932. Bonhoeffer wrote of his own childhood in the third person. The quotation is taken from Bethge, *DB*, 38–39.

21. Ibid.

22. Sabine Leibholz-Bonhoeffer, *The Bonhoeffers: Portrait of a Family* (Chicago: Covenant, 1994), 43.

Bethge dates to spring and early summer 1943, a grandmother is reading to "Little Brother" a story about a hunter stalking an animal:

> GRANDMOTHER (reading): ". . . The hunter had stalked the wonderful animal for many days and weeks. Several times he had it in his sights, but didn't shoot. He couldn't stop feasting his eyes on the magnificence of this creature. But one evening at sunset it so happened that the animal stepped out of the woods right in front of him, looked at him with very calm eyes, and stood there without fear. Never before had the hunter seen the animal like that. A wild longing seized him to have it, not to give it up, not to let it escape again. He loved the animal so much that he could not part from it anymore. Very slowly he lifted the gun, eye to eye with the animal, a long last glance, a long lingering; then came the shot. Afterward all was very quiet, and the last rays of the evening sun fell reconcilingly and peacefully on the fallen creature and its hunter." (She closes the book and puts it down.) This is where we stop today, Little Brother. The end of the story is not in the book. But it most certainly continues; as a matter of fact, it really begins at this point.[23]

Ruth Zerner has noted the autobiographical character of this fragment. "We may assume," she writes, "that God is the hunter and that Bonhoeffer is the creature."[24] In a letter to his parents, Bonhoeffer mentioned "the outlines of a play" he had recently written, adding that it was about the life of a family and that "there is a good deal of autobiography mixed up with it."[25] The words of Grandmother as she lays the book down call to mind the words attributed to Bonhoeffer the day before his death: "This is the end—for me the beginning of life." The "calm eyes" of the animal as it stood "without fear," the spirit of the "evening sun" falling "reconcilingly and peacefully," the security of the hunter's love: these elements suggest that death was just over the horizon and that Bonhoeffer was coming to terms with it.

From 21 July 1944 to the end of his life, death was more certain. In the September 1944 poem "The Death of Moses" Bonhoeffer found the analogy that Martin Luther King Jr. would find a generation later. He was like the tired Moses of old, to whom God had shown the land from afar and then taken prematurely in death. The poem closes with these lines:

> Sinking, o God, into Eternity
> I see my people's stride is proud and free.

23. Dietrich Bonhoeffer, *Fiction from Prison: Gathering Up the Past*, ed. Renate Bethge and Eberhard Bethge, trans. Ursula Hoffmann (Philadelphia: Fortress, 1981), 14.
24. Ruth Zerner, in ibid., 161.
25. From the letter dated 17 August 1943. See Dietrich Bonhoeffer, *Letters and Papers from Prison* (hereafter cited as *LPP*), 4th ed. (New York, Macmillan, 1972), 94.

God, who punishes and then forgives,
this people I have truly loved now lives.

It is enough that I have borne its sorrow
and now have seen the land of its tomorrow.

Hold me fast!—for fallen is my stave,
O faithful God, make ready now my grave.[26]

When Bonhoeffer penned these lines, his fate had already been
sealed by the Gestapo's investigations. But a clear line of expectation
for an early death runs through his entire life. The facts of his constant danger from 1939 onward, when he returned from New York
and entangled himself in conspiratorial activities, dismiss the early
and middle musings about death as some form of romanticism. In
such a context he had learned to see himself as a guest and stranger
in this world.

The Martyr Refuses to Flee

While Bonhoeffer wrote *The Death of Moses*, he was considering the
possibility of escape. His family had obtained a mechanic's uniform
and managed to get it to Dietrich's "most faithful guard," Corporal
Knobloch, who according to plan would escort him to the gate while
on duty and disappear with him in the first days of October. However,
the arrest of Dietrich's brother Klaus on 1 October, together with the
Gestapo's close watch on the Bonhoeffer family, apparently made the
escape plan a moral impossibility for Bonhoeffer. Knobloch reported
to the Bonhoeffers that Dietrich had given up the escape plan "so as
not to make things more difficult for his brother and not to expose his
parents and fianceé to an extra danger."[27]

The rejection of flight at this critical point reflects more than humanitarian sensitivities. The 21 July 1944 letter to Eberhard Bethge reveals
that Bonhoeffer had been thinking about his predicament in terms of
Jesus' final days in the grip of worldly powers. One "becomes human
and a Christian," he wrote, by "living unreservedly in life's duties, problems, successes and failures, experiences and perplexities." In this way
"we throw ourselves completely into the arms of God . . . watching with
Christ in Gethsemane."[28] In that same letter he revealed also that he

26. *ATTF*, 520.
27. Bethge, *DB*, 826–28.
28. *ATTF*, 510.

had been reflecting on his earlier work *Discipleship*,[29] which, though in hindsight contained certain "dangers,"[30] he was unwilling to abandon. In the chapter that arguably epitomizes the book, Bonhoeffer wrote:

> The acts of the church's first martyrs give witness that Christ transfigures the moment of the greatest suffering for his followers through the indescribable certainty of his nearness and communion. . . . Bearing the cross proved to be for them the only way to overcome suffering. But this is true for all who follow Christ, because it was true for Christ himself. . . . Jesus prays to the Father that the cup pass from him, and the Father hears the son's prayer. The cup of suffering will pass from Jesus—*but only by his drinking it.*[31]

The clouds of death that hung over Bonhoeffer in October 1944 gathered, so to speak, at his own invitation. In the summer of 1939, after coming to New York for a second time at the urging of some Confessing Church pastors and the arranging of Reinhold Niebuhr, as I have earlier related, Bonhoeffer was restless and dissatisfied, daily second-guessing his decision. Judging from his diary entries in those weeks, he concluded it was a mistake to have come to America. Through meditation on his Bible readings and prayer, as he told Niebuhr, God was urging him to "live through this difficult period of [his] national history with the Christian people of Germany."[32] The diary entries contain frequent references to biblical texts on which he was meditating at the time. Two of them are pertinent here. On 26 June he was dwelling on Paul's request to Timothy, "Do your best to come before winter," adding, "That has been in my ears all day." Two days before, he had been preoccupied with a saying from Isaiah—"The one who believes does not flee" (Isa. 28:16)—boldly applying it to his own situation.[33] These observations are intended neither to

29. I am avoiding where possible the older and popular English title *The Cost of Discipleship*. Following the new critical English edition of *Nachfolge* in *DBWE*, I revert to the simple title *Discipleship*, sometimes followed by the German title *Nachfolge* in parentheses when I wish to underscore the idea of "following after."

30. "Dangers" can here be understood as a set of problems that arise from a particular reading of *Nachfolge* which unduly emphasizes the disciple's break from the world. On this reading, one might conclude that faith is acquired by living a holy life somehow detached from life's duties and problems. A careful reading of the work, especially in tandem with Bonhoeffer's later writings, does not support that conclusion, which is why Bonhoeffer could say he stood by it. At the same time, the book's austerity tempts the reader toward that dangerous conclusion. Following publication of *Nachfolge* (1937) Bonhoeffer's understanding of faith continued to widen. By 1944 he wished to emphasize that one learns to have faith *only* by living completely in this world with its many duties and problems.

31. *DBWE* 4, 89–90.

32. *ATTF*, 479.

33. *ATTF*, 474.

dismiss altruistic motives altogether nor clinch theological ones. What they show is simply that amidst danger and threat of death, Bonhoeffer's decisions were made irrespective of his own safety, that he accepted whatever consequences would come of his actions, and that some measure of theological reasoning was involved in these decisions.

The Martyr Refuses to Retract

We do not know precisely how Bonhoeffer conducted himself during the court proceedings the night of 8 April 1945. It is doubtful that any form of retraction was requested of him—his words could alter nothing at that point—and inconceivable that he would have obliged if it were. The following texts, taken once again from the series of Bonhoeffer's letters to Bethge during his incarceration at Tegel prison, suggest just the opposite frame of mind:

> Now I want to assure you that I haven't for a moment regretted coming back in 1939—nor any of the consequences, either. I knew quite well what I was doing, and I acted with a clear conscience. I've no wish to cross out of my life anything that has happened since, either to me personally . . . or as regards events in general.

> I'm often surprised how little (in contrast to nearly all the others here) I grub among my past mistakes and think how different one thing or another would be today if I had acted differently in the past; it doesn't worry me at all. Everything seems to have taken its natural course, and to be determined necessarily and straightforwardly by a higher providence. Do you feel the same?[34]

He Increases the Offense by Repetition

Much of Bonhoeffer's career (1935 to 1945) was marked by continued resistance—passive and active—against the political powers. Though the "offense" varied from one period to the next, it was civil disobedience throughout. Practically from its inception the Finkenwalde Seminary had operated illegally. Even after its closure by the Gestapo in 1937, Bonhoeffer reorganized it under the guise of "collective pastorates" in remote regions of Pomerania, where illegally he kept preparing ordinands until March 1940.[35]

---

34. The first quote is from the letter dated 22 December 1943, the second from the letter dated 22 April 1944. *LPP*, 174, 276.

35. Bethge, *DB*, 587–96.

From August 1939 until his arrest in 1943, Bonhoeffer served as a civilian agent in the Abwehr. Despite being ordered to desist from public speaking and to report regularly to the police, from this position he strategized illegally to save Jews and eventually to participate in tyrannicide. His aiding and abetting Jews in the plan code-named "U 7," under which a group of Jews were smuggled successfully from Germany to Switzerland, was the precipitating cause of his arrest, incarceration, and trial in 1943. Bonhoeffer's participation in illegal activities crescendoed in his travels abroad to publicize the details of Hitler's anti-Jewish campaign, finally reaching its climax in the elaborate plans for a coup d'état that included the killing of Hitler and the temporary reconstruction of Germany's government. During this chaotic time, Bonhoeffer's crimes against the state had "resolved into a race between assassination and arrest."[36]

He Comforts His Disciples

During the period 1936–1942, before and after the shutdown of Finkenwalde, Bonhoeffer delivered systematic pastoral care and comfort to his seminarians through a series of circular letters. During the prison years he gave continual comfort to his friend Eberhard Bethge by means of his letters, many of them obviously written with just this aim in mind.

There were no "disciples" to comfort in the early months of 1945, but Bonhoeffer radiated a warm optimism and encouraged those who shared these final days with him. Bomb damage to the "house prison" at Prinz-Albrecht-Strasse forced Bonhoeffer's transfer to Buchenwald on 7 February 1945. As they waited together in handcuffs for the transport, Munich lawyer Josef Müller remembers, Bonhoeffer urged him, "Let us go calmly to the gallows as Christians."[37]

The stay at Buchenwald was brief. By early April, Admiral Canaris's complete diary and travel reports were discovered, arousing the wrath of Hitler, who summarily ordered the execution of all the conspirators. Bonhoeffer knew his end was imminent. By mistake he was shuttled with other conspirators to Schönberg, where on Sunday, 8 April, he held a service for his comrades, mostly Catholic, but among them the atheistic Russian Korkorin. According to Bethge, he had not wanted to ambush Korkorin with a Christian service, but when Korkorin showed support, Bonhoeffer prayed and unfolded the texts for the day: "With his

36. Ibid., 752.
37. For a detailed chronicle of the events of the final days, see Bethge, *DB*, 894–933.

stripes we are healed" (Isa. 53:5) and "Blessed be the God and Father
of our Lord Jesus Christ! By his great mercy we have been born anew
to a living hope through the resurrection of Jesus Christ from the dead"
(1 Peter 1:3), applying them to the thoughts and decisions captivity had
produced in all of them. Payne Best records that Bonhoeffer "reached
the hearts of all, finding just the right words to reflect the spirit of our
imprisonment."[38] That Bonhoeffer's words brought encouragement is
corroborated by the fact that other prisoners tried to smuggle him to
their room so that he could hold a service for them as well. But the
mistaken detour to Schönberg was rectified before he could oblige. The
door was opened and the summons given: "Prisoner Bonhoeffer, get
ready and come with us!" He was driven to Flossenbürg and executed
Monday morning.

The Martyr Pronounces His Fate Just

Just after Bonhoeffer forfeited the escape plan, he wrote the poem
"Jonah."[39] The timing and the theme secure its autobiographical nature.
Likening himself to the Old Testament prophet, Bonhoeffer contemplated his fate:

In face of death they scream and clutch the storm-drenched ropes,
Their hands stretch for the strands of fleeting, dying hopes.
Their horror stricken eyes see only torments of the night,
While raging waves and winds unleash their awesome, lethal might.

"O goodly eternal gods, but wrathful now," they shout,
"To us your help extend or that culprit single out,
Who unbeknown to us offends your lofty majesty,
With heinous murder, breach of oath, or scornful blasphemy.

"Who from us sins that soil our souls does hide,
To save the wretched remnants of his pride."
And tearful thus they pled 'til Jonah said, "'Tis I!
I've sinned against my God and now deserve to die.

"Away from you, cast me you must. God's anger flies at me alone.
The sinless must not precious lives give up to sinner's deeds atone!"

They trembled ever more. But strengthened now their hands, their
    hearts with purpose filled,

38. S. Payne Best, *The Venlo Incident* (London: Hutchinson, 1950), 200.
39. Dated sometime around 5 October 1944. See *LPP*, 407 (note 32).

The guilty one they seized and flung into the deep. The wind-churned
seas were stilled.[40]

With its obvious admission of guilt and acceptance of the consequences, the poem amounts to a confession of his sin and acceptance
of his death, the just desert of "heinous murder, breach of oath, or
scornful blasphemy." In the Old Testament story, Jonah's guilt resides
in his flight from God's will (Jonah 1:10); there is no mention of murder
or the breaking of oaths. Thus, coupled with the final line of the third
stanza, "I've sinned against my God and now deserve to die" *(Ich sün-
digte vor Gott. Mein Leben is verwirkt)*, this line refers to Bonhoeffer's
specific crimes against the state and his acceptance of the penalty. In
view of the typological connection between Jonah and Christ, Bonhoeffer
could also be construing his death as a vicarious one for the "innocent"
crew—righteous Christians guilty of inaction—or even looking forward
to resurrection.

The Martyr's Strength of Soul, Even Gladness

It would be easy to imagine Bonhoeffer's last months in confinement
as the worst time of his incarceration. Yet here, as before, he stretched his
roots deeper in the crucified Christ. The yield was an exciting freshness
and certainty both in the theological arena, where God's nearness was
seen anew in God's own sufferings with the world, and in his personal
experience of joy in suffering. Meditating on the life and death of Jesus,
Bonhoeffer wrote:

> It is certain that we may always live close to God and in the light of his
> presence, and that such living is an entirely new life for us; that nothing
> then is impossible for us, because all things are possible with God; that no
> earthly power can touch us without his will, and that danger and distress
> can only drive us closer to him. It is certain that we can claim nothing
> for ourselves, and may yet pray for everything; it is certain that our joy is
> hidden in suffering, and our life in death; it is certain that in all this we
> are in a fellowship that sustains us. In Jesus God has said Yes and Amen
> to it all, and that Yes and Amen is the firm ground on which we stand.[41]

In the final letter that found its way to Bethge, Bonhoeffer expressed
his personal disposition in the first person:

40. *ATTF,* 521. The German original can be found in Dietrich Bonhoeffer, *Widerstand
und Ergebung: Briefe und Aufzeichnungen aus der Haft,* 7th ed. (Munich: Chr. Kaiser
Verlag, 1956), 277.
41. Letter to Bethge dated 21 August 1944. *LPP,* 391.

Please don't get anxious or worried about me, but don't forget to pray for me—I'm sure you don't! I am so sure of God's guiding hand that I hope I shall always be kept in that certainty. You must never doubt that I'm traveling with gratitude and cheerfulness along the road where I'm being led. My past life is brim-full of goodness, and my sins are covered by the forgiving love of Christ crucified. Forgive my writing this. Don't let it grieve or upset you for a moment, but let it make you happy.[42]

Last Words, Pronouncement of Immortality, and Death of the Tyrant

"Das ist das Ende—für mich der Beginn des Lebens" (This is the end—but for me the beginning of life). Leaving Schönberg, Bonhoeffer asked Payne Best to relay this message to Bishop Bell.[43] These hopeful words distill Bonhoeffer's earlier reflections upon death to their bare minimum. They show the polyphonous nature of "life hidden in death" as he had put it earlier, plotting death directly along the axis of Christ's resurrection. With these words Bonhoeffer confidently pronounced his immortality, one of the recurring features of martyrdom according to Fischel. Also consistent to the pattern is the death of the unjust tyrant. Hitler's death followed Bonhoeffer's by a span of only three weeks.

Bonhoeffer's Reflections on Death and Martyrdom

Before a second party were to argue *anyone's* case as martyr, it would be helpful to know, to the extent possible, how that person may have conceived his own death. Since it is with a measure of freedom that martyrs take on the dangers of public confession, they often have

42. Letter to Bethge dated 23 August 1944. *LPP,* 393.

43. Bishop Bell gave a fuller account of the message Bonhoeffer entrusted to Best: "Tell him (he said) that for me this is the end but also the beginning. With him I believe in the principle of our Universal Christian Brotherhood which rises above all national interests, and that our victory is certain—tell him too that I have never forgotten his words at our last meeting." This was the way Bell remembered it, at least, in his Göttingen lecture of May 1957 (*GS* 1:412). David Mealand has raised what seem to be unnecessary questions about the discrepancy between Best's shorter message and the longer one by Bell. Bethge's explanation—that Best was not sufficiently familiar with the shared history of Bell and Bonhoeffer and therefore did not consider the latter portion of the message relevant to his aims when he wrote his book—is satisfactory. It is conceivable that unlike the second part of the message, the first ("This is the end—but for me the beginning of life") was not meant especially for Bell. See David Mealand, "The Text of Bonhoeffer's Last Message," in *The Modern Churchman* 20 (October 1976–July 1977): 121–22. See also Bethge's footnote in *DB,* 1022.

ample reason and opportunity to contemplate their death beforehand. In the vast majority of cases, martyrs' contemplations, especially those of theological ilk, are inaccessible to us. But in Bonhoeffer, a theologian who writes about death, we are fortunate enough to have them. It seems fitting, then, to gather up some of these reflections into our broader discussion and weigh them along with various kinds of external evidence.[44] How does one interpret that death which he must accept? This question will govern my subsequent handling of certain portions of his writings that deal, both directly and indirectly, with these themes. Then we will have to ask about the actual circumstances pertaining to Bonhoeffer's death and ask whether and to what extent, in the full light of the broader discussion, he can fit the profile of martyrdom in the Christian tradition.

It was Reformation Sunday 1934 when Bonhoeffer, preaching to his London congregation, distinguished two kinds of churches: the church that aims for success becomes "a slave to the powers of this world," while the church of faith lives solely by the past deed that God has done in the world, "the cross of Golgotha."[45] By this particular November Sunday, Bonhoeffer's mind was already leaping toward the future. Exactly five months earlier he had been approached with the possibility of taking on one of the newly forming seminaries of the Confessing Church, an option he had been weighing together with another: a trip to India where he might actively experiment with Gandhi's nonviolent resistance based upon Jesus' Sermon on the Mount. For a time he was, as he put it, "hopelessly torn" between these alternatives. Yet, as different as these two paths may have *seemed*, either of them might have sufficed to answer what became a burning question for him. Was it possible for a community gathered on the basis of Jesus' Sermon on the Mount to establish a base of resistance against tyranny?

To put it bluntly, Bonhoeffer was searching for a politically viable form of Christian community. Three years prior he had encountered Jesus' Sermon on the Mount in a highly personal way. He would testify in 1936 that since that fresh reading of it, "everything has changed." In his judgment he had "become a Christian." Shortly before leaving Lon-

---

44. A degree of caution is necessary to this endeavor. As Georges Casalis has said, Bonhoeffer is more a "martyr theologian" than a "theologian of martyrdom." This judgment, though true in a formal sense, must not be permitted to obscure the fact that Bonhoeffer's life and thought are permeated by the realities of death and martyrdom. Bonhoeffer's theology of death and martyrdom may not be immediately obvious, but one may recognize it between the lines. Casalis's reflection can be found in *Martyrdom Today*, ed. Johannes-Baptist Metz and Edward Schillebeeckx (New York: Seabury, 1983), 80.

45. From the November 1934 sermon "Only Love Keeps Us from Being Rigid," in *ATTF*, 250.

don, he hinted to his brother Karl-Friedrich that communities of this kind could be just the kind of power "capable of exploding the whole enchantment and specter [Hitler and his rule]."[46] Whether in India or Germany, it would be Bonhoeffer's growing fascination with this way of Christian life that was searching for concrete expression. When finally he decided to oversee one of the newly forming preachers' seminaries, he had at his disposal a means by which to negotiate "the powers of this world" and simultaneously to experiment with "a community of the cross."

After its first summer at Zingst, the seminary was moved to Finkenwalde, where, among other scholarly pursuits, Bonhoeffer undertook an intense examination of Matthew 5–7 with his students. Eventually his work culminated in the 1937 publication of *Discipleship (Nachfolge)*, at the heart of which stands his exegesis of the Sermon on the Mount. The German title, *Nachfolge*, contains more than a hint of imitation, closing, in fact, with an argument for holding together the twin themes of *imago Dei* and the *imitatio Christi*. Because of the personal circumstances and sociopolitical pressures out of which the work is written, it is a grave mistake to read it as a timeless, abstract treatment of Christian spirituality. Rather, the existential question exerts pressure from all sides: how must the follower of Jesus live in the Germany of the 1930s, where racism, nationalism, and a growing appetite for war have made themselves friends of the gospel of Jesus Christ?

Discipleship

As prelude to the theme of *Discipleship*, Bonhoeffer made a daring plunge into the difficulties of church-historical interpretation, a fact that has received only cursory treatment in the secondary literature. Bonhoeffer's reading of church history in this work is critical to its interpretation, for with it he imbues the metaphor of discipleship with

46. The difficult German original reads, "Die den ganzen Zauber und Spuk einmal in die Luft sprengen kann . . ." For the sake of clarifying the political intent, I reproduce here also a portion of the surrounding text: "Ich glaube zu wissen, dass ich eigentlich erst innerlich klar und wirklich aufrichtig sein würde, wenn ich mit der Bergpredigtwirklich anfange, Ernst zu machen. Hier sitzt die einzige Kraftquelle, die den ganzen Zauber und Spuk einmal in die Luft sprengen kann, bis von dem Feuerwerk nur ein paar ausgebrannte Reste übrig bleiben" (I believe I know that inwardly I shall be really clear and honest only when I have begun to take seriously the Sermon on the Mount. Here is set the only source of power capable of exploding the whole enchantment and specter [Hitler and his rule] so that only a few burnt-out fragments are left remaining from the fireworks). English excerpts from these letters may be found in *ATTF*, 424–25, and in Bethge, *DB*, 204–6. For the German original, see *GS* 3:25.

a distinctive, pre-Constantinian flavor. In so doing, it seems to me, he has chosen, implicitly if not explicitly, an important political horizon for his Finkenwalde community. Bonhoeffer was too sophisticated, of course, to have reprised the early church as a golden age to which all future ages must conform, and he warned constantly against the dangers of the "enthusiasts" *(Schwärmerei)*. But the sociopolitical *form* of the pre-Constantinian church—a minority community that spoke the claims of Christ to its age at great cost and on the margins, one might say, of public life—was apparently full of promise for him, and quite naturally so given the political skirmishes in which the Confessing Church was involved at this time. Thus one senses that Bonhoeffer quite deliberately invested the metaphor *Nachfolge* with the spirit of the age of the martyrs to prepare his church for the possibilities that lay ahead. He avoided the traditional German term *Jüngerschaft*, which was too laden with the idea of the original disciples *(die Jünger)* to fit his aims.

The term *Nachfolge*, which refers to the *act* of "following after," had a rich tradition dating back to the sixteenth-century Anabaptist martyrs, who plotted all Christian life along the curve of Jesus' journey to the cross. Bonhoeffer was well aware of this, of course, but he also had his own Lutheran heritage to draw upon. Luther had made suffering and the cross one of his seven "marks" of the church. In Bonhoeffer's judgment, the early church lived in a period when grace and discipleship went hand in hand. As an example he cites Peter, who twice hears the words from Jesus "Follow me," once at the start of his journey with Jesus and again after his denial of Jesus. The two occasions are worlds apart but convey the same grace. As Jesus consoled Peter in the wake of his failure, he "called the unfaithful Peter into the ultimate community of martyrdom and, in doing so, forgave him all his sins."[47] Bonhoeffer then concludes that Peter "received costly grace." With the dawn of the Constantinian era—which brought both a Christianization of the world and a secularization of the church—commitment to grace and its cost was diverted from the main current of Christianity into the eddies of monastic tradition, to form "a living protest against the secularization of Christianity, against the cheapening of grace."[48] What evolved was the "fatal conception" of a "maximum and minimum standard of obedience."

Bonhoeffer then argues that Luther's movement from the cloister back into the world was God's design for healing this double standard. For "following Jesus now had to be lived out in the midst of the world." By reentering the world Luther stitched the costly grace of discipleship

47. *DBWE*, 46.
48. Ibid.

together with a spacious freedom for living secular life. Yet the outcome of the Reformation, at least amongst the Lutherans Bonhoeffer targeted for criticism, was not the victory of costly grace. Rather it was "the alert religious instinct of human beings for the place where grace could be had the cheapest."[49] The costly grace of discipleship is Bonhoeffer's answer to what he perceived to be the weakness of organized institutional Lutheranism.

Against this historiographical horizon, Bonhoeffer then elaborates discipleship as a cruciform imitation of Christ. The cross is that form of suffering which comes to those whose exclusive devotion is to Jesus Christ.[50] Laid upon every Christian, the cross means "suffering and being rejected."[51] For those few whom God deems worthy of suffering in its highest form, the cross means "the grace of martyrdom."[52] Still, whether the disciple dies a martyr's death or lives to a ripe age, "his yoke and burden is the cross."[53]

As captured in the epigram with which Bishop Bell opens his introduction to *Discipleship (Nachfolge)*, the very trajectory of discipleship is death. For "whenever Christ calls us, his call leads us to death."[54] Though Bonhoeffer acknowledges that discipleship does not of necessity entail physical death, he remains adamantly committed to Jesus' call for simple, *literal* obedience. Even where spiritual interpretations of death are appropriate, such interpretations must always include the possibility of a quite literal obedience. This is true of all Jesus' demands. One is permitted to conclude, for example, that Jesus' command to the rich man—"Sell your possessions!"—speaks to the matter of our inner detachment from wealth. But one must not make "inner detachment" the abstract principle by which to interpret Jesus' words. Such amounts to an evasion of the obligation toward "simple obedience."[55] A person who wishes to follow Christ must come to terms with its literal costs, one of which may be death. For this reason, Bonhoeffer willingly acknowledges that the problem of discipleship is a problem of biblical exegesis and hermeneutics as well.[56]

49. Ibid., 49.
50. Ibid., 86.
51. Ibid.
52. Ibid., 87.
53. Ibid., 91.
54. Ibid., 87.
55. Ibid., 78.
56. Ibid., 82. Bonhoeffer clarifies the connection between spiritual and physical death in one of his circular letters (20 September 1939) to the Finkenwalde brethren: "Two things have become important to me recently: death is outside us, and it is in us. Death from outside is the fearful foe which comes to us when it will. It is the man with the scythe, under

Once baptized into a life whose structure is death, the disciple must carefully tend to the paradox of visibility and invisibility, which is said to mark the essential contrast between chapters 5 and 6 of Matthew's Gospel. On the one hand, disciples of Jesus have a high profile: "You are the light of the world. A city on a hill cannot be hid." As it is in the nature of light to shine, so it is in the nature of the disciple to make good works public. On the other hand, Jesus warns his disciples of practicing piety before others. When giving alms, he urges them, "do not let your left hand know what your right hand is doing." How can the follower of Jesus maintain this paradox? How can discipleship be public and hidden at the same time?

Bonhoeffer's answer discloses one of his most passionate commitments. The works of disciples are to be hidden from *themselves*, not from the world. Skeptical of that Reformation theology that prefers humble invisibility to Pharisaic visibility, Bonhoeffer says, "To flee into invisibility is to deny the call." When the disciples of Jesus flee into the invisible on the pretext of legalism, by default the hallmark of the church becomes *justitia civilis* (civil justice) instead of the kind of extraordinary visible community Jesus intends.[57] It becomes quite clear that for Bonhoeffer visibility entails the confession and performance of one's faith in the public sphere. When, as they must, disciples do come into the public sphere with their good works, they are called to do so under the constraining shadow of the cross:

> Does not a simple listener recognize quite clearly that precisely at the cross something extraordinary has become visible? Or is that all nothing but justitia civilis [civil justice]? Is the cross conformation to the world? To the shock of everyone else, is the cross not something which became outrageously visible in the complete darkness? Is it not visible enough that Christ is rejected and must suffer, that his life ends outside the city gates on the hill of shame? Is that invisibility?[58]

---

whose stroke the blossoms fall. It guides the bullet that goes home. We can do nothing against it, 'it has the power from the supreme God.' It is the death of the whole human race, God's wrath and the end of all life. But the other is death in us, it is our own death. That too has been in us since the fall of Adam. But it belongs to us. We die daily to it in Jesus Christ or we deny him. This death in us has something to do with love toward Christ and toward people. We die to it when we love Christ and the brethren from the bottom of our hearts, for love is total surrender to what a person loves. This death is grace and the consummation of love. It should be our prayer that we die this death, that it be sent to us, that death only comes to us from outside when we have already been made ready for it by this our own death." This translation taken from *ATTF*, 447.

57. *DBWE* 4, 114.

58. Ibid., 114.

Constraint is inherent in the works of the cross, which include poverty, meekness, peacemaking, and finally persecution and rejection. When these are done in the shadow of Christ's own cross, disciples come near to Christ and a "strange light" illuminates their good works, so that God rather than human beings might be praised."[59] Rooting himself in pre-Constantinian soil, then, Bonhoeffer parlays the cross into an enduring symbol of conflict between the world and the church:

> The world must be contradicted within the world. That is why Christ became a human being and died in the midst of his enemies.[60]

> If it engages the world properly, the visible church-community will always more closely assume the form of its suffering Lord.[61]

A cruciform confrontation with the world entails more than the passive acceptance of evil; it constitutes an assault upon the world and forms a subversive protest against those worldly powers that claim ultimacy for themselves. In freedom, says Bonhoeffer, Christians "are able to abandon the world whenever it prevents them from following their Lord."[62]

All this indicates that Bonhoeffer's phrase "the paradox of discipleship" attempts to name the mystery that characterizes those human beings in whom Christ himself is taking form. Christ the Crucified impresses his form upon the disciple. Hence, as if speaking to his detractors, for whom *Discipleship* and the entire Finkenwalde experiment were plagued by an onerous legalism and "methodism," Bonhoeffer insists that "to be conformed to the image of Jesus Christ is not an ideal of realizing some kind of similarity with Christ which we are asked to attain."[63] The image of God lost through Adam's fall is said to be recovered *only* by the disciple's conformation to the image of the Suffering Servant who was obedient to death. Despite the fact that Christian life is a life of crucifixion, disciples are not solely responsible for their death. Rather, Christ graciously baptizes them into the structure of death so that the new image of God, which Christ himself is, might emerge in them. Thus "it is by Christians' being publicly disgraced, having to suffer and being put to death for the sake of Christ, that Christ himself attains visible form within his community."[64]

59. Ibid., 114.
60. Ibid., 244.
61. Ibid., 247.
62. Ibid., 248.
63. Ibid., 284–85.
64. Ibid., 286.

From *Discipleship*, then, we carry forward several observations concerning Bonhoeffer's understanding of death. First, the reality of death is an intrinsic feature of Christian life and adequately describes its cost, even in the most literal way. Since the death of Christ was what it cost God to convey grace to human beings, human participation in that grace is costly in proportion to God's own cost. On this basis, it is reasonable for a disciple to construe her death not simply as "happenstance" but as the more or less expected result of a life of this kind. Second, the death of the disciple, like that of Jesus, can be seen as the quintessential occasion in which the "hidden" structure of Christian life, which is death, becomes uniquely "visible" to the public. Of course on such an occasion as this, what is made visible is not chiefly the disciple's death but Christ's, which undergirds it, supports it, and makes it what it is. Third, though the disciple's death by martyrdom may be taken as the consummate form of the *imitatio Christi*,[65] such imitation is always carried along by God's initiative and worked into the larger pattern of revelation and salvation. God utilizes the martyr's death to reveal the Crucified One and draw persons to him. In this way, martyrdom mirrors the rich, contrapuntal interplay between human and divine activity, wherein the human willingness to die is simultaneously a bestowal of grace, the "grace of martyrdom."

Letters and Papers

Outside *Discipleship*, Bonhoeffer's theology of death surfaces in other powerful ways. In one of the letters to Bethge he argues that it is concern for earthly life that marks the Old Testament idea of redemption. Whereas Nazi ideology had idolized and eroticized death—including the death of Christ!—along the lines of extrabiblical redemption myths, Bonhoeffer pointed to Christ's resurrection as the "decisive factor" for Christianity. In doing so, however, he stipulated that the meaning of Christ's resurrection lies not in "the far side of the boundary drawn by death" but in a renewed hope for life on earth. In this way he located an essential continuity between the Old and New Testaments, to be sure, but he also found a way to purge Christian death of any heroism or glorification. Unlike redemption myths, the Christian interpretation of death does not arise from human anxiety in view of the "boundary experience" but from Christ himself, who loved the earth by drinking the "earthly cup to the dregs."[66]

---

65. Interestingly, in the final weeks of his journey Bonhoeffer held in his possession a personal copy of Thomas à Kempis's *Imitation of Christ*, which can now be seen under glass at the Dietrich Bonhoeffer Kirche in Forest Hill, London.

66. *LPP*, 336–37.

Reflections like this reveal a new, deeper element in Bonhoeffer's thought. Considering the prospect of his own death, it appears that Bonhoeffer creatively bent the redemptive aspect of the *imitatio Christi* to touch upon the axis of creation, for participation in Christ's death is one avenue by which one comes humbly to love the earth as God loves it. Thus to be drawn into the structure of Christ's death is to be drawn into the very essence of earthly life:

> Socrates mastered the art of dying; Christ overcame death as "the last enemy" (1 Cor. 15.26). There is a real difference between the two things; the one is within the scope of human possibilities, the other means resurrection. It's not from an *ars moriendi*, the art of dying, but from the resurrection of Christ, that a new and purifying wind can blow through our present world. *Here* is the answer to δὸς μοὶ ποῦ στῶ καὶ κινήσω τὴν γῆν. If a few people really believed that and acted on it in their daily lives, a great deal would be changed.[67]

The Archimedean point in this citation is not death itself but a resurrection that leverages death in the interest of life. As one commentator concludes, "Bonhoeffer boldly reinterprets resurrection as the supremely this-worldly *denouement* of the Christian drama."[68] Baptized into the structure of Christ's death and resurrection, a martyr may become an instrument by which God communicates his abiding commitment to mend the creation.

---

67. Ibid., 240. The statement δὸς μοὶ ποῦ στῶ καὶ κινήσω τὴν γῆν (Give me somewhere to stand and I will move the earth) is from Archimedes.

68. Douglas John Hall, "Ecclesia Crucis," in *Theology and the Practice of Responsibility*, ed. Wayne Whitson Floyd Jr. and Charles Marsh (Valley Forge, Pa.: Trinity Press International, 1994), 68. In Bonhoeffer's *Ethics*, the cross marks the penultimate while resurrection marks the ultimate. Bonhoeffer explains: "The cross of Jesus is the death sentence upon the world . . . yet the crucifixion of Jesus does not simply mean the annihilation of the created world, but under this sign of death, the cross, men are now to continue to live, to their own condemnation if they despise it, but to their own salvation if they give it its due. The ultimate has become real in the cross, as the judgment upon all that is penultimate, yet also as mercy towards that penultimate which bows before the judgement of the ultimate." Dietrich Bonhoeffer, *Ethics*, ed. Eberhard Bethge (New York: Macmillan, 1955), 90.

6

The Distance between a Funeral and an Operation

Bonhoeffer and the Jews

For the sake of ten righteous people, God does not destroy the world. These are the Lamed Vavnik. They live scattered, in any nation under heaven, are members of any class, of any profession which may be imagined; and they are invisible to the world. Lo, not even they know the significance of their lives. Such ignorance *is* their righteousness. They merely live, so they suppose, as other people live. But heaven knows the difference. And this is the mercy of God: that when one of the Lamed Vavnik dies, God raises up another. I heard this from my friend. He said it was an old Hasidic legend. I believe it.

Walter Wangerin

Realism and Hope

It is important to keep before us the fact that Bonhoeffer's life and death are an interlocking piece of what has now become known as the Holocaust, or *Shoah*.[1] Is it too obvious to point out that Bonhoeffer met his end in a concentration camp? Burton Nelson has goaded Bonhoeffer

---

1. The term *holocaust* is the Septuagint's Greek rendering of the scriptural Hebrew term *Shoah,* or "burnt offering."

scholars to keep this horizon fully in view in order that in our "researching
and writing about Bonhoeffer . . . [we] bring together with *much* more
precision, *much* more insight and *much* more accuracy, the connecting
links between his theology and the historical chronicle of shame that
marked the Holocaust years."[2] Late in life, Eberhard Bethge confessed
that Bonhoeffer's concern for the Jews of the Holocaust was the most
important omission of his thousand-page biography. Apparently only
in the wake of new discoveries about Bonhoeffer's theological reflections did the possibility of handling the biographical material from this
perspective dawn on him.[3]

A full treatment of Bonhoeffer's link to the Jews of the Holocaust
would include elements not treated here, such as his family's frequent
association with Jews in the disproportionately Jewish Berlin Grunewald
district, his belief that the Jews would remain God's chosen people in
eternity, pressures he exerted on the Steglitz Synod to make a clear
statement condemning the Nuremberg laws, his fondness for the
verse "Open thy mouth for the dumb" (Eccles. 31:8), which appears
regularly in his writings from the London period onward, the extent of
his knowledge about the death camps, his cool treatment of a prison
guard after an anti-Semitic remark, and his newfound joy in the Old
Testament in the final period of his life. Since my chief intention is to
secure the link between Bonhoeffer's Jewish concerns and his political
decisions, I have selected primarily those elements that have a direct
bearing on this link.

Taken together, I think these carefully selected elements will also
paint a quite favorable impression of his theological disposition toward
Jews so long as we are able both to see them in the church context of
Bonhoeffer's day and to plot them along the curve of his own life development. Notwithstanding these caveats, I am aware that not all will
share my positive impression of his theology in this regard. Though in
the church context it may have been radical, one might still say that it
was too little and too late, and that Bonhoeffer never sufficiently understood the complex interrelation between theological and racial anti-
Semitism, certainly not in ways now obvious to us. We must remember,
however, that Bonhoeffer was a Holocaust, not post-Holocaust, figure.

---

2. F. Burton Nelson, "Dietrich Bonhoeffer and the Jews: An Agenda for Exploration
and Contemporary Dialogue," in *The Holocaust Forty Years After*, ed. Marcia S. Littell et
al. (Lewiston, N.Y.: Edwin Mellen, 1989), 89.

3. Eberhard Bethge, "Unfulfilled Tasks?" *Dialog* 34 (Winter 1995): 30–31. See also Eb-
erhard Bethge, "Dietrich Bonhoeffer and the Jews," In *Ethical Responsibility: Bonhoeffer's
Legacy to the Churches*, ed. John Godsey and Geffrey Kelly, *Toronto Studies in Theology* 6,
Bonhoeffer Series 1 (Lewiston, N.Y.: Edwin Mellen, 1981), and Bethge's comments in "The
Holocaust and Anti-Semitism," *Union Seminary Quarterly Review* 33, nos. 3-4, 146–7.

However much or little he grasped this connection, the fact that he—a theologian—died in solidarity with Jewish suffering could be considered a kind of theological response in and of itself. Could his martyrdom have been an answer to the anti-Semitic knot he was never able fully to disentangle intellectually?

Bonhoeffer's remarkable ethical instincts seemed often to guide him even while he was desperately groping for theological mooring. Hence it is common to encounter people who admire Bonhoeffer for his moral sensibilities and bold actions even while they lament his theology, though for a man who launched his theological career by trying to discern the relationship between "faith as act and revelation as being,"[4] such admiration seems hollow indeed. Emil Fackenheim, Jewish professor of philosophy and Sachsenhausen survivor, addressed the English Language Section of the Bonhoeffer Society in 1979 with these words: "I have heard it said (from Christians) that Bonhoeffer the man was better than Bonhoeffer the theologian . . . [But] of greater consequence for the future is Bonhoeffer *the theologian*."[5] Of course it was precisely Bonhoeffer the theologian that Eva Fleischner took to task, asking (and doubting) whether he had ever really repudiated the notion of a "divine curse" upon the Jews.[6] Rosemary Ruether, too, despite acknowledging Bonhoeffer as "the great figure of the resistance," finds him to display an element of that same "myopia" that rendered the Confessing Church unable to confront theologically the issue of anti-Semitism.[7] By contrast, Pinchas Lapide gives a largely positive assessment of his theology, calling Bonhoeffer a "pioneer and forerunner of a slow step-by-step re-Hebraisation of the churches in our days."[8]

In what follows it will be nigh impossible to say with precision just how Bonhoeffer's identification with the Jews of the Holocaust links up with his theology. His death in solidarity with Jews is tantamount to a theological position, but that is a matter that simply cannot be developed until we traverse his Christology and ethics. It will also be nearly impossible to exonerate Bonhoeffer in respect to some of his more controversial statements about the Jews. Nor should we try. Bonhoeffer was a man in development. What he became by his death was something greater than what he was at any stage along the way. If, however, we can substantiate the link between Bonhoeffer's political actions and "concern" for

---

4. *DBWE* 2, 28.

5. Bethge, "Dietrich Bonhoeffer and the Jews," 44.

6. Eva Fleischner, *Judaism in German Christian Theology since 1945* (Metuchen, N.J.: Scarecrow, 1975), 24.

7. Rosemary Ruether, *Faith and Fratricide: The Theological Roots of Anti-Semitism* (New York: Seabury, 1974), 224.

8. See Bethge, "Bonhoeffer and the Jews," 49–50.

Jews, we will have made sufficient progress. Along the way, I hope the reader can find an appreciation for how tenaciously and consistently Bonhoeffer took up the so-called Jewish question and also for his efforts to address the Jewish question along theological lines, however fumbling and inadequate those efforts may look in hindsight.

Response to the Events of 1933

Bonhoeffer was by most accounts the first theologian to recognize the theological importance of the Jewish question *(Judenfrage)*.[9] After the war, Karl Barth lamented somewhat his own position and in so doing paid Bonhoeffer a high compliment:

> New to me . . . was the fact that Bonhoeffer in 1933 viewed the Jewish question as the first and decisive question, even as the only one, and took it on so energetically. I have long felt guilty myself that I did not make this problem central, in any case not public, for instance in the two Barmen declarations of 1934 which I had composed. Certainly, a text in which I inserted a word to that effect would not have found agreement in 1934—neither in the Reformed Synod of January, 1934; nor in the General Synod of May at Barmen. But there is no excuse that I did not fight properly for this cause, just because I was caught up in my affairs somewhere else.[10]

Barth's admiration notwithstanding, critics like to point out that Bonhoeffer's April 1933 essay "The Church and the Jewish Question" is mired in that brand of Christian anti-Semitism that charges Jews with

9. The following description of the "Jewish Question" is lifted from the glossary of *ATTF* (p. 546): "The phrase 'Jewish Question,' or, alternately, 'Jewish Problem,' was used in publications, lectures, and statements of government policy to refer to the issues posed by the presence of a significant Jewish population within many Western nations. These included the place of the Jews within a so-called 'Christian' nation, the slanderous anti-Semitism and Jew baiting that aroused the hatred of and brutality toward Jews among the non-Jewish citizenry, the issue of the Jews as a Chosen People of God vis-à-vis the imperious claims of some Christian denominations to have replaced the Jews in God's covenant, the Jews as a 'nation within a nation,' the Jews as refugees, the Jews as a scapegoat for a nation's ills, and the alleged international 'Jewish conspiracy,' deriving from 'Protocols of Zion,' a virulent anti-Semitic document claiming the existence of a plot by the 'elders of Zion' to take over the world and establish Judaism as the sole religion, in essence a pretext for denying their civil rights within the nations."

10. This quote is taken from a May 1967 letter Barth addressed to Eberhard Bethge upon reading Bethge's biography of Bonhoeffer. A complete publication of this letter can be found under the title "To Rector Eberhard Bethge," in *Karl Barth, Letters 1961–1968*, translated and edited by Geoffrey Bromiley (Grand Rapids: Eerdmans, 1981), 250–53.

deicide, treats them as targets of Christian mission, and retains them under a curse for the killing of Jesus. One must admit the presence of these tendencies in this text. For instance, phrases like "forced exclusion of *baptized* Jews" (emphasis mine) or "prohibition of our mission to the Jews" seem to indicate the kinds of difficulties that might put the church in *status confessionis* (a state of confession). Where do we detect Bonhoeffer's concern for the Jews as a race? Shouldn't racial hatred be enough to put the church in a state of confession?[11] Upon closer inspection, we will see that racial hatred was just what Bonhoeffer had in mind when he wrote this essay.

"The Church and the Jewish Question" was written as an address for a group of pastors meeting to discuss the question that, following passage of the *Arierparagraph*[12] on 7 April, had come to dominate the day: how should the church respond to a law that excluded persons of Jewish descent from its own membership? As far as Bonhoeffer was concerned, by excluding Jews from the church on a legal basis the state had transgressed its God-given boundaries. He suggested three possible courses of action for the church: (1) "throw the state back upon its responsibilities" by asking it to legitimate its actions, (2) "aid the victims of state action," for "the church has an unconditional obligation to the victims of any ordering of society, even if they do not belong to the Christian community," or (3) jam up the spokes of the wheel of injustice itself through direct political action. The first two courses are "the compelling demands of the hour." Bonhoeffer thought the third course would require more careful treatment and a watchful eye on the future, but should it be necessary the ramifications are clear: the matter of baptized Jews will become irrelevant, for out of necessity this kind of action will mean direct political engagement and thus will have already traversed the threshold of ecclesiastical boundaries. These three "courses" caused such a stir among Bonhoeffer's colleagues that several left the assembly, ostensibly wanting nothing to do with revolutionary-type solutions.[13]

11. Dietrich Bonhoeffer, "The Church and the Jewish Question," in *ATTF*, 130–133. This early essay was written in view of the boycott against Jewish merchants and newly-passed *Arierparagraph* of 7 April, a section of the "Law for the Reconstruction of the Professional Civil Service, which banned persons of non-Aryan descent and those married to non-Aryans from public office. Naturally this included ministers and church officials. Franz Hildebrandt, who had wanted to begin a pastorate in East Berlin with Bonhoeffer, was thwarted by this law. For a critical Jewish response to Bonhoeffer's essay, see Stanley Rosenbaum, "Dietrich Bonhoeffer: A Jewish View," *Journal of Ecumenical Studies* 18:2 (1981): 301–307.

12. The *Arierparagraph* (Aryan Clause) denotes a clause within the "Law for the Reconstruction of Professional Civil Service" passed by the German Reichstag, which prohibited Jews and any person whose parents or grandparents had been Jewish from civil service positions.

13. Bethge, "Bonhoeffer and the Jews," 59.

In context, we can see that this essay signals a radical departure from the deep-cut categories of interpretation and biases present in his Lutheran heritage in respect to both its "two kingdoms" theory and latent anti-Semitism.[14] Helping to clarify Bonhoeffer's stance, Bethge writes:

> There were four keywords which caused unrest and reactions in the German Church under the attacks of the "German Christians" in the spring of 1933, namely "synchronization" (Gleichschaltung), "Reichs-church," "Führer principle," and "racial purity" (the Aryan clause). The last one (racial purity) caused at first the least alarm among church authorities and opposition movements.[15]

And as early as spring 1933, as a young man of twenty-seven, Bonhoeffer was in fact already moving the racial issue to the forefront of his own thinking while most of his older colleagues were languishing in these other problems and steeling themselves for the ecclesiastical skirmishes that lay ahead. As Bonhoeffer reflected on the rapidly changing political climate, he was scurrying to develop a Christian basis for humanitarian interest—aiding Jews as a race, not just as participants in the church—even while, ironically, he was still speaking in older ways of "forced exclusion of baptized Jews" and the "prohibition of our mission" to the Jews, phrases that can be taken to betray a latent theological anti-Semitism. The possible "third course," however, shows that Bonhoeffer comprehended the larger picture. Passage of the Arierpargraph left the church a twofold possibility: first, and most obvious, to consider its theological response to the matter of Jews in its membership, a consideration that would eventually involve the church in border disputes with the state; and second, to develop a responsible theological and ethical position on the state's aggression against the Jewish race itself. Of course, anti-Semitism had long been an issue in Western culture. Perhaps it was for that very reason that his colleagues could not seem to muster much concern. Yet Bonhoeffer quickly comprehended a difference between

---

14. Beginning about 1536, for reasons we cannot explore here, Luther made a dark turn in his attitude toward the Jews. This attitude is evident particularly in his two tracts "The Jews and Their Lies" and "Schem Hamphoras." In excoriating language he brought forward a set of charges: that Jews are poisoners, ritual murderers, usurers, parasites on Christian society, worse than devils, harder to convert than Satan himself, and doomed to hell. Luther advised the burning of synagogues, the confiscation of rabbinical books, and even the expulsion of Jews who would not be converted to Christianity. An excellent treatment of Luther and the Jews can be found in Heiko Oberman, *Luther: Man Between God and the Devil*, trans. Eileen Walliser-Schwarzbart (New York: Doubleday, 1989), 292–97. See also Edward H. Flannery, *The Anguish of the Jews: Twenty-three Centuries of Anti-Semitism* (New York: Macmillan, 1965), 152–53.

15. Bethge, "Bonhoeffer and the Jews," 57.

more general, mob-induced violence against Jews and state-supported racism. We might wish that he had taken one more step to realize that both have a common source. But careful investigation of this text reveals that, for Bonhoeffer, victimization of Jews *qua* Jews was enough to place the church in *status confessionis*. Without question, Bonhoeffer has the racial element in the foreground of his thought. Ambiguities in this essay are explainable in part by the fact that Bonhoeffer had begun but not consummated his transition out of the latent anti-Semitism of his German Lutheran heritage.

They are also explainable by the twisted racial ideology behind the Holocaust itself, which by 1933 was effectively erasing the distinction between theological anti-Semitism and racial anti-Semitism by reducing Jewishness to a racial monolith. Hitler himself responded to two bishops who had come to him complaining about Nazi racial policy by telling them he was only putting into effect what Christianity had preached and practiced for two thousand years.[16] It is a "critical yet perhaps poorly understood fact," writes Paul Hinlicky, that the Holocaust was racially motivated. Hinlicky expands:

> Race, as a biological and thus allegedly scientific category, did not exist before modern times. The idea of race depends on distinctively modern ideas of human evolution, genetic transmission of characteristics and sophisticated eugenic analogies derived from animal and plant breeding regimes. As such, race forms the basic category in the Nazi worldview in a way analogous to the market in a capitalist worldview or class conflict in a Marxist worldview. We may note here that the Bible by contrast gives us a picture of the derivation of the whole human race from one man and one woman; accordingly, any kind of serious racial thinking is foreign to the Bible. For just this *racial* reason, Nazi antisemitism was *also* religiously antijudaic, holding that the ideal of universal humanity under God in the Bible was a fiction created by Jewish religion to justify racial parasitism. . . . Consequently there could be neither a German Jew culturally nor a Christian Jew religiously. For by blood a Jew is a Jew is a Jew.[17]

If the root principle of Nazism is racial, and the *Arierparagraph* is an attempt to introduce that principle into public life, then I think the very ambiguities in Bonhoeffer's essay are themselves commendable, not to mention instructive. To home exclusively on the ecclesiastical repercussions of the Aryan paragraph, as most did, was to be "clear" about the issue but also to misread the dreadful logic behind it. To be caught in

16. See Ruether, *Faith and Fratricide*, 224.
17. Paul R. Hinlicky, "What Hope after Holocaust?" *Pro Ecclesia* 8, no. 1 (1999): 14.

ambiguity was to grasp in some way the massive, totalitarian power of Nazism's racial principle.[18]

By November 1933 one finds Bonhoeffer lamenting his decision not to conduct the funeral of Gerhard Leibholz's father, a Jew, who had died 11 April. He wrote to his brother-in-law:

> I am tormented by the thought . . . that I didn't do as you asked me as a matter of course. To be frank, I can't think what made me behave as I did. How could I have been so much afraid at the time? It must have seemed equally incomprehensible to all of you, and yet you said nothing. But it preys on my mind . . . because it's the kind of thing one can never make up for. So all I can do is to ask you to forgive my weakness then. I know now for certain that I ought to have behaved differently.[19]

Only rarely does Bonhoeffer admit his mistakes so candidly. This brief emotional display is especially interesting in view of the fact that Bonhoeffer made his decision after consultation with the general superintendent, who advised strongly against such a funeral in view of the theological and political tensions brought on by the events of April 1933. He could have hidden behind ecclesiastical responsibility. The fact that one detects in this letter no attempt to legitimate or excuse behavior by appealing to church authority shows how Bonhoeffer's thinking has changed. By his remorse, Bonhoeffer demonstrates that however inchoate or unconscious it may have been for him at that time, there was nonetheless an emerging rationale for his behavior toward Jews that pushed beyond the bounds of ecclesiastical or political expediency and should have resulted in a different course of action. His remorse also lends weight to Barth's judgment that by 1933 the Jewish question had become for Bonhoeffer, though clearly not for his church, the question above all others.

On 15 August 1933 Bonhoeffer, together with Hermann Sasse, began work on the original text of the Bethel Confession, envisioned as a means of confronting the *Deutsche Christen* (German Christians) who had been co-opted by the racist sentiments of the National Socialists. Bonhoeffer, in the article on Christology, had stressed the person of Jesus and

---

18. Interestingly, Bonhoeffer's exposure to racism in America may have prepared him for such an insight. Bonhoeffer took particular interest in the plight of American Blacks during his year at Union Theological Seminary. Paul Lehmann, a student friend at the time, recalls that "what was so impressive was the way in which he pursued the understanding of the problem to its minutest detail through books and countless visits to Harlem, through participation in Negro youth work, but even more through a remarkable kind of identity with the Negro community, so that he was received by them as though he had never been an outsider at all" (Bethge, *DB*, 155). By 1933 Bonhoeffer was already highly sensitized to racial prejudices.

19. Bethge, *DB*, 275–76.

his Jewishness so as to sharply criticize these racist political policies. However, as a harbinger of things to come, within just five days a spirit of "happy collaboration" had given way to skepticism:

> Our work here is enjoyable but very hard. We want to try to make the German Christians declare their intentions. Whether we shall succeed I rather doubt. For even if they admit the formulations officially, the pressure behind them is so strong that sooner of later it is bound to sweep away all promises. It is becoming clear that what we are going to get is a big, popular, national church whose nature cannot be reconciled with Christianity, and that we must be prepared to enter upon entirely new paths which we shall then have to tread. The real question is between Germanism and Christianity, and the sooner the conflict comes out into the open the better.[20]

By the time the original draft had gone through its revisions under the guidance of Friedrich von Bodelschwingh and Gerhard Stratenwerth, the power of the article on Christology had been emasculated and defused to the point that Bonhoeffer himself would not sign it when Martin Niemöller brought it to publication in November 1933. In its final form, the tone of the confession reflected more a desire to dialogue with than confront the *Deutsche Christen*.[21] Bonhoeffer's involvement in and disgruntlement with the Bethel Confession is important from various angles, but for our purposes here it reveals his firm grip on the Christian obligation toward Jews—an obligation rooted in Jesus the Jew. In one of the rare open references to Jews in his *Ethics*, written mostly in the period following the Wannsee Conference and thus during the execution of the *Endlösung* (Final Solution),[22] Bonhoeffer would bring

20. *GS* 2:78.

21. *DB*, 300–303. For an in-depth treatment of the Bethel Confession and its various drafts see Guy Carter, "Confession at Bethel, August 1933—Enduring Witness: The Formation, Revision and Significance of the First Full Theological Confession of the Evangelical Church Struggle in Nazi Germany," Ph.D. diss., Marquette University, 1987. Carter demonstrates how the *Deutsche Christen* sought to de-Judaize and dehistoricize Jesus, turning him instead into a heroic Nordic figure who revealed by his crucifixion the sin of the Jews, legitimating thereby their acceptance of the Nazi racist policies as part of the judgment of God. Therefore, in the Christology article Bonhoeffer countered by stressing Jesus' title "Son of David," his "mission to the lost sheep of the House of Israel," and his crucifixion as "the unique act of [God's] self-revelation." Pressures from others prevented the acceptance of these phrases in the final draft. See esp. 220–26.

22. The so-called Final Solution was a decision taken in a large retreat house along one of Berlin's beautiful lakes (the Wannsee). Hitler and Nazi leaders met there in order to conference over party policy regarding Jews. On 20 January 1942 they decided that extermination of the Jews would become official policy, although mass killings had already begun by this point.

the point forward with fresh vigor: "An expulsion of the Jews from the west must necessarily bring with it the expulsion of Christ. For Jesus Christ was a Jew."[23] A confession of Christ that ignores Jesus' Jewishness is no Christian confession at all.

Response to *Kristallnacht*

In the days surrounding 9 November 1938, Bonhoeffer was attending to his teaching duties, shuttling between the so-called collective pastorates in outer Pomerania. Thus it was only belatedly and from a distance that he learned the full scope of the new wave of terror associated with Kristallnacht (Crystal Night), the "night of broken glass," a Nazi pogrom of unbridled destruction directed at Jewish shops and synagogues. We should not allow Bonhoeffer's absence from Berlin to obscure the inner intensity of his lament. When he heard the news, he had been meditating on Psalm 74. He wrote in the margin of his Bible "9.11.38"; he then underlined a verse.[24]

In the next circular letter disseminated to the Finkenwalde brethren Bonhoeffer showed his sustained reflection on the plight of the Jews: "During the past few days I have been thinking a great deal about Psalm 74, Zechariah 2:12, Romans 9:4f, and 11:11–15. That takes us right into prayer."[25] His choice of these texts for meditation reveal that his theological views concerning Israel continued to evolve in a way that virtually rejected any curse upon the Jews or any punishment theory. More important, they show a new depth of solidarity with those Jews who were suffering.

Kristallnacht was the decisive event in a tumultuous string of events that marked the year 1938. According to Bethge, this constituted "the darkest hour" of the church struggle *(Kirchenkampf)*.[26] A few months earlier, the majority of Confessing Church pastors had acquiesced by swearing an oath of allegiance to Hitler, and it was becoming apparent that the kind of strong protest Bonhoeffer had hoped for would not materialize. The Sudeten crisis was worsening, which meant that war

23. Dietrich Bonhoeffer, *Ethics,* ed. Eberhard Bethge (New York: Macmillan, 1955), 27.

24. The penciled date is placed aside verse 8, "They said to themselves, 'We will utterly subdue them'; they burned all the meeting places of God in the land." Verse 9 is underlined, which reads "We do not see our emblems; there is no longer any prophet, and there is no one among us who knows how long" (Bethge, *DB,* 607).

25. *ATTF,* 444.

26. "Church struggle" *(Kirchenkampf)* refers to the struggle waged from within the German churches against the policies of the National Socialist Party under Hitler.

was imminent, and with it Bonhoeffer's draft. Just a few weeks earlier he had helped his sister Sabine's family, the Leibholzes, in their emigration from Göttingen to Switzerland and eventually to London.

This constellation of events forced Bonhoeffer into serious reflection about his future. As Bethge puts it, the result was that "Bonhoeffer had decided to answer for himself the Psalmist's question, 'how long, O Lord, how long?'—in a different and more active way."[27] Here at the end of the period of the Nuremberg Laws, in a most intense political climate, Bonhoeffer was beginning personally to come to terms with some form of the "third course" he had outlined earlier.[28] It is nearly impossible to say precisely when Bonhoeffer decided for conspiracy, but the escalation of Jewish suffering was a direct precipitating cause in the decision to extend his Christian confession by intervening politically for Jews.

"The Jew Keeps Open the Question of Christ"

In the fall of 1940 Bonhoeffer wrote a passage into the section of his *Ethics* called "Inheritance and Decay," which on account of its provocation I cite at length:

> Our forefathers are for us not ancestors who are made the object of worship and veneration. Interest in genealogies can all too easily become mythologization, as was already known to the writers of the New Testament (1 Tim. 1:4). Our forefathers are witnesses of the entry of God into history. It is the fact of the appearance of Jesus Christ nineteen hundred years ago, a fact for which no further proof is to be sought, that directs our gaze back to the ancients and raises in our minds the question of our historical inheritance.
>
> The historical Jesus Christ is the continuity of our history. But Jesus Christ was the promised Messiah of the Israelite-Jewish people, and for that reason the line of our forefathers goes back beyond the appearance of Jesus Christ to the people of Israel. *Western history is, by God's will, indissolubly linked with the people of Israel, not only genetically but also in a genuine uninterrupted encounter. The Jew keeps open the question of Christ.* He is the sign of the free mercy-choice and of the repudiating wrath of God. "Behold therefore the goodness and severity of God" (Rom. 11: 22). An expulsion of the Jews from the west must necessarily bring with it the expulsion of Christ. For Jesus Christ was a Jew.
>
> Greco-Roman antiquity, in quite a different way and very indirectly indeed, is also a part of our historical heritage. And we stand in yet another relation to our own, pre-Christian past. Classical antiquity stands

---

27. Bethge, "Dietrich Bonhoeffer and the Jews," 76.
28. See pages 99–101 above.

in a twofold relation to the appearance of Christ. It is the time when the
time of God was fulfilled, the time when God became man. And it is the
world which God took to Himself in the incarnation, the world of which
God made use in order to spread far and wide the Christian message. The
apostle Paul's appeal to his Roman citizenship and to the authority of the
Emperor makes it clear that Rome is placed at the service of Christ. But
it is at the same time also in the eyes of antiquity that the holiest token
of the presence of God, the cross, appears as the symbol of utter shame
and utter remoteness from God. *It is in this twofold relation to Christ that
antiquity becomes our historical heritage, in its nearness to Christ and in its
opposition to Him. It is the Roman heritage which comes to represent the
combination and assimilation of antiquity with the Christian element, and
it is the Greek heritage which comes to represent opposition and hostility
to Christ. While the peoples of western Europe, France, Holland, England,
and Italy sought in antiquity mainly for the Roman heritage, the relation of
Germans to antiquity has been determined primarily by Hellenism.*[29]

Though to my knowledge Bonhoeffer nowhere cites Adolf von Harnack's
work in the *Ethics,* it is readily apparent here that Bonhoeffer (a student of Harnack) has been mulling over the "Hellenization" thesis of
his teacher and appropriating it for his own use. In a free-wheeling bit
of metahistory, Bonhoeffer here makes a case not only for repealing
older Protestant anti-Semitic themes but for a fresh binding together
of the church with the Jews which will arrest the decay of Western
civilization.

Here Bonhoeffer depicts Hebraism and classical antiquity (broken into
Roman and Hellenic categories) as twinned forces struggling for their
existence within Christianity. The Christian West is littered with attempts
to reconcile antiquity with the essentially Jewish figure of the Messiah.
"Jesus Christ has made of the west a historical unit," says Bonhoeffer,
which implies he sees the coexistence of these forces as both possible
and desirable. However, whenever and wherever the Greek heritage is
conjured up minus the Roman interest in assimilation, it sets itself in
opposition to the Jewish heritage, sublimating it at best and expelling it
at worst. If Germany is truly the heir of the Greek world as Bonhoeffer
suggests, then there will be no room for the Jew. The Holocaust is something like the bastard son of classical Greek antiquity, bringing into the
bright light of day a hideous antithesis between Hebraism and Hellenism
that has been smoothed over by the dominance of the Constantinian
age. The analogy Bonhoeffer wants to draw seems fairly clear: as Jesus
the Jew was expelled from the world by means of the cross in the first
century, the Jews were expelled from Germany in the 1930s. What is

29. Bonhoeffer, *Ethics,* 26–27. Emphases added.

missing from the text is an analysis of the Greco-Roman aspect of Jesus' native Palestine. Here we might conjecture for Bonhoeffer that since by the time of Jesus the Diaspora Jews had been largely assimilated into the reaches of the Roman empire, and since even Jerusalem—earlier under the Seleucid kings and then later in 63 B.C.E. by the Romans—had come under Greek influence, the Greek spirit was instrumental in the death of Jesus.[30]

"The Jew keeps open the question of Christ" is therefore evidently not a statement about Christian supremacy. It does *not* mean the Jew exists for the sake of the Christian. Among other things, it reveals Bonhoeffer's ongoing search for a theological foundation upon which to establish his racial-ethical concern for Jews. By it Bonhoeffer is also making a statement about a Christian identity perpetually in danger of co-optation, namely that its Jewish Christ may be contorted into another figure altogether. Conversely, he is making a statement about Jewish identity, which by God's choice serves as a preservative leaven in his creation and forms a bulwark against the proliferation of other gods. It scarcely seems to bother Bonhoeffer that the messianic title ascribed to Jesus historically has been the sticking point between Christians and Jews, because the fundamental problem of Western civilization is not a Jewish versus Christian one. By more or less successfully winning the churches to its assumption that a particular *racial enemy* was responsible for Germany's ills, Nazism had exposed paradoxically that the Christian task of assimilating the Jewish element into German culture had not been completed. Bonhoeffer imagined that any genuine inheritance of classical antiquity must run through Jesus Christ the Jew, not around him. Therefore only the Christian who embraces Jesus Christ the Jew, and in him all Jews, is a true friend of Western civilization. The rest are enemies.

---

30. The reader is referred to an article by Anthony Beavers in which a similar interpretation is undertaken. Using Emanuel Levinas, Beavers draws the comparison between an Hebraic sense of ethical responsibility rooted in the face-to-face encounter with the local "other" and the highly prized value of the *polis* as intermediary between self and "other" characteristic of Hellenic culture. The Greek abstraction of "civic responsibility," he concludes, becomes a parasite on the concrete "social responsibility" characteristic of Judaism and depersonalizes the "other." In other words, "our civic responsibility has taught us to be irresponsible at home." In this line of interpretation one could find in Hitler's party the extreme application of the Greek *polis*, where every social relationship is mediated through the mechanism of the state. This provokes the following question: in his developing attraction to Jewish modes of thought, could Bonhoeffer have found the very lever that moves Christians toward their earthly responsibilities? Anthony Beavers, "Emanuel Levinas and the Prophetic Voice of Postmodernity," http://faculty.evansville.edu/tb2/trip/prophet.htm.

As Bonhoeffer explained to Reinhold Niebuhr in 1939, this creates an acute dilemma:

> Christians in Germany will face the terrible alternative of either willing the defeat of their nation in order that Christian civilization may survive, or willing the victory of their nation and thereby destroying our civilization. I know which of these alternatives I must choose; but I cannot make that choice in security . . .[31]

The language of inheritance and decay is admittedly impersonal, as is much of Bonhoeffer's writing in the *Ethics*. Since he was in continual danger while he wrote this work, most often his treatment of the Jewish problem gravitates either to academic prose or to cryptic expression. In this same chapter, however, there is a stirring confession of Christian guilt preceded by the admonition that the church's sin "is the entirely *personal* sin of the individual which is recognized here as a source of pollution for the whole community" (emphasis added). Bonhoeffer confesses, among other things, that the church is guilty of the loss of the Sabbath, of timidity and evasiveness, of being silent when the blood of the innocent was crying aloud to heaven, of desiring security, peace, possessions, and honor more than faithfulness. Further:

> The Church confesses that she has witnessed the lawless application of brutal force, the physical and spiritual suffering of countless innocent people, oppression, hatred and murder, and that she has not raised her voice on behalf of the victims and has not found ways to hasten to their aid. She is guilty of the deaths of the weakest and most defenceless brothers of Jesus Christ.[32]

That last phrase—"weakest and most defenceless brothers of Jesus Christ"—is one of those cryptic references to the Jews. This confession comes just at that time when Bonhoeffer is entering the conspiracy and taking up for himself, as an act of *metanoia*, the protection of Jewish life. As early as 1932 Bonhoeffer had speculated that his church would produce martyrs. Unlike the martyrdoms of early Christianity, however, he predicted that the blood of these martyrs would be stained with guilt.[33]

Guilt is what selfless love requires. "Jesus took upon himself the guilt of all men, and for that reason every man who acts responsibly becomes

31. *GS*, 1:320.
32. *Ethics*, 48–50.
33. *GS*, 4:71.

guilty."[34] Indeed, "real innocence shows itself precisely in a man's entering into the fellowship of guilt for the sake of other men."[35]

No doubt Bonhoeffer's attempt to make racial-ethical concern for the Jew an intrinsic feature of both Christianity and Western civilization was ambitious. It may have been easier for him to have interpreted the story of Western civilization along other lines. Yet Bonhoeffer longed to understand and experience God in the full spectrum of human life and history and to see Jesus Christ at its center. He could not overlook the fact that at the center of history, nature, and reality itself stood a certain Jew whose existence was oriented to others even if that meant a deep involvement in human guilt. He wrote:

> "Jesus is there only for others." His "being there for others," maintained until death, that is the ground of his omnipotence, omniscience and omnipresence. Faith is participation in this being of Jesus (incarnation, cross, and resurrection). Our relation to God is not a "religious" relationship to the highest, most powerful, and best Being imaginable—that is not authentic transcendence—but our relation to God is a new life in "existence for others," through participation in the being of Jesus. The transcendental is not infinite and unattainable tasks, but the neighbor who is within reach in any given situation.[36]

This is not the place to elaborate Bonhoeffer's Christology and ethics, but we must at all costs be clear that Bonhoeffer's interest in the Jewish neighbor does not amount to a humanitarian flight from theology. "The 'philanthropy' of God (Titus 3:4) that became evident in the incarnation is the reason for Christians to love every human being on earth as brother and sister."[37] Hence an attack even on the least of persons is an attack on Christ. The ontological merger of Christ and neighbor is critical here. For those same political acts that to others might have appeared most repugnant and distant from Christ were imagined by Bonhoeffer to be a movement into Christ. This is a vital and provocative feature of the "reasoned Christian conviction" upon which he engaged the political realm for the sake of the neighbor.

Operation 7

Under the pretense that they were needed by the Abwehr for reasons related to propaganda, Bonhoeffer assisted his brother-in-law Hans von

34. *Ethics*, 210.
35. Ibid.
36. *LPP*, 381.
37. *DBWE* 4, 285.

Dohnanyi in getting a group of fourteen Jews falsified papers so that they could cross the border to Switzerland. The Swiss were not in a good position to receive Jews at this time, and the Reich Security Office was very suspicious of the motives, which made for painstaking negotiations. Still, after a year of sustained effort they completed the operation successfully in 1942.

In view of the mass deportations of German Jews in progress at this time, the scope of this intervention seems trivial. Yet it became the basis for Bonhoeffer's arrest on 5 April 1943, when finally the Gestapo had begun to penetrate the secrecy of the Abwehr. The Gestapo had been investigating some alleged misappropriation of funds when they stumbled on the trail of "Operation 7," which led them in turn to Dohnanyi, the main target, but also to Bonhoeffer. During the ensuing trial, the prosecution hoped that Bonhoeffer would provide incriminating evidence against Dohnanyi. However, Dohnanyi had covered his tracks well. The prosecution could find no evidence of treason or subversion, only that the Abwehr spent too much money on Operation 7. Bonhoeffer's hopes for speedy release never materialized because, during the interrogations, questions raised about his travels abroad brought him under increasing suspicion. Thus his participation in this covert act to rescue a few Jews brought him into the clutches of the Nazi regime, from which he would never break free.

Why Bonhoeffer Really *Is* a Martyr

The objection to styling Bonhoeffer a true martyr of the church rests on legitimate concerns regarding his political activity. The concern is legitimate because when a confessor of the faith enters the crowded and complex arena of political causes, the clear association between confessing and dying seems inevitably to break down. In turn, this raises excruciating questions about whether the confessor may have sublimated faith to political ambition and by that corrupted her motivations. Then her death would be the *death of a Christian* but perhaps not *Christian death*.

Yet were the objection to Bonhoeffer as martyr founded solely upon the complexity of his political activity, one would expect to find a degree of tentativeness in the objectors' conclusions. Instead one finds the blatant and unapologetic separation of "true martyrs" on the one side from Bonhoeffer, a "political martyr," on the other. Assuming the objection is founded on a premise other than complexity, let us attempt to be more precise about it.

The objection to styling Bonhoeffer in the tradition of the church's true martyrs may rest upon *the fact of his political activity itself*. The objection could unfold in several ways: (1) The objector may stipulate that under no conditions whatsoever may Christian confession impinge upon the political sphere. (2) The objector may grant that Christian confession impinges upon politics, but find the particular form (conspiracy) of Bonhoeffer's political involvement either "morally wrong" or "morally right but outside the orbit of the church's martyr tradition." (3) The objector may grant that confession impinges upon politics and find Bonhoeffer's political action both "morally right" and somewhere within the orbit of the martyr tradition, yet inconsistent with his earlier beliefs such that the course of his political action does not square with his own confession. I will not address the third objection for two reasons: it begs the question of continuity in Bonhoeffer's life and thought, something I have assumed at the outset of the study, and it touches only tangentially upon the question of martyrdom.

I met the first objection by showing that (a) upon close examination of the early *acta*, Christian confession—and the death that follows—has a decidedly political dimension, (b) this political dimension is a feature of Jesus' own life and death, and (c) modern martyrs have brought the political dimension into the foreground again, albeit with the new element of solidarity with the neighbor. In the Holocaust context, the totalitarian encroachment of the state upon nearly all social institutions and relationships took from Bonhoeffer the decision *whether* to become political. Only the *form* of his political involvement was in question. As we saw, the Finkenwalde Seminary, where one might easily imagine a pious routine away from altercations, was politicized from the start by Bonhoeffer's aims for it, and along the way by the Gestapo's declaration of its illegality. The state, in other words, exposed and heightened the inherently political dimension of Christian existence.

Moreover, by pushing the racial principle to the fore and welding it to the future welfare of the nation, the Nazi state created the conditions under which Bonhoeffer could explore the meaning of Christian responsibility toward the state and for the Jews. When oppressive regimes target a race (Jew) or class (poor) of people, the neighbor's plight becomes an occasion for testing the limits of Christian confession. Under most circumstances those who confess are content to confine their action to written words or speech, but under certain oppressive conditions when freedom to write and speak is either taken away or proves powerless to mitigate the sufferings of the neighbor, Christian confession shows another side of itself, an active, ethical side. The state having already politicized the decisions of all its citizens and targeted some for persecution and death, the Christian who acts to defend the

neighbor *in any form whatsoever* is caught up in political resistance.
Thus I conclude that those who object to Bonhoeffer as martyr on the
grounds that Christian confession by its very nature does not impinge
on politics are resting Bonhoeffer's concrete case upon a distinction too
abstract for Bonhoeffer's, and perhaps any, context.

To Bonhoeffer's way of thinking, even though wanton racial hatred
may have thrust upon the church a sudden political responsibility to
act humanely for the neighbor, a confessional stance for the long haul
could not rest solely on a humanitarian ideal. His work on the Bethel
Confession together with his provocative historical-theological reflections about the place of Jews in Western culture, especially the Jew
Jesus, in whom racial and theological considerations merge, show that
Bonhoeffer sought and found what he took to be a Christian basis for
his political resistance. Moral action entwines with, or, even better, becomes an integral part of, theological work.

I have tried to meet the second objection in several ways. Whether
Bonhoeffer's actions were morally right or wrong is not directly a matter
of our concern, though as we have seen, some measure of innocence is
important in the consideration of martyrs. Bonhoeffer never attempted
to justify his conspiratorial activities (especially the plan to remove Hitler
by assassination) by appealing to ethical principles. I am not aware that
he tried to justify his actions at all. He certainly did not excuse himself
from guilt. Based on allusions in his poetry, it appears he saw his role in
the matter as sin in need of grace and forgiveness. Based on passages in
Ethics, he saw himself and his church as guilty long before the plot on
Hitler's life was set in motion. One cannot overemphasize the extremity
of the situation in Germany, which played havoc with ordinary ethical
concepts, such that both those who acted for the neighbor and those
who did not incurred guilt. Bonhoeffer submerged himself in the shame
of the Holocaust as one of those "guilty martyrs" he had premonitorily
forecasted years earlier. If guilt was endemic to life in Bonhoeffer's situation—one must remember the deep sense of guardianship *(Stellvertre-
tung)* that came with his bourgeois family, and the sense of class guilt
in allowing the barbarism of Hitler to strangle democratic ideals—then
his bold intervention for Jews was but the trading of one kind of guilt
for another, the guilt of inactivity for guilt of activity. There could be no
"guiltless" martyrs in Bonhoeffer's Germany.

In any case, in the course of the discussion I suggested that innocence
is always a matter of degree, save for Jesus Christ, who, as the anony-
mous writer of Hebrews indicates, was like us in all respects except sin.
The point of paramount importance is that the martyr bears witness to
Christ in life and death. The more innocent the martyr, the more clearly
Jesus' innocence comes into focus for those who look on. A "guilty

martyr" paradoxically may still be said to bear witness to Christ, his guilt the blemished background against which the innocence of Jesus is set in relief. But he may also bring into focus the paradox of Christ himself, who, though "he committed no sin" yet "bore our sins in his body on the cross" (1 Peter 2:22, 24) and thus assumed fully the guilt of the world. If it is Jesus Christ himself, or his truth, to which the martyr's life and death bears witness, then a facet, but not necessarily the whole, of Christ's life-to-death movement must be evident in the martyr. Some will be transparent to the Innocent Lamb, still others to the One who by following the downward trajectory of the incarnation emptied himself in service of others, bore their grief, and became their sin (2 Cor. 5:21). Like Christ's, Bonhoeffer's willingness to die is inseparable from his readiness to incur guilt.

Against those who grant Bonhoeffer's moral justification but find him too distant from the martyr tradition, I attempted to show that at the core of the Christian martyr tradition lies the belief that followers of Christ must not end their imitation of the Master at death's door. Rather they must be ready to walk through it when and if faithful confession requires, and they must do so in a manner sensitive to the delicate dialectic of freedom and constraint: "willing but not too willing." Under the concept of discipleship Bonhoeffer cut a channel through which the *imitatio Christi* tradition could irrigate his own life and the lives of his ordinands. His occasional comments as he neared death (e.g., "watching with Christ in Gethsemane . . .") and general readiness for death even while still vitally participating in the storm of events reflect a responsible application of Christ's life in his own self-understanding. As Bonhoeffer put it, "faith demands an elasticity of behaviour," taking care to practice both resistance and submission. "We must confront fate," he said, "as resolutely as we submit to it at the right time."[38]

Aside from the *imitatio Christi*, I pointed out the plausible connection between the narrative structure of Bonhoeffer's death and that "formal pattern" culled by Fischel from Jewish and early Christian *acta*. Bonhoeffer's deathward journey fits the "formal pattern" in most ways, but certainly not all. In the final analysis, comparing Bonhoeffer to the classical understanding of martyrdom yielded mixed results. His conscious appropriation of the *imitatio Christi* with its various nuances is

---

38. *LPP*, 217–18. For this idea Bonhoeffer is most surely indebted to Kierkegaard, who, in his discussion of Abraham, elaborates the dialectic or "double movement" of faith. There is first the movement of "infinite resignation" through which, in pain and discomfort, one reconciles oneself with God's will. This movement is the necessary precondition of faith itself, wherein one fully grasps the possibilities of one's existence before God. See *Fear and Trembling*, trans. Walter Lowrie (Princeton, N.J.: Princeton University Press, 1941), 38ff.

perhaps the most convincing correlation. But the most serious departure from the classical understanding is the quite ambiguous connection between Bonhoeffer's confession and his death.

Were this the sum of the argument, it would be difficult to say with confidence that Bonhoeffer deserves to be considered a martyr in the traditional sense, because one of the most important and dramatic features is missing. Images of brave Christians standing heroically before the worldly powers giving unequivocal, lucid confession of their faith before being consigned to beasts, burnings, and boilings are forever etched in popular memory. The pointed encounter between persecutor and persecuted, between executor and executed, makes absolutely clear *why* these persons went to their deaths: they confessed Christ! Yet given the eccentric nature of the Roman context, it is more likely that these conspicuous encounters derive from the vicissitudes of history than from the essence of martyrdom. Confessing Christ is surely the obligation of every Christian generation, but confession may assume a variety of forms, dependent on the rich texture of God's creative Spirit and human response.

In the political overtones of the twentieth-century martyrs, it might be said that the Spirit of God is illuminating both the continuity of Christian confession through the centuries and the variety of its forms. The political elements in the early *acta* went largely unnoticed in Christian history because from the inception of the Constantinian era, religious existence and political existence were integrated in the concept of Christendom. The breakdown of Christendom has once again thrown this dimension into the open, so that we now grasp the affinity between contemporary and ancient martyrs. The fresh element in our time can also be traced to the end of Christendom. In a Constantinian world, confessions of faith may be enough to call worldly powers to account before God. Luther could appeal, for example, to the German princes to act justly vis-à-vis the citizens, fully expecting that as administrators of God's created order they would carry out his will. In a post-Christian context, or one that cloaks itself in Christian garb to hide its anti-Christian soul, such pleas are likely to fall on deaf ears—deaf ears truly, for religious confession is not considered essential for unity in the *polis* and can therefore be easily filtered out. The political powers of our day do not seem overly agitated by strong verbal confessions, unless and until those confessions lead to actions, or better yet, until those confessions find their active voice. When verbal confession spends but buys no results, confession must change its form in order to achieve its fruit. In germ, this explains how the martyrs of our age have gotten themselves entangled in politics. They confess Jesus Christ by acting for those "others" who have been marginalized in the *polis*. Living in an age of disorder, Bonhoeffer himself walked to the precipice of this conclusion as he considered the beatitude of Jesus, "Blessed are those who are persecuted for righteousness' sake, for theirs is the kingdom of heaven":

> This beatitude puts those Christians entirely in the wrong who, in their mistaken anxiety to act rightly, seek to avoid any suffering for the sake of a just, good and true cause, because, as they maintain, they could with a clear conscience suffer only for an explicit profession of faith in Christ; it rebukes them for their ungenerousness and narrowness which looks with suspicion on all suffering for a just cause and keeps its distance from it. Jesus gives His support to those who suffer for a just cause, even if this cause is not precisely the confession of His name; He takes them under His protection, He accepts responsibility for them, and he lays claim to them. And so the man who is persecuted for the sake of a just cause is led to Christ. . . . This, too, is not an abstract deduction, but it is an experience we ourselves have undergone, an experience in which the power of Jesus Christ became manifest in fields of life where it had previously remained unknown.[39]

At this point one might still object that Bonhoeffer's action was motivated as much by politics as by love for the marginalized others in the *polis*. It is abundantly clear that his family's high social standing and rigorous support of the liberal aims of the Weimar Republic played an enormous role in Bonhoeffer's ethical sensibilities. The Bonhoeffer family lost four members—two sons and two sons-in-law—in the conspiracy, a fact hardly explainable by chance. In the Nazi era, those who acted consciously for the cause of Christ were persecuted alike with those for whom the cause was justice, truth, and goodness. In Bonhoeffer's own judgment the latter were acting for Christ whether they knew it or not,[40] but it was only *as theologian*—one who had come to see the relationship between God and the world in a certain way—that Bonhoeffer could arrive at such conclusions.

And so I return repeatedly to the rather mundane fact that Bonhoeffer was by choice a theologian, that he wrote theology in the Holocaust context, that he labored incessantly to understand his own behavior from the Christian point of view and drew out the connections between faith and action from his *Habilitationschrift* (Bonhoeffer's inaugural dissertation, *Act and Being*, by which he qualified as a university lecturer) to his *Ethics*. Along the way his concerns for Jews, even if quite personal, were always secured on a specific basis as we have seen, and they intensified proportionate to watermarks left by the tide of escalating pogroms and atrocities. In short, because Bonhoeffer was a theologian, we have the opportunity to construe his action differently from that of others in his family, or the conspiracy in general.

---

39. *Ethics*, 181–82.
40. Ibid.

Part Two

Interpretive Prospects of Martyrdom

7

Toward a Hermeneutic
of Martyrdom

The pastor should visit the cemetery as often as he is able. This is whole-some for him personally, for his preaching, for his spiritual care, and also for his theology!

Bonhoeffer, *Spiritual Care*

I have now finished my painstaking argument for Dietrich Bonhoef-fer as martyr. The reason for the argument will become clear in this chapter and the next, where I propose martyrdom as a "reading key" for Bonhoeffer's life and thought. What I want ultimately to "read" is the *relationship between his theology and his ethics*, with martyrdom functioning as the lens. Or, to use a slightly different metaphor, I want to illumine the *passageway* between belief and behavior with the use of martyrdom.

Forging martyrdom into an interpretive tool requires some philosophi-cal investigation. As we will see, martyrdom amounts to a theological interpretation of one's life. It also converges upon the larger mystery of human death. For these reasons it will be expedient to consider mar-tyrdom as the expression—indeed the epitomizing expression—of what might be called a Christian theology of death.

In the pages that follow, Bonhoeffer recedes into the background until the hermeneutical aspect of martyrdom is sufficiently developed. In the foreground sits an analysis of a key portion of Martin Heidegger's monumental work *Being and Time* and some insights gleaned from the writings of Karl Rahner. Taken together, the works of these individuals establish an ontological-theological foundation for what I am calling a "hermeneutic of martyrdom." Before examining them in detail, however, I think it will help to sketch out broadly the vision I have in mind.

Martyrdom as an Interpretive Category

Martyrdom implies a standpoint "after the fact," as it were. As we noticed in the Lyons martyrs, who in advance of their deaths would not permit others to call them martyrs but only humble confessors, the very ascription *martyr* was attributable only after their lives were over. That is, martyrs do not name themselves but must *be named*, posthumously, by those who in one way judge them worthy of the term. In the most simple, chronological sense, it ought to be obvious that martyrdom is inherently an interpretive category. But *why* is it so?

A martyr's death may be seen as one's last ethical act—an *act* because it could have been avoided had the martyr chosen differently, and *ethical* because it is an act cast against a horizon more compelling than narrow self-interest—performed with the intent of remaining true to one's religious confession (and thus true to one's self). The appellation *martyr* might then be considered a postscript that ratifies, vindicates, and asserts continuity between belief and behavior in the life of the deceased. Must it necessarily be others who make these ascriptions? Should it not be possible for the confessors themselves, through the sheer force of their good life, to assert this continuity *before* their death? Certainly confessors may construe their own lives as continuous, and often do, yet their assertions lack a ring of finality, for their end has not yet come. Framing a whole life with finality requires all its various parts to be accessible. So long as the confessor is living, such an assignment remains quite unattainable; only those who survive the confessor's death have the requisite vantage point from which to make this judgment. Martyrdom, therefore, is not unlike the memorial wreaths the living place respectfully upon the graves of the dead.

In any case, it is unlikely that confessors near death will be preoccupied with the continuity of their own lives. More often than not, at the end they aspire only to be transparent to Christ, directing their own and others' gaze only toward him. Like John the Baptist, they are witnesses to a truth much larger than themselves. Even so, however much martyrs may transcend themselves and witness to truth, they remain *witnesses* to it, and as such "subjects" of their own actions. In martyrdom the last "ethical act," though not specifically intended, proves itself inseparable from the larger series of previous acts (words and deeds) that are undertaken in a calculated manner. The final act of the martyr is related to its antecedents not like the last apple placed into a bushel but like the last note of a melody or the closing stanza of a sonnet. This final act completes and configures what has gone before. Indeed, the term *martyr* would be vacuous were there not a coherent matrix of belief and action preceding it.

In the strictest sense, of course, only in the case of suicide can persons be the exclusive subjects of their own death. However, martyrs may be called subjects in a special sense. Their death holds the power to summarize their entire existence in a way ordinary deaths do not, because in the very manner of their dying a constitutive facet of Christ's death is dramatized in the present moment. For Christ *offered* his life in free obedience to the Father's will. On this basis we must contend that while the postscript *martyr* is surely a retrospective ascription of continuity—that is, "after the fact"—it is also an ascription that is in a most real sense elicited by the martyr as actor. In turn, this means that the attribution *martyr* cannot be affixed by mere interpretation, or mere description, but interpretation tinged with recognition, approval tinged with affirmation. *Martyr* is an attribution that marks a touching of horizons, a signal of resonance between the faith of the living and the faith of the dead.

My contention that martyrs contribute substantially toward eliciting their title requires the supposition that death is an act performed in freedom. In everyday experience, where death is envisaged as an unexpected, intruding thief that takes away life, the active and free dimensions of death are not readily apparent. Death "happens." Death is the "actor" while the dying are "acted upon." Even when death is expected, it is not expected imminently, and therefore its definite quality frequently eludes the realm of ordinary experience. As long as one's death remains segregated from everyday existence, when at last it bursts into the foreground it will take the appearance of an accident, or at the very least a gruff interruption to the presumably normal course of events. Yet, this is only because one's own death has not really become one's own. Only when the brute fact that all *must* die, that *I* must die, is reckoned with at last will it be possible to grasp death's active aspect. If I *must* die, then my life is the life of a dying person, at which point the questions "How shall I live?" and "How shall I die?" prove one and the same. Carl Jung conveyed the idea poetically when he said,

> From the middle of life onward, only he remains vitally alive who is ready to *die with life*. For in the secret hour of life's midday the parabola is reversed, death is born. . . . The negation of life's fulfillment is synonymous with the refusal to accept its ending. Both mean not wanting to live; not

wanting to live is identical with not wanting to die. Waxing and waning make one curve.[1]

The martyr's choice to live in a certain way, to confess in a risk-laden manner, is simultaneously a choice to *die* in a certain way. That is, the martyr chooses a *course toward death* that others do not and thus, in effect, chooses to die differently.

Virtually from the cradle of Western philosophy death has been an imperative horizon for life. It is still the case today, though that fact may be less clear than in preceding historical epochs. In medieval Europe the dead coexisted more plainly with the living, symbolized perhaps by the placement of cemeteries in the plaza square of the church, where one could be visually reminded that life is lived toward death, or the public nature of the dying person's bedchamber visited regularly by relatives and friends. In a secularized world life and death do not dialogue as openly as they once did. Instead the tendency is to suppress death wherever possible and make it into a private affair. The late Joseph Cardinal Bernardin of Chicago tried to remedy this situation when he vowed to die a public death. "My decision to discuss my cancer openly and honestly," he said, "has sent a message that when we are ill, we need not close in on ourselves, or remove ourselves from others."[2]

Socrates, whose voluntary acceptance of death influences the Christian view of martyrdom in subtle ways,[3] labeled his philosophy the "practice of death."[4] True to his deepest convictions, Socrates held no pretense to knowledge concerning death. For "no one knows," he said, "whether death, which men in their fear apprehend to be the greatest evil, may not be the greatest good."[5] Nor did he waver at the suggestion that he could evade death simply by consenting not to promulgate the way of life that brought him into conflict with his accusers. Socrates would not trade his life for freedom, because by his own measure he had already attained it. He had come to terms with his own ignorance—that is, with himself—and in doing so was prepared to face his death freely.

---

1. Carl Jung, quoted in Christopher E. Mooney, *Man without Tears: Soundings for a Christian Anthropology* (New York: Harper and Row, 1973), 105–6.

2. For coverage of Bernardin's death, see Kenneth L. Woodward and John McCormick, "The Art of Dying Well" in *Newsweek* (25 November 1996): 61–67. For philosophical and historical treatments of death, see Philippe Ariés, *Western Attitudes toward Death: From the Middle Ages to the Present,*trans. Patricia M. Ranum (Baltimore: Johns Hopkins University Press, 1975).

3. Arthur J. Droge and James D. Tabor, *A Noble Death: Suicide and Martyrdom among Christians and Jews in Antiquity* (San Francisco: HarperSanFrancisco, 1992).

4. Albert B. Hakim, *Historical Introduction to Philosophy,* 3d ed. (Upper Saddle River, N.J.: Prentice-Hall, 1997), 30.

5. Ibid., 40.

Socrates has long been a model for human dying, and for reasons that transcend stoic courage. To unlock the riddle of his resolve in the face of death, one must note that his way of life had already become the practice of death. This was his secret: the dialectic of life and death had been concretized and personalized in his own experience to such a degree that the meaning of life and death had been forged together. Or, to put it more succinctly, for him *living was dying*.

We should note that the manner of Socrates' death left an indelible stamp upon his life. Today he remains for us the Socrates who died for the truth he taught. When the martyr steers her life into the narrow shoals and risks death, she connects the actual terminus of death to the wider narrative of her life, such that the terminus is at the same time a fulfillment of her existence.

The notion that martyrdom completes a life is a noteworthy feature of the anthropology of Irenaeus, for whom martyrdom was an acme of growth wherein Christians were brought into communion with the dead Christ and therein formed finally into the *imago* of God.[6] This conspicuously active dimension of the martyr's death is detectable in the church's linguistic symbols. Often we say that martyrs "seal" their confession by means of blood. If the martyr's death were not in some profound sense an *act* of freedom, it would be difficult to see how a "martyr" could be distinguished from a "victim."

At this point, it is becoming obvious that fashioning martyrdom into a hermeneutic device requires a theological treatment of the larger mystery of human death and the various ways one might meet it. So far I have sketched only the barest outline of a working model; it will need further detailing and honing to become useful in our quest to illumine the passageway between belief and behavior in Bonhoeffer's life. Even when the model is better defined, however, I will follow Alfred North Whitehead, who suggested it was more important for a proposition to be interesting than for it to be true. Much of my subsequent work will be done in this spirit. Yet I am interested in truthfulness as well as usefulness, and for that reason I must direct the current of the present discussion closer to the shores of ontology.

Heidegger's Being-unto-Death

As Heidegger began part 2 of *Being in Time*, he summed up what had already been found and what he was yet seeking. He had established in

6. Gustaf Wingren, *Man and the Incarnation: A Study in the Biblical Theology of Irenaeus* (Edinburgh: Oliver and Boyd, 1959), 35.

part 1 the structure of *Dasein*'s[7] being-in-the-world in its various manifestations by means of a "preparatory analysis."[8] In part 2 Heidegger
sought to lay bare the structural whole of Dasein by examining its "hermeneutical situation," that is, its total structural context as a temporal-
historical entity with a "beginning" and "end." In this fashion Heidegger
wanted to consummate his interpretation of Dasein's being begun in
part 1, but he also wanted, precisely by that means, to gain access to
Being in general. His endeavor in part 1 was carried out by an *existential*
analysis of Dasein, a mode of analysis that, by his own admission, could
not lay claim to primordiality.[9] If Dasein is to become a foundation for
the basic question of ontology as Heidegger intends, then the mode of
analysis in part 2 must become more directly ontological.

Heidegger's framing of the matter in this way is vital to our project,
because it offers a defensible ontological ground. Yet the potential for
confusion is obvious. Because part 2 is still in the mode of existential,
even if "more ontological," analysis, Heidegger's readers may be tempted
to restrict his insights to the realm of individual existence and miss their
broader metaphysical relevance.

The overlapping nature of Heidegger's existential-ontological analysis
seems to derive from the nature of existential analysis as such, where
existence defines essence. Existential analysis thus always stumbles upon
a thorny problem: an individual existing entity cannot be examined in
its totality so long as it still exists. To put the problem as a question, how
can Dasein come into view as a whole when something essential to its
being, namely its end, lies yet in front of it? Heidegger writes, "As long
as Dasein is, there is in every case something still outstanding, which
Dasein can be and will be."[10] Until Dasein's existence closes up, so to
speak, what it can be and will be is not resolved. That is, Dasein's Being
is chiefly a potentiality—"potentiality-for-Being-a-whole." When finally
Dasein's Being is resolved, its potentiality having become actual by its
completion, it disappears over the horizon and becomes unobservable:

7. *Dasein* is the term by which Heidegger refers to the concrete, individual instance of
the existing entity of the human. In philosophical discussions, the term is brought directly
into English. Translated literally, *Da-sein* is "there-being." With this term Heidegger meant to
break away from the kind of ontology that had long characterized the Western philosophical tradition. For him, "Being" was not a category to be considered in the abstract—that
is, as a *concept* standing prior to the one who considers it. Rather it must be examined as
a feature of the inquirer herself, who is "there" within the world. As such, every question
about Being is necessarily a question about being human. *Dasein* (hereafter employed
without italics) thus represents Heidegger's fundamental ontological standpoint.
8. Martin Heidegger, *Being and Time*, trans. John Macquarrie and Edward Robinson
(New York: Harper and Row, 1962), 274.
9. Ibid., 276.
10. Ibid.

"As long as Dasein *is* as an entity, it has never reached its 'wholeness.' But if it gains such 'wholeness,' this gain becomes the utter loss of Being-in-the-World. In such a case, it can never again be experienced *as an entity*."[11]

How ever can one grasp the whole of Dasein? How is it possible with a discrete instance of existence to decipher the realm of Being?

Here Heidegger takes an intuitive step. He surmises that Dasein's Being, by its very structure, may disclose Being as such. The structure of Dasein's Being is *toward death (Sein zum Tode)*. Heidegger argues that Dasein may become aware of its own death, grasp it, assimilate it into its existence, and thereby achieve "authenticity." The argument proves circular, as Heidegger himself admits, but circularity seems unavoidable in existential analysis, for the question of what it means to be itself ushers one into the hermeneutic circle. As Michael Gelven explains it,

> To question what it means to be operates in the hermeneutic circle; it begins with a consciousness of what it means to be, and through the analysis of the various ways of existence reveals more specifically and more ontologically the true meaning of Being. This consciousness of Being, of course, is itself a way of existing.[12]

When Dasein grasps its own Being it latches onto Being Itself, of which it is a particular instance. But it can do this only vis-à-vis death, and that is why Heidegger's analysis pivots on the notion of death. In a gesture of grace, death holds out to Dasein the chance to drop anchor in the tumultuous seas of its everyday existence. It provides access to the ontological totality of Being. Yet how must Dasein arrange itself vis-à-vis death? Let's trace the discussion in more detail.

Heidegger says that death is something toward which Dasein *comports* itself. For Dasein, death is something that stands before it, something impending. It does not impend in the manner of a storm, which may be endured and thus survived. Dasein's death impends in a way utterly distinct from the endless variety of "events" that characterize life. Since Dasein cannot survive its own death, at issue is nothing less than its very Being-in-the-world. "Death is the possibility of the absolute impossibility of Dasein," and for this reason it manifests itself as "that possibility which is one's ownmost, which is non-relational, and which is not to be outstripped."[13] Unlike routine affairs of life that involve persons with

11. Ibid., 280.

12. Michael Gelven, *A Commentary on Heidegger's "Being and Time,"* rev. ed. (DeKalb: Northern Illinois University Press, 1989), 140.

13. By "ownmost" *(eigenst)* Heidegger means the death that is very much my own, my own death. Because it is my own it cannot be shared, hence it is "non-relational"

others in myriad ways, death must be faced individually. Death may be a familiar element of human experience—it happens around us as a matter of course—but it retains its uniqueness in respect to each individual Dasein. Heidegger rejects the notion that Dasein conjures up on its own the uniqueness of its death and projects itself into this situation. Rather, Dasein is "thrown" into the conditions of existence.

Now it is important to note that comporting one's self toward death has nothing to do with a romantic idolization of death or some other fascination with it, morbid or otherwise. Nor does it have to do with one's psychological disposition toward death, much less one's state of mind while dying. Just when the reader's attention is fixed unflinchingly on the terminus of existence, Heidegger redirects the focus to accentuate existence itself. For when one realizes what it means to be something that will one day cease to be, disclosed is precisely the significance of one's *life*. What it means not to be is always inseparable from what it means to be. Potentially at least, awareness that one is going to die is greatly beneficial because it enables one to focus on being-able-to-be.[14] Impending death floods life with meaning.

Except when it doesn't. One may comport one's self to death either authentically or inauthentically. In average everyday Being-toward-death, the self takes refuge in the anonymous "they" of public interpretation,[15] masking the individuality of Dasein's death. In mainstream public opinion death is a considered a "mishap" that regularly occurs to others, an indefinite something that arrives as a fugitive but is not yet *mine*. "Dying," says Heidegger, "which is essentially mine in such a way that no one can be my representative, is perverted into an event of public occurrence which the 'they' encounters." The result is that death as one's ownmost possibility of Being is conveniently hidden from view, softened, tranquilized.

"Anxiety," not "fear," earmarks an authentic comportment toward death. Unlike fear, anxiety has no object. It is the positive and appropriate human response to the threat of nonbeing. But public opinion intervenes to mitigate "anxiety." It construes death as a social inconvenience or an event against which people are to be protected. When Dasein succumbs to the public interpretation of death, it is alienated from its ownmost potentiality for Being, because in the last analysis "everyday Being-towards-death is a constant *fleeing in the face of death*. Being-*towards*-the-end has the mode of *evasion in the face of it*—giving

---

(unbezügliche). And because it cannot be avoided it is not to be "outstripped" *(unüberholbare)*. See ibid., 148.

14. Ibid., 156.

15. Heidegger, *Being and Time*, 296.

new explanations for it, understanding it inauthentically, and concealing it."[16] The problem with everyday Being-toward-death is not that it rejects the reality of death out of hand or even by some daydream imagines it to be "uncertain." Flight does not in this case imply outright denial. At one level, those living in "everydayness" understand perfectly well that death is real. They may be "certain" of it in fact, but their "certainty" is itself inauthentic since, in their concern to alleviate death's discomfort, they keep it at bay and thus conceal it from their present life. In the end, by relegating death to the future they fail to realize its existential importance in the present moment.

We arrive now at a crucial point. For Heidegger, authentic comportment toward the possibility (a *certain* possibility) of death happens in the mode of *anticipation*. When Dasein anticipates its own Being-unto-death, it simply remains faithful to the kind of Being it is: one for which something always lies out ahead. Since the very Being of Dasein has the structure of anticipation, it follows that in order to be true to itself, or authentic *(eigentlich)*, it must grasp its own structure of existence as Being-toward-death.[17] Unlike inauthentic comportment toward death, which conceals the structure of Dasein, anticipation reveals it. When Dasein approaches death in anxious anticipation, its ownmost possibility (its individuality) is "wrenched away" from the public "they," and it faces the unavoidable "mineness" of death with this result: *it frees itself for accepting death.*

Freedom, then, is the fruit of an authentic confrontation with death. Heidegger expands:

> When, by anticipation, one becomes free *for* one's own death, one is liberated from one's lostness in those possibilities which may accidentally thrust themselves upon one; and one is liberated in such a way that for the first time one can authentically understand and choose among the factical possibilities lying ahead of that possibility which is not to be outstripped. Anticipation discloses to existence that its uttermost possibility lies in giving itself up, and thus it shatters all one's tenaciousness to whatever existence has been reached.[18]

Notice the emphasis here. The genuine possibilities that lie ahead of one's death—those pertaining to one's life—are illumined precisely in the authentic encounter with the quite certain possibility of death. Faced in the mode of anticipation, death throws a light back across one's life so as to illumine the whole of Dasein in advance.[19] Once this breakthrough

16. Ibid., 298.
17. Ibid., 307.
18. Ibid., 308.
19. Ibid., 309.

occurs, one should cultivate anticipation so as to maintain one's self in this truth.[20]

The conscience, rooted in the structure of guilt and responsibility, plays a special role in Heidegger's description of authentic existence. As a form of self-discourse it has four dimensions, each of which involves the self: it is the self that *calls;* it is the self that *is called;* the call is *about* the self; and it is the self *toward* which the self is called. As a call from self to self, conscience alerts individual Dasein to the "must" of its decision either for or against authenticity. Guilt is implied by conscience, since there is something that the self should be but as yet is not, though in Heidegger's existential analysis guilt is not evidence of moral transgression but rather an indication of Dasein's thrownness into the conditions of finitude. Its negative aspect—the self not being what the self might be—amounts to a revelation that the self may in its decisions both include and exclude possibilities pertaining to its Being. Thus the conscience, "this reticent self-projection upon one's ownmost Being-guilty,"[21] affords Dasein a state of "resoluteness" in which it is poised for that anxiety which, vis-à-vis death, leads to authenticity.

Being-unto-Death and the Continuity of a Life

I break momentarily from my analysis of Heidegger to clarify my use of him and to take stock of the interpretive possibilities *Being and Time* contains. The path that will soon open before us is lined with narrative possibilities to the side and supported by a metaphysic beneath. It is my hope that along such a path creativity and soundness might mingle profitably. On the basis of the analysis so far we can recognize in the distance some intriguing convergences between Bonhoeffer and Heidegger, among them Bonhoeffer's evident inner freedom toward death, his determination not to evade it, his willingness to incur guilt along the way, and a concomitant "resoluteness."

Bonhoeffer wrote *Act and Being* (1929) directly in conversation with *Being and Time* (1927), a fact that provokes the imagination in sundry ways.[22] It is possible, no doubt, to overemphasize the impact of Heidegger upon Bonhoeffer, especially since Bonhoeffer criticized

20. Ibid. At this point Heidegger reminds his readers that *"the state-of-mind which can hold open the utter and constant threat to itself arising from Dasein's ownmost individualized Being, is anxiety"* (see 310).

21. Ibid., 343.

22. The index of the new English edition of *Act and Being* reveals that Bonhoeffer's most frequent references are distributed evenly among Heidegger, Luther, and Barth (see *DBWE* 2:214).

Heidegger's project at several key points. Nevertheless, some important threads of correlation may be followed across Bonhoeffer's life.[23] It is both possible and justifiable, I think, to examine Bonhoeffer's life and thought as an authentic comportment toward death, since, as I have shown, freedom toward death is one of the distinguishing marks of his life and that of martyrs in general. True, neither Bonhoeffer's relation to Heidegger nor his "authenticity" is directly under consideration here, but we *are* seeking a entrance point into Bonhoeffer's life and thought that satisfactorily illumines the whole. If it could be shown that Bonhoeffer projected the unity and wholeness of his own life in a Heideggerian tone, or consciously authored it with Heidegger's notion of authenticity in mind, then the case would be all the more interesting, whatever their theological and philosophical differences. Such an approach would insert the interpreter into an imaginary viewpoint within Bonhoeffer's experience and flesh out the relationship between his thought and actions accordingly. It is within the scope of this work to explore this avenue, and it will be attempted in various ways in succeeding chapters, though not directly in Heideggerian terms. For the present, however, my primary task is to locate the interpretive potential of martyrdom. I am not using Heidegger in order to show that Bonhoeffer is Heideggerian. It will be remembered that what Heidegger contributes to the project is a launching point from which to organize the thought-action relation from the perspective of martyrdom. Naturally I desire my reading of this relation to be roughly continuous with Bonhoeffer's self-understanding, but insofar as the postscript *martyr* is, strictly speaking, a matter of after-interpretation, not self-interpretation, I do not consider such continuity obligatory.

Building on our discussion, the death that Bonhoeffer could only anticipate—his own—in advance has now become part of the complex nexus of history which needs to be reflected upon and configured from a more comprehensive perspective. As the title *Being and Time* conveys, Heidegger could not have finished his work without extrapolating his

---

23. Charles Marsh describes the importance of the Bonhoeffer-Heidegger connection this way: "In an attempt to shape reflection in a way that is not determined by the totality of the self-reflective subject but emerges from a source prior to and external to the individual, Bonhoeffer finds certain themes in Heidegger's fundamental ontology congenial to his theological purposes. Bonhoeffer subjects these themes to christological redescription, and thus does not appropriate existential analysis *tout court.* Nonetheless, Heidegger's notions of potentiality-for-being, authenticity, and being with others push Bonhoeffer in his thinking about human selfhood and sociality to recognize specific social-ontological distinctions and concepts critical to his developing christology." See Charles Marsh, *Reclaiming Dietrich Bonhoeffer: The Promise of His Theology* (New York: Oxford University Press, 1994), 112.

analysis of Dasein into the domain of temporality and historicality. Having asserted that the structure of Dasein is organized around its future death, by implication Heidegger has already plotted Dasein historically. Dasein is a Being *in* time, a being stretched out temporally. Therefore the question of wholeness and authenticity, indeed the entire matter of Being-toward-death, cannot be torn away from the garment of history. Being-in-Time, as it turns out, is the supporting structure for the kind of existential analysis of Dasein that Heidegger has given. That is, temporality is what must be presupposed if Dasein is to grasp its Being by way of anticipation.

Heidegger chose to unfold this discussion of temporality in dialogue with Wilhelm Dilthey, who concerned himself with the various problems of history, and of whose work Heidegger calls his an appropriation.[24] Like Dilthey before him, Heidegger declared his interest in the historical nature of existence, and in particular the "connectedness of life" *(der Zusammenhang des Lebens)* through its temporal duration.[25] The prospect of a connected life, or for that matter the lack of one, raises a provocative question: how do the nearly infinite sequence of experiences that comprise a life from birth to death get thematized? Or, how might the history of a life be written? Though individuals may and do gauge their own lives, organizing and reorganizing sundry disparate elements, as subjects they can never project themselves as the total object of their reflection, and hence as subjects they cannot answer the question definitively. In Heidegger's philosophy the subject-object structure already presupposes a more comprehensive "world" to which both subjects and objects belong. Therefore all questions of coherence or connectedness must be answered with recourse to that "world" in which the individual Dasein finds itself.[26]

Authentic history, individual and social, must seek to rise above the mere chronicle of facts, because facts must translate into meaningful possibilities in regard to human existence. This means that history is always subject to reinterpretations and fresh appropriations. Michael Gelven explains:

> An interesting consequence of Heidegger's theory of history is something that Heidegger himself does not comment about but that merits consideration. If history is grounded in one's fate and destiny, then history must

---

24. Heidegger, *Being and Time,* 449. Pannenberg says of Heidegger's work that "as a matter of fact, not only his section on the historicity of Dasein but the entire conception of *Being and Time* drew incisive inspiration from Dilthey." Wolfhart Pannenberg, *Metaphysics and the Idea of God* (Grand Rapids: Eerdmans, 1990), 74–75.

25. Heidegger, *Being and Time,* 439.

26. Gelven, *Commentary,* 200.

constantly be *reinterpreted;* not only because of each generation, but indeed each individual adds his own unique perspective to the understanding of his fate and his people's destiny, and hence the historical perspective must be changed to fit that aspect of human existence which asserts itself as most important in a particular era or group, or even in a single man.[27]

To go a step further, one might venture that it is more than necessary to surrender history to constant reinterpretation, because with each successive interpretation a new whole of a life or people comes into view. In this vein, Dilthey had suggested that a biographer was privileged over his subject because he came along after the death of the subject and could assess the whole.[28] Dilthey understood, of course, that there could be no final assessment of even an individual life until the end of history, when all material was available in hindsight. No boisterous claims to finality are heard here. Yet taken together, the temporal nature of individual existence, its link to the larger whole of temporized human existence, and the demand that history be significant precisely for human existence impose upon the interpreter a task that is more than necessary because it is a task grounded in the nature of reality itself. If we recall that for Heidegger individual Dasein discloses the nature of Being, then the question of *its* wholeness vis-à-vis *its* end is a particularized instance of an ontological wholeness-in-view-of-the-end. That is, the death of a particular Dasein reveals the general significance of death for life.

The interest of our investigation is of course the significance of Bonhoeffer's death for Bonhoeffer's life, but whatever that significance turns out to be, it must be defensible on some deeper ground. Just as the totality of a human life cannot be assessed within its peculiar history, neither can total historical description of that life be realized within history. The meaning of a life cannot be pinned down in its temporal trajectory but must be "settled," as I put it earlier, from a standpoint "after the fact." Now, however, it is becoming obvious that this standpoint does not denote a fixed point of reference, as in a view from the bank of a stream, but one that is simply farther downstream in the temporal flow of human existence.

Dilthey's influence on Bonhoeffer deserves to be noted as well. Ernst Feil has tracked Dilthey's impact through several of the key prison letters to show that the seminal ideas behind Bonhoeffer's "world come of age"[29] emerged directly from his reading of Dilthey. Popular "Bonhoefferian" phrases such as "religionless Christianity,"[30] "even if there were no God"

27. Gelven, 214.
28. David Carr, *Time, Narrative, and History* (Bloomington: Indiana University Press, 1986), 77–78.
29. *LPP*, 342.
30. Ibid., 282.

(etsi deus non daretur),[31] and "the movement towards human autonomy"
begun in the thirteenth century,[32] among others, can all be traced directly
to his reading of Dilthey.[33] Bonhoeffer's personal attempt to understand,
assess, and narrate modern intellectual history—an immensely creative
endeavor admired by nearly all his readers—was catalyzed by just the
kind of interpretive impetus I am developing. Bonhoeffer's actual connections with the ideas of Heidegger and Dilthey are incidental to my
argument. But they deserve mention nonetheless, because they show
that the interpretive framework I am proposing for reading Bonhoeffer's
life was not alien to the man himself.

In the course of the present discussion I have been drawing out narrative possibilities for the "connected life" which martyrdom brings
to view, because I am seeking a way of telling Bonhoeffer's story, or at
least an important segment of it. Commensurate with our discussion
so far, a narrator differs from a chronicler by arranging and selecting
material according to her adventitious grasp of the whole. Whereas
chroniclers are mainly concerned with the factual sequence of events
and are obliged to include all that is known, narrators assemble the facts
that are amenable to a certain point of view and seek to work them into
a thread or pattern that achieves coherence for their audience or wins
them to an appreciation of the narrator's viewpoint. Naturally, narration
is more complex than chronicle, and fraught with problems. Yet without
it the set of occasions that comprise a life cannot be rescued from the
nakedness of sheer temporal sequence. Without narration facts cannot
rise to significance. For this reason my preoccupation with Bonhoeffer's
martyrdom has less to do with his death than with its significance for
his life, and perhaps for the more inclusive realm of "Christian life."

If narrative really is this important, then it cannot be left to biogra-
phers and storytellers, for it is the very texture of human experience
itself. Inasmuch as human beings desire their own life to be coherent, to
mean something, to be *for* or *about* something, they engage in a repeated
interpretation of their life, massaging the ever-widening array of events
and stitching them together. To be sure, disjointed elements lurk in the
background of every life, perhaps as so much "white noise," and occasionally they may storm to the fore and dominate the story itself, making
it one of chaos instead of integration. But even the disparate elements

31. Ibid., 359.
32. Ibid., 325.
33. Bonhoeffer's own references to his reading of Dilthey are scattered through the
late letters from prison. For an in-depth treatment of the theological connection, see
Ernst Feil, *The Theology of Dietrich Bonhoeffer*, trans. Martin Rumscheidt (Philadelphia:
Fortress, 1985), 178–84.

are what they are only in reference to the story that they do not support or do not make. Perhaps it belongs to the genius of great thinkers that they are able to weave even disparate elements into their personal narrative. And perhaps it is part of the cunning of Christian faith that the disparate elements can be treated in one fashion or another in terms of sin and thus be sunk into the heart of the passion narrative. One thinks of the way Augustine, in the *Confessions,* was able to work the aberrancies of his earlier years into the larger mystery of God's electing grace, much as he had unified the whole panorama of history by means of the eternal God. Augustine's *Confessions* may mark the best of the genre, but the prevalent human interest in autobiography, written and oral, demonstrates a near compulsiveness for narration. *Der Zusammenhang des Lebens* (the connectedness of life) is an innate task of human existence as such that does not lighten its load at death but only increases its burden by placing itself into the lap of those who follow.

Edmund Husserl, to whom Heidegger dedicated *Being and Time* in order to acknowledge his indebtedness, attempted to demonstrate the connectedness of experience through the example of a melody.[34] He noted that the hearing of a melody is, strictly speaking, not possible, since only one note of the melodic sequence can be heard at a time. Yet people speak confidently of hearing a melody, because in the act of listening a horizon of the "just-passed" is retained together with a horizon of "just-ahead." Experience has a "temporal thickness" that stretches backward by "retention" and forward by "protention," such that the whole melody—the entire continuum of notes—becomes an object of awareness despite its stubbornly serial nature. In Husserl's example, each note of the series presents the whole melody, each note a hidden feature of the whole. Conversely, awareness of the whole shapes the experience of each note in the series.

One could examine the same theme in reference to spoken language. Though speech is fragmented into a series of consecutive syllables, by retention and protention human experience can grasp these syllables in ever larger wholes, from words and phrases to paragraphs and entire speeches. It might be objected that melodies are naturally suited for this kind of description because of their substantial duration. But even a much shorter event like a sneeze is not without temporal thickness, the constricted inhalation protending the oncoming exhalation and the exhalation retaining a "memory" of the inhalation just passed. By analogy, an elongated event such as a human life, composed of a lengthy series of smaller events, can be experienced melodically from within

34. I am relying on the fine treatment of Husserl's example found in Carr, *Time, Narrative, and History,* 21–30.

and without, its various parts being forged together to form themes, and then broader themes, until the whole is configurable as a unity.

Bonhoeffer himself resorted to musical terminology when in May 1944 he wanted to express the continuity of life amidst seeming chaos. Eberhard Bethge, who at this time had been frustrated repeatedly in his personal travel plans and had been preparing for his own imprisonment and the full weight of its implications, communicated his frustration to Bonhoeffer. From his cell at Tegel, Bonhoeffer responded:

> There's always a danger in all strong, erotic love that one may love what I might call the polyphony of life *[die Polyphonie des Lebens]*. God wants us to love him eternally with our whole hearts—not in such a way as to injure or weaken our earthly loves, but to provide a kind of *cantus firmus* to which the other melodies of life provide the counterpoint. . . . Where the *cantus firmus* is clear and plain, the counterpoint can be developed to its limits. The two are "undivided and yet distinct," in the words of the Chalcedonian Definition, like Christ in his human and divine natures. May not the attraction and importance of polyphony in music consist in its being a musical reflection of this Christological fact and therefore of our *vita christiana?* Do you see what I'm driving at? I wanted to tell you to have a good, clear *cantus firmus;* that is the only way to a full and perfect sound, when the counterpoint has a firm support and can't come adrift or get out of tune, while remaining a distinct whole in its own right. Only a polyphony of this kind can give life a wholeness and at the same time assure us that nothing calamitous can happen as long as the *cantus firmus* is kept going. . . . Rely on the *cantus firmus*.[35]

Despite the abstruseness that accompanies this playful invention—*die Polyphonie des Lebens*— it is possible to locate within it one of Bonhoeffer's core interests: life is construable as a continuity of events on the basis of Christ. The *cantus firmus* symbolizes the continuous narrative thread that Christ makes possible for every Christian life. With his sure grasp of music, Bonhoeffer understands that the *cantus firmus* can be

---

35. *LPP,* 303. In an earlier letter Bonhoeffer expressed the same idea in nonchristological terms. It is equally compelling: "The important thing today is that we should be able to discern from the fragment of our life how the whole was arranged and planned, and what material it consists of. For really, there are some fragments that are only worth throwing into the dustbin . . . and others whose importance lasts for centuries, because their completion can only be a matter for God, and so they are fragments that must be fragments—I'm thinking, e.g., of the *Art of Fugue.* If our life is but the remotest reflection of such a fragment, if we accumulate, at least for a short time, a wealth of themes and weld them into a harmony in which the great counterpoint is maintained from start to finish, so that at last, when it breaks off abruptly, we can sing no more than the chorale 'I come before thy throne,' we will not bemoan the fragmentariness of our life, but rather rejoice in it" (219).

what it is only by virtue of the other melodies that compete against it. As in a fugue, the other melodies may be enjoyed but must not be permitted to dominate the score. At times they tempt the hearer to delight in the polyphony itself and thus present a certain "danger," but even so they remain the presupposition for the listener's experience of unity. Joy and pain, reunion and separation, the individual in community, life and death: all the tensions of life prove complementary when referred to the Christ who in his own being manifests unity in differentiation.

For Bonhoeffer, the continuity of life is both task and gift. On the one hand the Christian, precisely because she is one who *thinks*, is able to preserve life's multidimensionality and hold open possibilities for integration.[36] On the other hand, if the full profile of Bonhoeffer's Christology and ethics is kept in view, it is difficult to maintain in any final sense the Christian person as the source of her own continuity, for being birthed into the structure of Christ, who constitutes the center of reality itself, her activities have been made a function of Christ's own. Ultimately, then, amid her own renderings of continuity, the Christian must refer the many facets of her existence to God, who coordinates them christologically.

It is obvious from this discussion that the categories of "part" and "whole" play a prominent role in the coordination of human experience. It has been argued that their function in the human sciences is analogous to that of "law" in the natural sciences, especially where they impinge upon historicophilological investigations,[37] where it is common to begin with the smallest parts and progress toward more comprehensive wholes. Each part holds a unique and unexchangeable place with respect to the whole of which it is a part. Conversely, the whole is composed precisely of its particular parts. Wholes and parts stand in dynamic dialectical relation. However, this relation cannot be static so long as history is still unfolding, because the perspective possible on that relation changes as the actual occasions of history come to be. No whole can be frozen and semantically settled while the most comprehensive whole—history itself—remains undecided. It may be, for example, that an author's words always derive their meaning from the larger wholes of the work of which they are a part, the entire corpus of works of which that work is a part, the whole of the author's life in its sociocultural context, and the whole historical epoch in which he lives. Yet inasmuch as our perspective on the whole of his historical epoch

36. Ibid., 311.
37. Wolfhart Pannenberg, *Metaphysics and the Idea of God*, trans. Philip Clayton (Grand Rapids: Eerdmans, 1990), 136–38.

may and must shift in the passage of time, the various whole-part relationships, even the most seemingly settled ones, surrender themselves to reconfiguration and reinterpretation.

Happily, this does not require the conclusion that a hopeless relativism attends all hermeneutical endeavors. Every new interpretation is at least a prophetic assertion of truth, even if the data upon which it rests are historically conditioned. This is why the mode of *anticipation* proves so important in Heidegger's analysis, for by it one is able in some way to engage the "whole" that thematizes the chaos of temporality. It might seem that anticipation in this sense is a vapor too diffuse to hold any real content, a mode only externally related to the anticipated whole. But one must remember that in such an ontology anticipation shares structurally in the whole of reality, such that content of the anticipated in some way enters the present temporal nexus.

Implicitly this book's consideration of Bonhoeffer as martyr has already taken into account the categories whole and part. I pointed out that the whole of the church's martyr tradition necessarily includes the exceptional developments of twentieth-century martyrs. Evaluating Christian martyrdom today requires us to deal with a more diverse body of literature and a more nuanced set of individual cases. We gained new insights and in retrograde fashion put them to use in assessment of the earlier tradition. Our newly configured whole of the tradition now presents its parts somewhat differently. Burton Nelson's appeal that we frame Bonhoeffer's life and thought in the Holocaust context (and by implication we must broaden this to the whole sphere of Jewish-Christian relations) is something of a plea to move our interpretation of the man and his life into an avenue that twentieth-century history has itself suggested. With the twentieth century behind us, we are able better to assess the significance of the Holocaust for our epoch and the wide sweep of Western history. We are also better equipped to handle one whose life and death were so consciously and inextricably bound up with it. Ascertaining the meaning and significance of Bonhoeffer is an ongoing project.

8

Christian Life as the Practice of Death

The fickle-minded man is merely a witness to the constant border warfare between life and death . . . but the serious man has entered into a treaty of friendship with the opposing forces, and his life has in death's earnest thought the most faithful of allies.

Søren Kierkegaard

In traversing Heidegger's fundamental ontology we found that death contains prospects for the coherence of a life extended in time. It has not yet been made clear, however, how and what *martyrdom* contributes to the coherence of a life extended in time. How and what martyrdom contributes cannot be derived convincingly from the following syllogism:

Death offers possibilities for the coherence of a life.
Martyrdom is a type of death.

Martyrdom must also contain these possibilities.

The truthfulness of the second premise is questionable. If in the above syllogism we were to replace the noun *martyrdom* with *suicide*, it would still be possible for us to construe a life coherently in view of its particular end by finding a correlation between the life actually lived and the act of suicide that ended it. For, tragically, a troubled life is consistent with suicide. It "hangs together." Arguably, suicide brings a life before us in a way similar to martyrdom, as can be seen in the subsequent desire to identify and understand the "cause" or locate the "signs" of a troubled soul. But the fact that suicide can be substituted for martyrdom in this argument reveals a difficulty with the second premise. Surely martyrdom is related to death and must be understood together with it, but can it be assumed justifiably that martyrdom is a *type* of death that can be placed alongside others?

The question is a serious one. In the Christian perspective, martyrdom implies not just the bare fact of consistency between life and death, but a specific *kind* of consistency whose theme is the life and death of Christ. Because martyrdom, by virtue of its character as "witness," brings before us the image of Christ's death, the death that above all deaths is constitutive for the meaning of the Christian faith, there may be more to learn about death *qua* death through the lens of martyrdom than the other way round. In making such a statement, I am assuming that the meaning of human death has been taken into God's triune life by virtue of the Son's death, which according to the Christian faith was a profoundly human one and therefore unthinkable apart from this basis. This being the case, in Christian martyrdom we are dealing not with a species belonging to a genus but with the very essence of what might be called a *Christian* death. This is not to say that martyrdom is the only bona fide form of Christian death, only that it illumines more brightly than any other what the essence of a Christian death is. Our argument, then, should proceed like this:

> Death offers possibilities for the coherence of life.
> Martyrdom epitomizes death from the Christian point of view.
> ───────────────
> The death of martyrdom offers the highest potential for understanding the coherence of Christian life.

Death as Fulfillment

Karl Rahner, who linked his theology of martyrdom with Heidegger's philosophy under the twin notions of *freedom* and *act*, defined Christian death as "the freely exercised liberty of faith, which in reality and truth disposes the whole of life, by accepting the incalculability of this mortal existence as a meaningful and loving disposition of God."[1] For Rahner, freedom is not the capacity to change one's physical course this

---

1. Karl Rahner, *On the Theology of Death*, trans. C. H. Henkey (New York: Seabury, 1973), 96.

way and that, though, as we have seen, that can and must play a part in a theology of martyrdom. Rather, freedom is

> the power to decide that which is to be final and definitive in one's life . . . the power to bring into being from one's own resources that which must be, and must not pass away, the summons to a decision that is irrevocable. . . .

> If, therefore, man is personal freedom, then it follows that he is one who uses the resources of his own innermost nature to form himself by his own free act, for by the exercise of this freedom of his he can definitively determine the shape of his life as a whole, and decide what his ultimate end is to be, the ultimate realisation of his own nature, beyond all possibility of revision.[2]

We see here that for Rahner the human person is endowed with, or better, constituted by, a self-directing freedom, the freedom to become a self in the fullest sense of the term, to develop toward the realization of the self's own nature. For the Christian, attaining fulfillment requires death, because only at the end of this temporal existence does God bring to pass the promise of glorification, but also because the existential situation of the human being—mortality—is itself linked to freedom in the Genesis narrative. If human freedom aims at what is most basic and fundamental to human nature, and if death is the occasion par excellence in which this aim reveals itself, then freedom is inextricably bound up with death.

Death is the breaking in of finality upon mere transience—that finality which is the concretization of freedom come to its maturity.[3] The Christian person, then, will perceive in death an invitation to completion, a challenge concerning his own nature in which he is to gather life up and place it freely into God's hands. Paradoxically, the same death that is truly *free*, and thus a consummating inward *act*, is also a cessation of all freedom and activity.

Dying is the ultimate act of freedom because it is the act in which one "either *willingly accepts or definitively rebels against* his own utter impotence."[4] When every last vestige of human power and possibility threatens to shut down, can one accept the fact that she is totally within the control of another? Will she yield everything up to God willingly, or will it be taken from her by force? Freedom comes down to this single,

---

2. Karl Rahner, *Theological Investigations* 7, trans. David Bourke (London: Darton, Longman and Todd, 1971), 287.

3. Ibid., 289.

4. Ibid., 290.

all-encompassing decision. The one who accepts impotence before God and leans upon him in faith dies a death of human fulfillment by presenting the whole self to God, whereas the one who rebels against her impotence dies a death of prideful autonomy. In the final analysis, both modes are a fall into the unfathomable depths of God, says Rahner, but while the one is an act of faith, the other is a mortal sin.[5]

Though here we speak of death as the final act, we must remind ourselves once again that we are more concerned with the *life of death* than the *death of death*. Knowing that freedom comes to maturity with our last act—the death of death—as a matter of necessity, it is tempting to project our present faith into a completed state and derive from it some comfort. Yet in the life of death freedom cannot achieve a resolution "beyond the possibility of all revision." Hence no one knows for sure whether the death he is dying with his life is that of courageous and trustful faith or the death of absolute autonomy and despair.[6] Which kind of fall our death will be remains largely hidden from view. It will become clearer when our lives of death are over, yet despite the relative clarity of deaths died in faith (i.e., Christian deaths), a veil of ambiguity still surrounds them. This is because Christian death is itself ambiguous. Quoting Rahner now at length:

> Even though this death is personal and unique to the individual in this sense, still it is the death which has been ushered into this world of the embodied spirit . . . by the rebellion of the first man. And at the same time it is the death which the Son of Man freely takes upon himself. Our death is modeled upon the death of both of these. For it was precisely the death of Adam that the Son of Man willed to die in order to redeem this death. And because it is never possible for us to say of ourselves with complete certainty which exercise of life we commit ourselves to with the ultimate decision of our free will, we cannot ultimately know either whether it is possible for us to say which of the two deaths we are dying, the death of perdition or the death of Adam which has been redeemed; in other words whether the death of Christ imports life for us or judgment, whether it is the death of despair that we are dying or the death of faith. Both modes of dying are *concealed beneath the surface* in the everyday process of dying.[7]

Elsewhere Rahner courts this same ambiguity, this time, however, raising the critical question of a death that may break through to greater clarity.

5. Ibid., 290.
6. Ibid., 291.
7. Ibid., 291–92.

The ambiguity of all freedom in fact reaches its supreme and unique culmination in death. Any other act in this world leaves behind part of its reality which, to the doer and his fellow-men, offers the possibility of at least a partial judgment in regard to the whole of the action. In death, however, deed and doer disappear from the range of observation of doer and spectators into the mystery of God's sole judgment. . . . [But] is there a death which can expose its dark, veiled essence to us and so enable us to know how a particular man really died? Is there a death in which the appearances disclose the reality? If there is such a revealing and patently evident Christian death, then it would constitute the Christian witness as such, because the act integrating all that is Christian and perfecting a life, would also manifest what it is.[8]

Martyrdom, he concludes, is such a death. It really is the prototype of Christian death, expressing "that ultimate beauty which is born of the perfect harmony between interior reality and external appearance."[9]

By freely accepting a death that they could also have freely avoided, martyrs evince what is necessary for Christian death in every case, for Jesus said of his own death, "I lay down my life" (John 10:17). Every genuinely Christian death is said to be marked by a submission to the will of God. One might say that free submission of one's life-unto-death to God is the expected result whenever and wherever the structure of Christ's life-unto-death has been assimilated into the life of faith. This active freedom of submission to God's will is often invisible to the onlooker. Rarely, if ever, will it give the appearance of an "act." On an empirical basis, it may even be disdained as the absence of the free act.[10] Thus while persecutors are wielding earthly power over their victims and bringing about their death, they may see only foolish passivity. But in the end, the violence that *appears* to place the martyr in a passive posture, reduce her to a mere victim, and steal her freedom is in truth a God-granted opportunity for the exercise of freedom. Indeed, just when the external forces are most dominant the believer may become most free toward death, because its possibility at that moment is a God-given one.[11] Rahner pushes on to what is for us the most pertinent point:

8. Rahner, *On The Theology of Death*, 97.

9. Ibid.

10. According to the Gospels, Jesus' general silence and confounding refusal to perform brought taunt and mockery from those leaders who instigated his death and those soldiers who meted it out, such as, "He saved others; let him save himself if he is the Messiah of God, his chosen one!" and "If you are the king of the Jews, save yourself!" (Luke 23:35–36).

11. In T. S. Eliot's *Murder in the Cathedral*, Archbishop Thomas à Becket, anticipating his own martyrdom, preaches these provocative words: "A martyr, a saint, is always made by the design of God, for his love of men, to warn them and to lead them, to bring them back to His ways. A martyrdom is never the design of man; for the true martyr is he who

In a violent death, which could have been avoided and which is, never-theless, accepted in freedom, the freedom of a whole life is gathered into the one burning moment of death. Then the death of life (in its totality and freedom) enters into the death of death, in an act of complete freedom affecting the totality of life and so life's eternal finality. The death of mar-tyrdom is a death of genuine liberty. By it is disclosed what is elsewhere hidden under the veil covering death's essence. By it the enigma and veil of death (is it a death of enforced freedom or real liberty?) receives a definite answer.[12]

Drawing upon my earlier discussion of martyrdom as the consummate form of the *imitatio Christi*, I now submit that the free act of martyrdom has the power to sum up one's whole existence *as Christian*. Interestingly, Ignatius, in his letter to the Ephesians—a people who lived along the trade route to Rome and thus on "the highway of God's martyrs"—wrote that he was "not yet perfected in Jesus Christ." On the way to his own martyrdom, in a spirit of free submission, he confessed to them, "I am now but being initiated into discipleship."[13] The martyr's end that lay just ahead was already imparting to him a sense of consummating clar-ity and concreteness. He was at the precipice of something summative for his life. By summing up life *as Christian*, martyrdom contains the inherent powers of thematization we need for positing coherence among the various thoughts and acts that compose Bonhoeffer's life.

But equally important, if Rahner is correct then martyrdom is a *revela-tion* of death in the Christian sense, that is, a revelation of death in faith. Martyrs participate uniquely in God's self-revelation within the temporal process, helping us to locate God's work among us.[14] To anticipate some

---

has become the instrument of God, who has lost his will in the will of God, not lost it but found it, for he has found freedom in submission to God. The martyr no longer desires anything for himself, not even the glory of martyrdom." See T. S. Eliot, *The Complete Poems and Plays* (New York: Harcourt, Brace, 1952), 199–200.

12. Rahner, *On the Theology of Death*, 98.

13. Johannes Quasten and Joseph C. Plumpe, gen. eds., *Ancient Christian Writers* (New York, N.Y./Ramsey, N.J.: Paulist Press, 1946–present), vol. 1: *The Epistles of St. Clement of Rome and St. Ignatius of Antioch*, trans. James A. Kleist, 61.

14. An interesting application of the idea can be found in David M. Matzko, "Hazarding Theology: Theological Descriptions and Particular Lives," Ph.D. diss., Duke University, 1992. Matzko, who is less interested in martyrs than in saints and saint-making, examines the life of martyred bishop Oscar Romero and renders the interesting conclusion that his life provides a guide "for interpreting the world and locating God's activity" (85). His conclusion is then widened to show that when upon the death of an extraordinary life, the church takes up the task of "naming" that life, the saint may be said to disclose "ways of seeing, acting, and what to live, hope, and die for" (93). I think one could also consider this from the opposite perspective: that *God* uses the scandal of martyrdom as means of locating the ship of his true church in the vast seas of the "religious."

terminology from Bonhoeffer's *Ethics,* in them the crucified Christ is "taking form" concretely. Like Christ, they have bonded their life with their death such that neither can be considered without recourse to the other. This is what Rahner means when he says, "The death of life enters into the death of death."[15] The motif of Christian death that permeates their life—the death that they *live* by virtue of their submission to the will of God in Christ—is in one sense an extended preparation for the death that lies ahead of them. Rahner consciously appropriates that prolonged death *(prolixitas mortis)* of which Gregory the Great spoke when trying to describe the life that is subject to suffering and death.[16] Life is a long, drawn-out death. In comporting themselves favorably to their finitude, martyrs have allowed the reality of death to permeate their very life, such that the movement from life to death, ordinarily considered the break-off point of existence (a terminus), has become for them also a moment of consummation and fulfillment.

This explains in part why many martyrs have exuded joy in their parting moments. The reality of Christ's death, which has given a density to their life and which has often been hidden from public view, is at last being made visible and concrete in their own suffering. They are brought into synchrony with Christ the Crucified and enjoy, as Paul the apostle put it, "the power of his resurrection and the sharing of his sufferings by becoming like him in his death" (Phil. 3:10). As if a secret told on the occasion of their death, the stigmata of Christ that lie embedded in the ambiguities of everyday actions emerge, for martyr and interpreter alike. Like light passing through a prism, the actual death of the martyr, the "death of death," splashes before us the full spectrum of the "life of death" that they practiced as a matter of faith.

Bonhoeffer, too, could consider death a fulfillment. He conveyed the idea in christological terms, as was so characteristic of him. To my

---

15. One might object that since Rahner was steeped in Heidegger we have here only a theological restatement of Heidegger's idea of "anticipation." But interestingly this idea of death entering life can be developed from within the Christian context without the influence of Heideggerian existentialism. For example, the Greek theologian Archimandrite Vasileios, *Hymn of Entry: Liturgy and Life in the Orthodox Church,* trans. Elizabeth Briere (Crestwood, N.Y.: St. Vladimir's Seminary Press, 1984), writes: "The believer's whole life becomes a spiritual increase inasmuch as it is an offering. Instead of being exhausted it is regenerated, because before time and old age and illness can exhaust it, he has given his strength and his life to God. . . . The death and bodily burial of the believer in the earth is his last earthly act of universal offering. . . . Thus even the final death which has come upon his body has been accepted by him as the visitation of God's fatherly love, the purpose of which is total cleansing, resurrection and freedom. . . . *As death becomes voluntary, so the inevitable death that comes to us is conquered. As it is an act of freedom, so it transforms the ultimate constraint into eternal freedom*" (pp. 65–66). Emphasis added.

16. Rahner, *On the Theology of Death,* 76.

knowledge, he never enfolded the idea in a larger conceptual framework or even developed it beyond a single paragraph, but the following passage bears remarkably upon our present theme:

> In life with Jesus Christ, death as a universal fate which comes to us from outside is contrasted with death that is from within, one's own death, the free death of dying daily with Jesus Christ. Anyone who lives with Christ dies daily to his own will. Christ in us gives us over to death so that he can live in us. So our inner dying grows up against death from outside. In this way, Christians accept their real death; physical death in the true sense does not become the end, but the consummation of life with Jesus Christ. Here we enter the community of the one who could say at his death, "It is accomplished."[17]

Death as Collapse

This idea of death as fulfillment or completion is not without its critics. Bartholomew Collopy, for example, rejects Rahner's thesis. According to Collopy, Rahner and others like him (e.g., Ladislaus Boros) who, following Heidegger, construe death as a positive and consummating personal act by which human beings opt for what they really are, do not give death its due. He prefers instead a "dark model" wherein death signifies a "final fall into the weakness of being human." Death is an event of disintegration, an "optionless" and "untheological" event "totally without resonance to religious faith or theological concern" that gives "no clue about survival, continuance, 'inner' victory, deliverance, [or] personal salvage of any sort from what is, empirically, unconditional loss."[18]

In deference to Collopy, we may grant that death itself shows little promise for fulfillment. Death seems to pull a blanket of smothering silence over life. What is immediately apparent, at least, is nothing like resolution, completion, or fulfillment, but more like negation, nullification, and judgment.

Collopy's dark model has merit. Death as fall is a critical feature of the Christian story, where death is connected irrevocably to sin (Rom. 6:23), albeit in complex and nuanced ways. Whether biological death is to be considered a consequence of sin is not the most important issue here. Death seems to be a part of nature, and therefore of human nature as well. Helmut Thielicke describes the matter with unique clarity:

---

17. Bonhoeffer, circular letter dated 15 August 1941. See *ATTF*, 455.

18. Bartholomew J. Collopy, "Theology and the Darkness of Death," *Theological Studies* 39 (March 1978): 22–54.

> When the Bible . . . relates death to sin and to the *fall* from order, this
> rules out at once the misunderstanding that death is a result of sin on its
> *biological* side. Instead, Scripture shows that human dying is something
> that is indeed executed in the medium of biological death but still has to
> be differentiated from this medium. Human death is qualitatively different
> from the purely biological death of animals. The opposite of biological
> death is biological life. The opposite of human dying (executed in the
> medium of biological life) is life from God: "We live even though we die"
> (John 11:25ff).[19]

The importance of the connection between biological death and sin
lies in the fact that sin, as a contradiction of God's purposes for human
life, alters the human comportment toward death. Since sin interrupts
the entire ontological structure of human existence, the limit of that
existence becomes a threat.[20] To face that limit is to face the terrifying
fact that I am entirely subject to the control of God. According to the
author of Genesis, my life *should* have been entirely under God's control throughout. Ostensibly, this would have given my biological death
a nonimposing character. However, when now I approach the boundary of my existence, I am thrust back upon my own responsibility as a
sinner. I must deal with the fact that the threatening character of my
temporal limit is self-imposed, or perhaps imposed by God as a natural
consequence of my sin.

Whatever the biological necessity of death means, it cannot mean
death in the most serious and final sense. In Eve's reply to the serpent's
temptation she repeats the divine prohibition "You shall not eat . . . or
you shall die," to which the serpent offers the rejoinder, "You will not die;
for God knows that when you eat of it your eyes will be opened, and you
will be like God" (Gen. 3:2–5). Clearly one form of death is being played
off another here. The serpent's temptation—eat and become like God—is
an inducement for the creature to push beyond the divine limit. Once the
limit has been violated, what death is becomes clear as the creatures come
to recognize their precarious position before God. They now experience
in dreadful austerity the boundary between Creator and creature.

Sensing that creatures who once transgressed their limitations could
exacerbate the situation, perhaps break even their biological limits,[21]

---

19. Helmut Thielicke, *Living with Death*, trans. Geoffrey W. Bromiley (Grand Rapids:
Eerdmans, 1983), 33–34.

20. Anticipating the final victory of God in the temporal order, when death will be
"swallowed up" in victory, Paul gauges the difficulty of the present situation in the phrase
"the sting of death is sin" (1 Cor. 15:56 NRSV).

21. "Then the LORD God said, 'See, the man has become like one of us, knowing good
and evil; and now, he might reach out his hand and take also from the tree of life, and
eat, and live forever'" (Gen. 3:22).

God reinforces the existing boundary: dust shall return to dust. Life shall henceforth be lived in consciousness of this boundary. Life chafes against death to reveal at any and every moment the fault line between Creator and creature. Under this pressure, the sin and guilt of the creature will always be visible.[22] Pain in childbirth and sweat over the soil stand as fitting symbols of life unto death. In these symbols of the "curse," God is imbuing the biological limit with a new meaning, an enduring message, which he encodes in the structure of his relationship to human beings. Biological life continues on onerously, struggling against the hidden gravity of death in this final sense.

In some fundamental way, then, our sin is a refusal to accept the God-ordained limits that accompany finitude, yet God continues to employ his creativity as the saga of human life unfolds. In fact God utilizes precisely the natural limit of death to chasten his creatures toward self-reflection. It is no longer finitude, merely, with which we must deal, but our share of personal responsibility for sin. Perhaps like the prodigal we must come home to ourselves here in the far country before we can come home to God. Could our sin, guilt, and death function graciously as catalysts in this regard? As the story of Babel indicates, God continues to contravene the heavenward aspiration of human beings. God answers our aspirations for transcendence by stretching a canopy over our existence beyond which he will not let us ascend,[23] not because God is a stingy deity intent on reinforcing boundaries between himself and his creatures, but because his creatures have not yet understood the one thing needful, not yet come to the requisite self-knowledge for engaging authentically in the God-human relationship.

In our death, then, we might venture to say that God is contradicting us in the most forceful way imaginable, confronting us with our limitations a final time so that we might come to terms with ourselves and be reconciled to him. God wants to meet us just there at the boundary of our existence, where the self ends and God begins. Calling once again upon Thielicke:

22. "For I know my transgressions, and my sin is ever before me" (Ps. 51:3).

23. Within his larger treatment of human estrangement from God, Paul Tillich opened a masterful discussion of *hubris* and showed how in the etymology of the term lies the notion of human self-elevation into the sphere of the divine. He concluded, "*Hubris* is not one form of sin beside others," but "it is sin in its total form." As self-elevation *hubris* depicts aptly the human usurpation of its creaturely structure, for humans are not contented with finitude. Paul Tillich, *Systematic Theology* (Chicago: University of Chicago Press, 1957), 2:49–55.

> A personal relation means that I must not complain against God when death comes. God is telling me something by it. In my death he is reacting to me. There is a message in it. I see God's hand and word aimed at me.[24]

In part, the message is that we are guilty before God and have become targets of his judgment. For the Christian, sin, guilt, and judgment, even if we assign them a penultimate rather than ultimate status, are constitutive elements of death and dying. Once again, death throws us finite beings back upon our creatureliness to be sure, but at the same time it confronts us with the numerous choices, conscious and unconscious, we have made against God and therewith against our own humanity. Parenthetically, I might suggest that death has such immense moral efficacy that its denial necessitates immense moral consequences.[25]

If all I discovered at the boundary was God's inviolable limit I might manage to be thankful for having had my illusions stripped away, and perhaps I could take minimal comfort in having plumbed the depths of life's tragic dimension—a tragic reality may be preferable to a comedic illusion—yet, being unable to survive this boundary situation, I should find hope quite impossible. The cunning of God resides in the fact that my temporal limit is simultaneously a message and a means of grace. By establishing this limit God, ever the respecter of my freedom, encourages me in the strongest way possible to come to terms with that limit, remember him, and resolutely present this earthen vessel back to him. I must not complain when death comes, because wrapped within the sobriety of my sin and guilt before God is also a summons to my final and most important episode of faith. For the Christian, death is the final act of faith wherein one casts one's whole self into the hands of God. In every other act of faith the self survives the act. In dying, however, one is presented with a unique and infinitely more difficult challenge, for, as Rahner put it, the act and the actor disappear together.

If I meet the challenge, I die a Christian death. If I fail to meet the challenge, that is, if I cannot consummate the free and faithful act of submitting to God in this way, then I have twice stormed the boundary God has given. Elaborating upon Rahner, I propose that the essence of *Christian* death, then, lies in this: it is an *act* in which one *freely accepts*

24. Thielicke, *Living with Death*, 125.

25. In the judgment of Christopher E. Mooney, "The modern avoidance of death, both socially and psychologically, is really a denial by man of his sinfulness. For to accept death as part of one's life is to integrate it into those free moral decisions which determine life's quality. And this cannot be done without an acceptance of one's finitude and need of help, without an acknowledgment of moral weakness at the heart of one's freedom." See *Man without Tears: Soundings for a Christian Anthropology* (New York: Harper and Row, 1973), 115.

one's precarious position before God, a position stamped with sin, guilt, and the threat of judgment, and nevertheless trustingly yields to him. In terms of our life-death dialectic, when one's final act assumes this form it forges a bond with that running stream of acts, whether committed in faith or unfaith, that compose a human life. For a Christian death is an all-summarizing act.

From this discussion it is manifest that the standpoint from which death is seen as the unnatural and tragic terminus of human life must then be given its due without being absolutized. By stressing only the collapse of the human, this view configures the matter one-sidedly. Death amounts to God's judgment upon the human situation, but it contains only meager epistemological significance with reference to the human. Death chastises without instructing; death judges without mercy. Against this view, I want to maintain that death is a severe form of the divine mercy, a "teacher of earnestness," as Kierkegaard proposed.[26] It may

26. The reader is referred to a lesser-known but provocative reflection given upon the death of his father. I excerpt here three passages from Søren Kierkegaard, "The Decisiveness of Death: At the Side of a Grave," in *Crucial Situations in Human Life: Three Discourses on Imagined Occasions,* trans. David Swenson (Minneapolis: Augsburg, 1941), which have particular bearing on our theme: one in which he describes death as the "teacher of earnestness," another in which he suggests death's retroactive power for life, and a third that highlights its ethical significance. "For death is the teacher of earnestness, but its earnest instruction is to be recognized precisely by the fact that death leaves the individual to search out himself, so as to learn earnestness only as it can be learned in and through the man himself. Death attends to its task in life; it does not run about . . . sharpening the scythe and scaring women and children as if this were earnestness. No, it says 'I exist; if anyone wishes to learn from me, let him come to me'" (81). And then, commenting on the misguided explanations (that death is a transition, a transformation, a suffering, a punishment and so forth) that humans customarily give to the riddle of death, Kierkegaard says that in such explanations "the decisive feature. . . . which prevents death's nothing-ness from making the explanation a mere nothing, is that it requires retroactive power and reality in the life of the living, so that death becomes a teacher for him, and not one who treasonably assists him to a self-appraisement which makes the explainer out to be a fool" (108). Or again, "Let death then keep its power, 'that it is over'; but let life also keep the right to labor while it is day; and let the earnest man seek the thought of death as an assistance to this end. The fickle-minded man is merely a witness to the constant border warfare between life and death, his life is merely doubt's reflection of the relationship, the outcome of his life is a delusion; but the serious man has entered into a treaty of friendship with the opposing forces, and his life has in death's earnest thought the most faithful of allies. If there is, then, one likeness for the death, that it is over, there is nevertheless one difference, my hearer. A difference that cries aloud to heaven, the difference in what kind of life it was, which now with death is over" (92–93). Finally, in an ethical vein, "Earnest-ness does not waste much time in guessing riddles, it does not sit sunk in contemplation, it does not seek paraphrases for the expression, it does not consider the ingenuity of the metaphors, it does not discuss. It acts." Thus, "if death is a night, then life is a day, and if it is not possible to labor in the night, then it is possible to work while it is day; and the brief but stimulating cry of earnestness is like death's brief cry: yet today" (90).

indeed set the inviolable limit to creaturely life, but in doing so it offers an opportunity to assess and enrich the very life it limits.

Christian Life as the Practice of Death

If, as I have suggested, living is a matter of dying, then we should expect to apprehend the deepest significance of human life only by means of a dialogical encounter with death. In Martin Buber's *Tales of the Hasidim* he tells the story of Rabbi Baumann, who as he lay dying saw his wife weeping over his impending death. He responded: "What are you crying for? My whole life was only that I might learn how to die."[27] The rabbi's statement reveals his commitment to work death into his life's narrative. He would not permit the unfolding episode of his death an alien status, as if he were meeting a stranger, but instead managed to incorporate it into his personal story. In doing so he understood that within death the whole mystery of his creaturely existence was contained, that in this particular episode of experience there lay some profound and necessary truth about himself which could be grasped in no other way.

The psalmist pleads for a similar understanding when he prays that God will "teach us to count our days that we may gain a wise heart" (Ps. 90:12). Here God is petitioned to provide an awareness of death in order that life may be lived with greater insight and understanding. In Psalm 39:4–6 the plea is elaborated:

> LORD, let me know my end,
>   and what is the measure of my days;
>   let me know how fleeting my life is.
> You have made my days a few handbreadths,
>   and my lifetime is as nothing in your sight.
> Surely everyone stands as a mere breath.
>   Surely everyone goes about like a shadow.
> Surely for nothing they are in turmoil;
>   they heap up, and do not know who will gather.

Why does the psalmist appeal to God to *know* his end? Certainly he is not asking to know *whether* there will be an end. The fact of his destiny is abundantly clear, for he understands his life already as but "a few handbreadths" and a "shadow." What he seeks is an alertness toward

27. Martin Buber, *Tales of the Hasidim: The Later Masters,* trans. Olga Marx (New York: Schocken, 1961), 268.

this destiny by which he can unlock the mystery of his being as a creature before God.[28]

In Ecclesiastes the teacher of wisdom sums up his prolix consideration of life's temptations and pleasures by appealing to death: "The dust returns to the earth as it was, and the breath returns to God who gave it." The wise will remember their Creator[29] in the days of their youth. Such remembrance is brimming with prospects for life, for the "end of the matter" is a renewed moral vigor: "Fear God, and keep his commandments; for that is the whole duty of everyone" (Eccles. 12:1–13).

From the Christian perspective, however, Jesus Christ plumbed the dialectic of life and death in a way that holds particular promise for those who follow him. As the great hymn quoted by Paul suggests, his incarnation was unto death (Phil. 2:6–11). Paul says elsewhere that Christ descended into hell (Eph. 4:9–10), where ostensibly he shared fully the fate of the dead. This nadir marks a logical, divinely intentioned culmination of the kenotic movement—"and being found in human form, he humbled himself and became obedient to the point of death." Though we may tie the particular details of Jesus' life-unto-death to the accidentals of history, if we were to treat his *comportment* toward death in this way we would alter the entire structure of Christian revelation and reconciliation. The Jewish rabbi who got entangled in Roman politics and suffered crucifixion outside Jerusalem could well have tangled with some other powers and some other means of torture in some other city had God initiated a history with some other people. Yet if in Christian revelation we are dealing with the revelation of God's very self, a *self-unveiling*, then it is nigh to inconceivable that the Son's approach toward death could have been substantially different. Under the surface details of his death, there moves a current of divine purpose. Each act that hastens his death, which he suffers passively, must be seen as an external response to the current of his own activity that is already flowing in the direction of death.

---

28. In a 15 January 1936 funeral oration for his grandmother Frau Julie Bonhoeffer, Dietrich Bonhoeffer made an interesting allusion to this text: "And it is not only her life that is to become a lesson for us, but precisely her death as well. Lord 'teach us to number our days that we may get a heart of wisdom.' Even a life so meaningful and aware is subject to the law of death, which oppresses all that is human. We must also go one day, together with all our ideals, goals and work. To get a heart of wisdom; that means to be aware of one's boundary, one's end, but even more, to be aware of the other side of this boundary, to be aware of the God who is from all eternity, in whose hands we fall whether we want to or not, in whose hands she is now well cared for through all eternity." See *ATTF*, 270.

29. Some commentators believe that "Creator" is a glossator's insertion for the term *cistern* or *well*, in which case "Remember your grave" would be the more accurate rendering. O. S. Rankin, *Ecclesiastes, Song of Solomon, Isaiah, Jeremiah*, vol. 5 of *The Interpreter's Bible*, ed. George Arthur Buttrick (New York: Abingdon, 1956), 83.

Christian conviction has always been that Jesus seized hold of death, grappled with it, made it his own. This is why, in the Christian tradition, his death has always been seen to be redemptive: because his total acceptance of ultimate darkness and dread was precisely a total negation of human selfishness and sin, a free transfer of Jesus' existence to the Father in obedience, hope and love: "Father, into your hands I commend my spirit."[30]

To the last Jesus retains control of his death. Death cannot be inflicted on the one who has already died.

Because the career of Jesus winds irrevocably through death, death itself is imbued with new possibilities. Since death has been "baptized" into the triune life and thereby leveraged in the interests of divine life, those who follow Jesus the Son are likewise baptized into his death so that they may share his life.[31] In light of our larger discussion, baptism can be seen as an entrance into fellowship with the martyr's death of Jesus. In baptism, that critical point at which one falls under the mark of the cross, the lines of human death and divine life converge. To be sure, God answers the humility of the baptized with exaltation, their frailty with a new power of the Spirit. But this is no mere exchange of goods. Humility, frailty, and the entire cloud of impotence that hangs over human life remain. Instead God sets the death of Christ *alongside* our natural death[32] and makes it, in effect, our death. For this reason Christian life may be understood as a revitalization only to the extent that it is at the same time understood as a vital loss. New life is not a possession but adherence to the life of God through the death of the Son. On the thin yet strong cord of Christ's death the entirety of Christian life hangs.

Therefore Christ's death, which, as I have shown, includes the biological-physiological aspect of Adam's death, permeates the new life Christ gives, and this as a matter of *metaphysical* as well as practical necessity. Paul's rationale for putting his life in danger—for standing, shall we say, at the brink of martyrdom—is that he is already dying daily (1 Cor. 15:30–31). It is the death of Jesus that he carries with him bodily through affliction and persecution, "for while we live, we are always being given up

---

30. Mooney, *Man without Tears*, 108.

31. "Do you not know that all of us who have been baptized into Christ Jesus were baptized into his death? Therefore we have been buried with him by baptism into death, so that, just as Christ was raised from the dead by the glory of the Father, so too we might walk with him in newness of life" (Rom. 6:3–4). Noteworthy also is the fact that Paul adduces the Christ hymn (Phil. 2:6–11) to enjoin upon the church "the same mind that was in Christ Jesus."

32. "I have been crucified with Christ" (Gal. 2:19).

to death for Jesus' sake, so that the life of Jesus may be made visible in our mortal flesh" (2 Cor. 4:10–11). No one could gainsay that in Paul's theology baptism meets Jesus' followers at the beginning of their life with him, as it did for Paul himself, but its effect extends in time over their life as a matter of course. In faithfulness to Christ, they must grapple with death as a defining feature of their revitalized existence. Baptism is a sign that anticipates death. If the authentic life of true freedom arises only in conversation with death, and if by that conversation we are brought to an anticipatory grasp of our whole self, then we may regard baptism as a Christian means of conversing with death. In baptism one grasps the entire trajectory of one's future life by anticipation.[33] *Christian life then becomes the practice of death.* Insofar as baptism signals God's initiative, such a life is simply received—the image of Christ is impressed upon us (Rom. 8:29); insofar as baptism is a willing response to God, such a life is an obedient surrender, a free movement into the cruciform impression left by Christ (Phil. 3:10–12).

In the following chapter we will need to pay special attention to this contrapuntal movement, because in the *Ethics* Bonhoeffer stresses repeatedly the simultaneity of human and divine action. At present that issue is best left open so as to stress what is most important: however the matter of divine initiative and human response is traversed, under the sign of baptism and the whole set of images and actions that make the rite, Christ's followers are made vividly aware of their own death.

Though martyrdom falls to relatively few of Christ's followers, its possibility lies embedded in the meaning of baptism. The chronological separation of baptism and martyrdom is a quite trivial matter that devolves on historical conditions. Structurally they are of a single piece. This recognition was secured in the early Christian doctrine that catechumens martyred before their baptism were in fact baptized in their own blood. While certainly this was a solution to the practical problem of how to assess the souls of those who died for Christ outside of water baptism, at the theological level it is tantamount to proclaiming that a martyr's death is the hidden meaning of baptism. In any case, the clear association of baptism and martyrdom often was drawn without deference to the special case of catechumens.[34]

---

33. For a discussion on baptism that emphasizes this point, see Wolfhart Pannenberg, *Systematic Theology*, trans. Geoffrey W. Bromiley (Grand Rapids: Eerdmans, 1998): 3: 239–244. Pannenberg works baptism into his proleptic understanding of reality. This text serves as a sample: "This means that the sign of baptism, as a summary of the individual future Christian life, covers the whole historical course of this life in each case and establishes the unity of this new life in its individuality" (243).

34. For example, after arguing against the Jewish practice of repeated washing, Tertullian extols the virtue of the *one* Christian baptism, but then adds "We *have* indeed,

Eight Theses on Martyrdom's Hermeneutical Prospects

I have been considering a diffuse constellation of perspectives on death. Some pieces orbit tightly, and others more loosely, the Heideggerian ontology of being-unto-death, but all their trajectories have been charted in service of the main goal: to fashion the death of martyrdom into a hermeneutic lens for illumining the passageway between Bonhoeffer's theology and his ethics. The final chapters will judge my success. However, I wish here to arrange these perspectives in a set of theses to mark as clearly as possible the key movements in this pivotal discussion.

Thesis 1: *The totality of a human life and its identity is graspable only when death is entertained as a constitutive feature of that identity.* Humans are incurably historical creatures, always in the process of becoming. That means that their revelation, whether to themselves or others, is a matter of time. At death their "becoming" gives way to "being," which is to say that their identity is there settled upon with finality. For this reason every attempt to apprehend the totality of a human life, that is, not its becoming but its being, requires consideration of the temporal boundary that circumscribes it. The term *circumscribe* must not here be used to denote an external boundary that marks off an internal reality. That would render death external to human identity. To the contrary, the boundary that circumscribes the human is that without which its proper nature could not be ascertained. While including the temporal boundary within the circumference of human life would appear to render impossible any talk about human being as such, in traversing Heidegger's fundamental ontology we saw that the temporal future of death can become a factor in present existence by means of anticipation.

Thesis 2: *Subjectively, or existentially, in the midtemporal experience of one's own death by anticipation the posttemporal whole of a life may be grasped in advance and become a significant catalyst for life.* In the experience of anticipating death, the dawn of an entire being breaks into the twilight of its becoming. Death is imported into the structure of life, whole meets part, future acts upon present, with this result: life is tended to more carefully. No doubt this comes in the form of intensified awareness of self and world, whose concomitant ethical ramifica-

---

likewise, a *second* font (itself . . . *one with the former*), of *blood*, to wit; concerning which the Lord said, 'I have to be baptized with a baptism,' when He had been baptized already. For He had come 'by means of water and blood,' just as John had written; that He might be baptized by the water, glorified by the blood; to make *us*, in like manner, *called by water, chosen* by *blood.*" See Tertullian *On Baptism* 15 (*ANF* 5:677) and the *Anonymous Treatise on Re-baptism* (*ANF* 5:676).

tions could be followed out as a matter of course. But so what? Why should my personal anticipation of my death be considered meaningful to the kind of project here undertaken? Because the revelation that accompanies my own being-unto-death is simultaneously a revelation of Being itself. In the particular vibrations of my own being a universe of meaning makes itself known. Whole extends to part, future reaches to present, death quickens life: these are the metaphysical underpinnings that coordinate reality. This, at any rate, is Heidegger's claim, and it is the chief reason I chose to construct a hermeneutic of martyrdom on his foundation.

Thesis 3: *Objectively, the postmortem vantage point, though excluding the subject of death by definition, is one in which the totality of a life appears to others as an object for consideration and reconsideration.* The objective vantage point works itself out at two levels. First, at the individual level it can ask retrospectively about the relationship between the subject and its own impending death, and thereupon seek to describe the subject's life in view of its newly birthed totality. Inasmuch as it is a whole life that comes to view, coherence among its parts will be an essential task of that description. When a whole life, bounded by birth and death, lies before us, the elements composing its temporal sequence are now what they are in relation to their temporal whole, such that something like a life story becomes possible. Second, at the social level it can ask about this life as an individual totality within successively larger historical totalities, which, in conversation with the individual totality, serve to illumine still more facets of it. At each level temporality governs the description, the historical whole lending significance to the various parts and the parts to the whole.

Thesis 4: *The quality of that totality of life which now appears as an object for consideration and reconsideration is fixed neither by the end point of its death nor by continuity as such, but by its evident comportment toward death, and hence, by the kind of end and the kind of continuity achieved.* Here lies the segue between Heideggerian ontology and a Christian theology of death and martyrdom. By its very nature, temporality lends order to human experience. One can imagine a baseball game, for example, marred by an abundance of physical and mental errors, rain delays, and other stoppages, all of which threaten the game's continuity. And yet in the passage of time the ninth is played and the game ends. Upon their return home, those who witnessed it will speak about "last night's game"—a horrendous game full of discontinuities but a game nevertheless. Describing the meaning of a life from the Christian perspective entails something beyond sheer temporal closure and sheer continuity. It requires careful consideration of a life's synchrony with Christ. Does the emergent whole of a life-unto-death qualify as a life conformed to Christ's life-unto-death? Heidegger, Dilthey, and Husserl could not help us at this point, and so we had to rely upon others, like Rahner, to pioneer a Christian appropriation of their contributions.

Thesis 5: *A Christian death is one that consummates a life into which Christ's death has been assimilated.* Amidst the ambiguities that shroud fallen existence, a Christian death is an act of free and utter submission to God that arrives as the external manifestation of the internal assimilation of Christ's death into life. To the extent that such a death carries God's sentence it is a collapse, yet it is a fulfillment too, for the final act of freely giving over one's existence to God encapsulates a long train of acts in which the self was freely surrendered. As one friend and admirer said of the late Joseph Cardinal Bernardin of Chicago, "His way of death confirms that this man did not have two faces . . . he was inside with his outside, and outside with his inside."[35]

Thesis 6: *The process of assimilating Christ's death into one's life begins at baptism.* As a burial with Christ, baptism vividly symbolizes the interdependence of life and death for the Christian. It is one of God's good gifts that he should provide his people this gracious means of confronting their own death, for Christ's death is therein established as the ontological foundation of the Christian's death, which opens for her a new possibility: she may now die the death of fellowship with Christ. The *degree* to which her death manifests Christ's is not settled at baptism, however, but depends upon the degree to which, in the mystery of God's sovereignty and human freedom, her life is sunk into the passion of Christ.

Thesis 7: *Martyrdom is the quintessential form of that assimilation of Christ's death begun at baptism, whose possibility is contained embryonically within it.* Because this act of surrender comes in the fullness of life, it maximizes human freedom before God. Unlike the death that is accepted in old age as the dissolution of biological processes, martyrdom lays life down midstride. In so doing it dramatizes Christ's life-toward-death, indeed his whole disposition before God, for all those willing to consider it. It reveals with unparalleled power because the means of the witness aligns most perfectly with the object of the witness, or the medium of the revelation with the message of revelation. Yet—no trivial matter—martyrs also clarify other things for those who pay attention, like the oft-hidden meaning of Christian death, and, not least, the meaning of the now-finished project of their own life, which was theretofore obscured by the ambiguities of temporality.

35. Kenneth L. Woodward and John McCormick, "The Art of Dying Well" in *Newsweek* (25 November 1996): 63.

Thesis 8: *The quintessential Christian death called martyrdom may serve, then, as a powerful lens for observing various aspects of the life it encapsulates.* Having been thematized by the omega point of martyrdom, the vast array of temporal occasions, and their interrelations, yield themselves to retelling but never in isolation from the martyr's own narrative accomplishment, for the martyr has in martyrdom mastered the narrative of his own life and thematized it for those who follow.

These theses can be summed up in a single proposition: Bonhoeffer's martyrdom should be a significant factor in the interpretation of his life and thought. It would be a task too large for this study to retell the complete story of Bonhoeffer's life under the theme of martyrdom. In any case it is not biography that concerns me most, as interesting as it is, but the connection between theology and ethics which his martyr's death portends. Having examined the hermeneutic value of death and martyrdom, we have now at our disposal a way of magnifying certain aspects of his theology and ethics, aspects that, so magnified, appear to have martyrological importance of their own. To put it another way, if we consider the chain of Bonhoeffer's activities in the Holocaust context to be the natural outworking of his academic work in theology and ethics, even in a somewhat loose sense, as I think we must, then we will find that a structural affinity exists between his martyrdom and his theology. Cautiously I advance the claim that the systematic framework of Bonhoeffer's theology and ethics is structurally open to the possibility of martyrdom. Or, more boldly, we might contend that martyrdom is the hidden *telos* of his theology and ethics.

Part Three

Bonhoeffer
in Martyrological
Perspective

9

Pushing Back Christendom to Christ

The encounter with Jesus is fundamentally different from that with Goethe or Socrates. . . .

There are only two ways possible of encountering Jesus: man must die or he must put Jesus to death.

Bonhoeffer

I have now completed two phases of my study. In the first phase I clarified the concept of martyrdom, sketched its place in the study of Bonhoeffer, and elaborated the traditional sources for understanding martyrdom. In the second phase I elaborated a theoretical foundation for employing martyrdom as a hermeneutic key for interpreting Christian faith, theology, and life. Now we are ready to test the hermeneutic key's ability to interpret Bonhoeffer's Christology and ethics.

Though ethics and Christology intertwine in Bonhoeffer's thought, for clarity's sake this chapter will treat his Christology as a discrete sphere of study. This pragmatic division should not obscure the point that Bonhoeffer's Christology and ethics belong together and ought not to be isolated from each other. Faithfulness to Bonhoeffer's own intentions demands this. For to him a Christology that is not also a social ethic is no Christology at all. The ontology he develops, an ontology in which Christ is virtually synonymous with the structure of reality itself, also demands it. In particular, I will examine Bonhoeffer's Berlin lectures of 1933 together with *Discipleship* (1937), works that jointly define the primary shape of his Christology.

In chapter ten I will take up the *Ethics* and attempt to develop the themes of death and martyrdom as the hidden *telos* of Bonhoeffer's work. Let me be clear at once that I do not think Bonhoeffer sought directly to die a martyr's death. The term *telos* is meant here to convey something more than the bare structural openness of his thought to martyrdom and yet something less than a clear martyrological trajectory. Certainly I do not see martyrdom as the inevitable outcome of his Christology and ethics. Bonhoeffer's Christology and ethics have a *certain yet loose* teleology toward martyrdom, fittingly so, because orthodox voices of the church consistently reject martyrdom as the literal goal of Christian life. Long ago, Augustine, for example, rejected in clarion voice the opinion of the Donatist Petilianus that Christ "ordained" Christianity to be a movement that "makes progress by the death of its followers."[1] Who could consider the loss of church leaders in their prime, marked by unique gifts and talents, an unqualified gain? As I noted earlier, too much zeal for death is an illegitimate application of the *imitatio Christi*. In any case, fidelity to my vantage point demands that I be ready at all points to see the man Bonhoeffer together with his thought, a challenge that I try to meet from the start by setting the Berlin lectures, and indeed all the developments that follow, in the larger *Sitz im Leben* of Bonhoeffer's personal discipleship.

1933 Berlin Lectures

In the summer of 1933 Bonhoeffer's academic career was at its summit. He had been lecturing since 1931 and had already won for himself an enviable popularity. Nevertheless, in a letter to Erwin Sutz, he drew upon a sixth sense and remarked concerning the impressions of his teaching colleagues: "My theological extraction is gradually becoming suspect here, and they seem to have the feeling that perhaps they have been nourishing a serpent in their bosom!"[2] His suspicious colleagues may have kept their distance, but Bonhoeffer's unconventionality and noticeable youth were practically a billboard of invitation to the students at Berlin. When nearly two hundred students gathered in the early

1. Augustine, *The Writings Against the Manicheans, and Against the Donatists*, ed. Philip Schaff, vol. 4 of *Nicene and Post-Nicene Fathers*, First Series (Peabody, Mass.: Hendrickson, 1994), 2:90–196 (576–77). Petilianus had made his case on the basis of John 12:24, "Unless a grain of wheat falls into the earth and dies, it remains just a single grain; but if it dies, it bears much fruit."

2. *ATTF*, 384. This letter was dated 25 December 1931.

morning to hear his Christology lectures, it was with a clear sense of expectation. As student Otto Dudzus remembered it:

> He looked like a student himself when he mounted the platform. But then what he had to say so gripped us all that we were no longer there to listen to this very young man but we were there because of what he had to say—even though it was dreadfully early in the morning. I have never heard a lecture that impressed me nearly so much.[3]

After attending several of Bonhoeffer's seminars—among them "Creation and Sin" *(Schöpfung und Sünde)* and "Recent Theology" *(Jüngste Theologie)* in winter 1932–1933, and the summer course "Christology" *(Christologie)* under consideration here—another student gave a more detailed description:

> He was an extremely inspiring personality and quite absorbed by the problems he was dealing with; therefore there was no room for sentimentality or rhetorical artifices. What attracted more and more students to the lectures of this young scholar was his Kierkegaardian depth, his Harnack-like ability for analysis, the profound way in which he saw things in their context, like Troeltsch, his knowledge of his material, in which he resembled Holl, and his Barth-like singleness of mind. We followed his words with such close attention that one could hear the flies humming. Sometimes, when we laid our pens down after a lecture, we were literally perspiring.[4]

For all the students knew, Bonhoeffer had always been like that. Yet as Bethge reminds us, there was a distinct change in him that occurred commensurate with the beginning (1931) of his work at the university.[5] Bonhoeffer later ascribed that change to his powerful encounter with the Jesus of the Sermon on the Mount, a change that made him noticeably more fervent in his piety[6] and occasionally even offensive. One student in Bonhoeffer's inner circle recalled, for example, that he put to his class the uncomfortable question "whether we loved Jesus,"[7] and he surprised

---

3. *DB*, 219.

4. Ferenc Lehel, "Seen with the Eyes of a Pupil," in *I Knew Dietrich Bonhoeffer* (hereafter *IKDB*), ed. Wolf-Dieter Zimmermann and Ronald Gregor Smith, trans. Käthe Gregor Smith (New York: Harper and Row, 1966), 68.

5. *DB*, 202–3.

6. Several marks of this change include regular church attendance, systematic meditation, frequent talk of oral confession, community life, obedience, and prayer, and his conviction that the Sermon on the Mount was to be acted upon rather than held up as a mirror to one's shortcomings. See ibid.

7. Ibid., 204. Bethge received this account from J. Kanitz, the larger portion of which reads: "There, before the church struggle, he said to us near the Alexanderplatz, with the

his audience with prayers in the lecture hall. Though Bonhoeffer disliked talking about it, many others testified to a momentous change in him. Paul Lehmann, whom Bonhoeffer had met earlier at Union Seminary, was struck by it when he visited Bonhoeffer in April 1933 just prior to the Christology lectures.[8]

On rare occasions Bonhoeffer did reflect on this "conversion" and its effects. I quote here significant fragments of three letters written respectively to brother Karl-Friedrich, a girlfriend, and brother-in-law Rüdiger Schleicher, in which he tries to articulate the change that came upon him in 1931:

> It may be that in many things I seem to you to be somewhat fanatical and crazy. I myself sometimes have anxiety about this. But I know that, if I were more reasonable, for the sake of honor, I should have to, the next day, give up all my theology. When I first began theology, I imagined it to be somewhat different—perhaps more like an academic affair. Now it has become something completely different from that. And I now believe I know at last that I am at least on the right track—for the first time in my life. . . . I believe I know that inwardly I shall be really clear and honest only when I have begun to take seriously the Sermon on the Mount.[9]

> I plunged into work in a very unChristian way. An . . . ambition that many noticed in me made my life difficult. . . .
> Then something happened, something that has changed and trans-formed my life to the present day. For the first time I discovered the Bible. . . . I had often preached, I had seen a great deal of the church. . . . but I had not yet become a Christian. . . .

> I know that at that time I turned the doctrine of Jesus Christ into something of a personal advantage for myself. . . . I pray to God that that will never happen again. Also I had never prayed, or prayed only very little. For all my abandonment, I was quite pleased with myself. Then the Bible, and

---

simplicity that was perhaps used by Tholuck in the old days, that we should not forget that every word of Holy Scripture was a quite personal message of God's love for us, and he asked us whether we loved Jesus." Tholuck (1799–1877), one of the leading pietist theologians of the nineteenth century, was born in Bonhoeffer's native Breslau and lectured at Berlin. He propounded a *Vermittlungstheologie* that stressed personal piety and downplayed confessional dogmas. See R. V. Pierard, "Tholuck, Friedrich August Gottreau" in *Evangelical Dictionary of Theology,* ed. Walter A. Elwell (Grand Rapids: Eerdmans, 1984), 1089–90.

It is worth noting that in one of his letters Bonhoeffer remembered to Barth an ad hoc statement the latter made during one of his regularly held discussion evenings. Barth apparently confessed to his students his temptation to become like "old Tholuck" and ask, "How goes it with your soul?" (*ATTF,* 431). In this letter Bonhoeffer is justifying his Finkenwalde experiment to Barth by showing that he has taken his advice!

8. *DB,* 204–5.

9. Letter to Karl-Friedrich dated 14 January 1935. *ATTF,* 423–424.

in particular the Sermon on the Mount, freed me from that. Since then everything has changed. I have felt this plainly, and so have other people about me. It was a great liberation. It became clear to me that the life of a servant of Jesus Christ must belong to the church, and step by step it became plainer to me how far that must go. . . .

My calling is quite clear to me. What God will make of it I do not know. . . . I must follow the path. Perhaps it will not be such a long one.[10]

If I am one who says where God shall be, so I will always find a God there who corresponds in some way to me, is pleasing to me, who belongs to my nature. If it is, however, God who speaks where God chooses to be, then that will probably be a place which does not at all correspond to my nature, which is not at all pleasing to me. But this place is the cross of Christ. And the one who will find him there must be with him under this cross, just as the Sermon on the Mount demands. This doesn't suit our nature at all but is completely counter to it. This, however, is the message of the Bible, not only in the New but also in the Old Testament (Isaiah 53!). In any event, Jesus and Paul intended this: with the cross of Jesus is the Scripture, that is, the Old Testament, fulfilled. The whole Bible will, therefore, be the Word in which God will allow the divine self to be discovered by us.

. . . I also want to say to you quite personally that since I have learned to read the Bible in this way—and that is not so very long ago—it becomes more wonderful to me every day. I read it every morning and evening, often also during the day. And every day I take for myself a text that I will have for the entire week and attempt to immerse myself entirely in it, in order to be able to really listen to it. I know that without this I would no longer be able to live properly. Or, even before that, to believe in the right way.[11]

In each of these fascinating texts Bonhoeffer makes reference to an encounter with the Sermon on the Mount, or rather an encounter with the Jesus who preached it. He also conveys a sense of what might be termed Kierkegaardian inwardness and suggests a new set of spiritual exercises that followed in its wake.[12] Not coincidentally, the themes of prayer, meditation, and devotion to Jesus' teaching in the Sermon on the

10. Letter to a woman to whom Bonhoeffer had been engaged, dated 1 January 1936. *ATTF,* 424–25.

11. Letter to Rüdiger Schleicher dated 8 April 1936. *ATTF,* 425–26.

12. In the lecture series *Schöpfung und Sünde* (Creation and Sin), which dates closer to the time of this change, Bonhoeffer had urged his hearers in the introductory lecture to consider the fact that listening to the word of God involved *"exercitium,"* a term which, rooted in the mystical tradition, appears in both Thomas à Kempis's *Imitatio Christi* and the *Spiritual Exercises* of Ignatius of Loyola. Bonhoeffer was familiar with both books. Later, referring to this work on the Sermon on the Mount he told Erwin Sutz "I am busy

Mount later became, under Bonhoeffer's careful direction, distinguishing features of the Finkenwalde experiment, which was already under way by the time these last two letters were penned.[13] They also became distinguishing features of *Discipleship*, which epitomized that period.

What should the interpreter make of this collection of reflections by Bonhoeffer and his students? It may seem odd to open a discussion of Bonhoeffer's Christology by sifting student reactions to his lectures and self-appraisals of "conversion," but it is by any and all means essential to grasp that by summer 1933 Bonhoeffer was following a new course whose impetus derived from a personal-type encounter with Jesus. Clearly, he carried into his academic work that summer an unusual sense of purpose and intentionality which, in retrospect, might be said to characterize his work from that point onward. One receives the impression that quite beyond the natural curiosity new professors evoke, his burgeoning popularity was riding to a great extent on the students' perception that the soul of the man was welded to his theological work. As testimony to Bonhoeffer's lure, a number of his Berlin students would join up with him again at Finkenwalde. Apparently Bonhoeffer had been gripped by Jesus' teaching in a way that flooded his previous theological training with a fresh earnestness, not negating it but working it toward a higher plane.

Theologically speaking, the tone of these texts hints at the *kind* of encounter he had with Jesus. In respect to his previous life it is described, curiously, as "liberation." Who could take the Sermon on the Mount seriously and at the same time consider it liberating? How could confrontation with Jesus' difficult ethic there yield freedom? One might

---

with a work that I would like to call exercises (*Exerzitien*)." This reinforces the impression we are dealing with here, viz., that Bonhoeffer had been thinking about theology in an active, not purely academic mode. For comments on *exercitium* see *DBWE* 3, 155–56. The letter to Sutz can be found in *GS* I, 41.

13. It might be objected that Bonhoeffer's reflections upon his "conversion" date to the period following his brief academic career at the university, with the result that at that time he was throwing a negative spin on his previous life so as to justify his current course beyond the ambit of the university. As the objection might go, a theologian soured on the university can be expected to frown upon theology as an "academic affair." If Bonhoeffer's own reflections were all we had our disposal, such an objection might stand, but we still have the witness of those "others about me" to whom Bonhoeffer appeals. No doubt some of the Finkenwalde spirit is present in these letters (especially those to his anonymous girlfriend and Rüdiger Schleicher), but this only serves to reinforce the point: because the kind of changes witnessed in him during 1931—an intensified life of prayer and Bible meditation—are precisely the spiritual exercises that came to distinguish the Finkenwalde years, we have strong reasons for imagining a line of steady development from 1931 onward which runs straight through the period when Bonhoeffer was preparing the Christology lectures.

expect, in fact, just the opposite. The answer lies in Bonhoeffer's threefold apprehension that Jesus' Sermon on the Mount stands in sharp contradiction to the natural impulses of the human,[14] that the cross marks the logical culmination of this contradictoriness, and that Jesus' followers are bound to live out such contradiction in their own lives. When Bonhoeffer calls Jesus' sermon a "liberation," I believe he is offering the reader a cipher by which to understand the nature of his conversion. In exposing the truth that the momentum of fallen life runs, quite literally, at cross-purposes with God's aims, the cross seizes God's creatures and impels them toward an either-or decision: a decision either for God, which demands the death of self, or for the self, which demands the death of God. The cross chews up all neutral ground. One must stand on one side or the other. When it came to Christ, and therefore when it came to *Christ*ology, Bonhoeffer had made an either-or decision. If, as a result, he had to appear the awkward religious fanatic to his brother, that was necessary to his new course, for to retreat to something else would mean the end of his theology. If he must die early along this path, as was his premonition, it is to be taken as the expected extremity of his new course. If he would surrender his new mode of personal Bible reading, that would spell the end of his entire theology.

Liberation lay in the relative clarity of his new life, which aimed at something more or less tangible and specific along the lines of Jesus' experience before God. To render a decision with one's whole life—what in *Discipleship* he would call "singleness of heart" (and what Kierkegaard had called purity of heart, "to will one thing")—rescues a person from the illusion that serving two masters is possible. Jesus presents the choice for or against him in the starkest possible way so that one stands naked, as it were, before one's self and before God. Simplicity and freedom emerge when from this tension a person commits the whole of himself to God. These themes are worked to maturity in *Discipleship (Nachfolge)*, but let me here state categorically that these quotations we have considered, while revealing of Bonhoeffer's personal faith, yield a strong theological impression of his belief concerning the figure of Jesus and his authority.

The point of this narrative entrée to Bonhoeffer's Christology and ethics can be summed up as follows: I submit that the Christology lectures lie along a curve of development from 1931 to the Finkenwalde years and beyond, years in which, by the testimony of both Bonhoeffer and those who knew him, "everything had changed." Many are understandably reticent to press Bonhoeffer's experience into an evangelical, born-again mold—admittedly a hazardous move, given his own reticence about it,

14. One should note here that Barth's theology had already made a lasting impression.

his theological moorings in the Lutheran tradition, and the profoundly continuous construal of his life given at other points. Yet that reticence should not be permitted to obscure the obvious point that something significant had changed for him both personally and theologically.

Combining two findings at this juncture will sharpen the point into a question. First, we know by extant testimonies that Bonhoeffer the lecturer seems to have invested a large portion of himself in his academic work, and as we will see momentarily, he desired this for his students as well. Second, we find in Bonhoeffer's self-disclosure concerning the change of 1931 numerous hints of anticipation that the road ahead was lined with dangers. These hints are strewn throughout Bonhoeffer's writings, many of them coming long before he made the dangerous decision to entangle himself with Hans von Dohnanyi and the other conspirators. Together these findings give rise to the question whether we might locate in the theological works of this period a current that flows in the direction of a martyr's death.

To be fair, the Christology lectures purport to be a course in Christology, not the Christology of Dietrich Bonhoeffer per se, much less a sort of spiritual autobiography. To that end Bonhoeffer worked many of the traditional themes—the problem of the two natures, the docetic and ebionitic heresies, and the relationship of Christ's person and work, for example—into the lectures in ways not easily surrendered to our question. But especially in those portions where his unique contributions surface we will find a clear resonance with his own life commitments, even if they lie buried in lofty academic style.

Christ Cannot Be Assimilated

Judging from students' notes,[15] Bonhoeffer began the course with a twin appeal to Kierkegaard's admonition "Be still, for that is the absolute" and Cyril of Alexandria's epigram "In silence I worship the unutterable." He was trying to describe therewith the theologian's humble posture in respect to the subject matter of Christology. Since Christology deals with Christ's person, who is also the Logos of *God*, it deals directly in the transcendent: "Christology [is] the science *par*

---

15. The Berlin lectures of summer term 1933 are not available from Bonhoeffer's hand. Bethge culled student notes and reconstructed them. Bonhoeffer's plan for the course fell into a three-part structure under the headings The Present Christ, The Historical Christ, and The Eternal Christ. There was also a substantial introduction. Since no notes were attainable on The Eternal Christ, it is presumed that, as often happens to professors, the course ran out before the content. In English these notes are collected in *Christ the Center*, trans. Edwin H. Robertson (New York: Harper and Row, 1978).

excellence because it comes from outside study itself."[16] As such, it has no proof by which it can establish the transcendence of its subject. Christology must simply presuppose transcendence. In the domain of theological method this means that revelation suggests its own epistemology, one that operates something like this: the wish to know God is fulfilled only where the theologian conforms to the form of God's revelation, that is, where the humility of the theologian meets the humility of God. The theologian must allow Christ to function as the presupposition of theological thought. It follows that "only a discipline which understands itself in the sphere of the Church is able to grasp the fact that christology is . . . the unknown and hidden center of the university of learning."[17]

This auspicious beginning reveals Bonhoeffer's essentially Barthian commitments, though as the lectures roll on there is mounting evidence also of important disagreements with Barth, most of which devolve upon Christ's relationship to the world. The issue of any Barthian Christ-imperialism aside, Bonhoeffer is preparing to battle any and all who wish to approach Christology on a strictly scientific basis. He draws the contrast between the Logos of God on the one hand and the "classifying logos" of the human on the other. Again, if we projected this into the province of theological method, it would approximate the common contrast between revelation and reason. The human "classifying logos" approaches its subject matter with the question "How?" because it is programmed to ascertain the *causes* for things. As it approaches the figure of Christ it recognizes the claim of deity embedded within the very title, and it follows its habituated pattern by asking "How is such a claim possible? How can it be contained within its structure?"[18] But the habitual human quest for causes is prone to exceed its limit, and for that reason the question "How?" may become insidious.[19] Indeed, the question "How?" may indicate a recalcitrant refusal to accept the claim Christ makes on the human logos and its dominion.

Confronting the human "classifying logos," Bonhoeffer asks:

16. Ibid., 28.

17. Ibid.

18. Ibid., 29.

19. Bonhoeffer explains that the question does not always spring from the hard-boiled rationalism of the Enlightenment, where human reason defends itself protestingly against the divine. The question may also indicate a more subtle course of assimilation, as with Hegel. For this reason Bonhoeffer is unequivocal in his choice of terms. The Logos is not an Idea but a *person*. Whereas the Idea of Christ can be assimilated into the structure of human reason, Christ as person always stands as "Other" and resists assimilation. See *Christ the Center*, 29–30.

What happens when doubt is thrown upon this presupposition of his scientific activity? What if somewhere the claim is raised that this human logos is superseded, condemned, dead? What happens if a counter-logos appears which denies the classification? What if the old order of the first logos be proclaimed as broken up, superseded and in its place a new world has already begun? When the human logos is addressed like that, what answer can it give?[20]

At this point Bonhoeffer makes a noteworthy terminological shift. Christ is hereafter depicted as the *Counter-Logos*, the One who contradicts the human logos and makes a claim upon it. The Counter-Logos does not present itself as an Idea for consideration, or an object of human thought, but as the incarnate, personal, spoken Word of God. And what does the Counter-Logos say to the logos?

> "I am the way, the truth, the life," "I am the death of the human logos, I am the life of the Logos of God," "Man with his logos must die; he falls into my hands; I am the first and the last."[21]

The Counter-Logos demands death, and in so doing shows the logos that all possibility of assimilation is gone. The question "How?" is rendered inappropriate by the very claim of Christ. The only question that remains, the "question of dethroned and distraught reason," is "Who?" *This* is the question of Christology. "How?" is now shown to be the "serpent's question," while "Who?" is oriented toward transcendence and proves its asker ready to hear.

Bonhoeffer now ripens the transcendent question:

> The question, "Who?," expresses the strangeness and the otherness of the one encountered and at the same time it is shown to be the question concerning the very existence of the questioner. He is asking about the being which is strange to his being, about the boundaries of his own existence. Transcendence places his own being in question. With the answer that his logos has reached its boundary he faces the boundary of his own existence. So the question of transcendence is the question of existence, and the question of existence is the question of transcendence. In theological terms: it is only from God that man knows who he is.[22]

Only in a confrontation with the contradicting Counter-Logos does human existence come fully to light. Here and only here may humans learn their limits and come to understand their status relative to God.

---

20. Ibid., 29.
21. Ibid., 30.
22. Ibid., 30–31.

This confrontation is experienced as both life and death, beginning and end—a beginning because the meaning of human life is first illumined there at the boundary, and an end because something of the human is extinguished there too. Above all else, it is a dangerous confrontation, because at this boundary the logos must exercise freedom for or against the Counter-Logos. One of the two will give way. Either the logos will kill the Counter-Logos or it will submit and be killed.[23] In the final analysis, this is the confrontation that delineates everyday life with God.

But it is only an everyday question because of the historical work of Christ. Historically, the logos could not bear the encounter with the Counter-Logos. It refused to die. So "the one who compelled the dangerous question must be killed."[24] Elaborating the point, in the face of the logos's refusal to die the Counter-Logos dies *so that* the human logos might live on with its unanswered question of existence and transcendence. By crucifixion, the Counter-Logos succumbed to the logos as a penultimate movement. However, the Counter-Logos then rose up against its murderers—the Crucified showed himself the Risen One—and thereby sharpened the question "Who?" to an extreme point, where "it remains a living question for ever, over, around and in man, as also does the answer."[25] God permits the human logos to struggle against the Crucified One, but it remains impotent against the Risen One. The question now reverses, flinging itself back upon the human logos with immense force. The human logos may and must ask the question "Who?" as Bonhoeffer said, but first and foremost it must give an answer to the Risen One concerning *itself*.

This is precisely why, as the epigraph over this chapter conveys, an encounter with Jesus is fundamentally different from an encounter with Socrates or Goethe. Jesus *lives*. And thus he cannot be avoided. Every encounter with the risen Christ forks off necessarily into two possibilities, says Bonhoeffer. Either "man must die or he must put Jesus to death."[26]

In my judgment we are getting in Bonhoeffer's introductory lectures—as in any good introduction—those personal assumptions and biases of the speaker that serve to contextualize the content that follows. In other words, we are peering into the story of Bonhoeffer's encounter with Christ, dressed in the acceptable symbols of theological-philosophical discourse. Bonhoeffer's encounter with Jesus was different from his encounter with Socrates and Goethe; Bonhoeffer hung between

23. Ibid., 33.
24. Ibid.
25. Ibid., 33–34.
26. Ibid., 35.

the questions "How?" and "Who?"; Bonhoeffer's life forked into one of two possibilities. And it is to himself that Bonhoeffer speaks when he adds:

> It is the same temptation for the theologian who tries to encounter Christ and yet to avoid that encounter. Theologians betray him and simulate concern. Christ is still betrayed by the kiss.[27]

Theologians too easily become Judases among the true disciples, wishing that Christ would conform to some humanly contrived agenda instead of putting themselves completely at his disposal.

The source of Bonhoeffer's passion and presence in the lecture hall, and even the occasional provocation "Do you love Jesus?" lies not primarily in academic curiosity—though his academic curiosity was immense—but in the deeply personal nature of his engagement with Christ. Preparing to leave Berlin later in 1933, as a parting gift to his students Bonhoeffer wrote the brief essay "What Should the Student of Theology Today Do?" ("Was soll der Student der Theologie heute tun?"). In that essay he urged theologians in no uncertain terms to take Christ's passion into their work. Speaking of and to the theological student, Bonhoeffer wrote:

> He may accept into his theological study his philosophy, his ethics, peda-gogy, culture, and social passion; they belong to him as a whole person, and as a theologian he really should be a whole person (certainly he would be a worse theologian were such passions not driven into his study), but he should learn and know as a theologian that the power of his life and thought can come from nothing other than the passion of Jesus Christ, the crucified Lord. . . . The proper study of sacred theology begins at the place where the person in his questions and searchings encounters the cross, where he recognizes in the suffering of God that is caused by human hatred the end of all his passions, and receives judgment of his entire vitality.[28]

---

27. Ibid.

28. The above is my translation of the German original, which reads as follows: "Er mag in sein theologisches Studium seine philosophische, seine ethische, pädagogische, völkische, soziale Passion mit heineinnehmen; sie gehört zu ihm als ganzem Menschen, und er soll als Theologe wahrhaftige ein ganzer Mensch sein–gewiß ein schlechter Theologe, den nicht auch gerade solche Passionen in sein Studium hineingetrieben hätten–aber er soll dann als Theologe lernen und wissen, daß der Antrieb seines Lebens und Denkens als eines Theologen nirgends anders herkommen kann als von der Passion Jesu Christi, des gekreuzigten Herrn. . . . Das rechte Studium der theologia sacra beginnt dort, wo der Mensch in seinem Fragen und Suchen auf das Kreuz stößt, wo er im Leiden Gottes unter der Menschen Haß das Ende aller seiner Leidenschaften erkennt, das Gericht über seine ganze Vitalität vernimmt." *GS* 3:244.

Christ's Presence

At a relatively early date in the history of Bonhoeffer studies, Jaroslav Pelikan penetrated the central theme of the Christology lectures when he emphasized the moniker *Christus praesens*,[29] which may still be regarded today as one of Bonhoeffer's distinct contributions to Christology.[30] The significance of Christ's presence as an entrance point into Christology derives as much from what, or who, is rejected thereby as from what, or who, is affirmed. Bonhoeffer brings his proposal into the arena with such notable figures as Friedrich Schleiermacher, Albrecht Ritschl, Wilhelm Hermann, and Adolf von Harnack, each of whom, he concludes, has bypassed the truly important thing in Christology.[31] "Jesus is the Christ present as the Crucified and as the risen one," and "that is the first christological statement." Such presence is to be understood *in space and time, here and now,* for it is in the nature of a person to be present in this way. Hence "the understanding of the Presence opens up the way for the understanding of the Person."[32] This is what these theologians have missed, for they construe the presence of Christ either as the *influence* that emanates from his historical person, as with Ritschl, or they retreat from the historical altogether to focus instead on an *image* of the inner life of Jesus, as with Hermann. Schleiermacher is said to participate in both errors. To understand Christ in terms of his influence attributes to him a power, and to understand him in terms of an image attributes to him a value, but in neither case is Christ permitted to be a person who confronts us *hic et nunc.* It hardly needs to be said that Bonhoeffer is promoting here a kind of high Christology that Harnack could not have endorsed, a wry move from a pupil of Harnack who, as Pelikan noted, less than two months earlier had delivered the master's funeral oration and was about to become a *Dozent* at his own university!

According to Bonhoeffer, the shortcomings of this prestigious group can be summed up by their decision not to consider the resurrection, which alone makes possible the presence of the living Christ. Bonhoeffer

29. Jaroslav Pelikan, "Bonhoeffer's Christologie of 1933," in *The Place of Bonhoeffer: Problems and Possibilities in His Thought,* ed. Martin E. Marty (New York: Association Press, 1962), 145–64.

30. Though not without precedent, the choice to unfold Christology from the standpoint of the *present* Christ is rare among Protestant theologians. For Bonhoeffer, however, it was an easy extrapolation of his prior work on the sociality of the church, *Sanctorum Communio,* in which he pioneered the idea of "Christ existing as the church."

31. Whether Bonhoeffer treats them fairly is an open question, and I shall not pursue it here. In the context of Bonhoeffer's lectures his treatment of them *appears* to have been cursory. Most likely these figures are set as buoys to mark off the channel of his own interest.

32. *Christ the Center,* 43.

thus rests his thesis *Christ's presence opens the way to his person* squarely on the premise of the resurrection.[33] Stopping at the cross, these others are left trying to explain Christ's person solely in terms of his work.

Bonhoeffer chooses Luther as his theological predecessor in this regard, for "Luther tried to interpret the presence of Christ from the Ascension."[34] In this way Luther was able to speak of Christ as our contemporary. Though Bonhoeffer does not directly acknowledge it, Luther left his mark upon him in yet another way. The presence of the Crucified and Risen One in space and time, *hic et nunc*, means that even today Christ participates fully in the ambiguities of human life. That is, just as his historical presence "in the likeness of sinful flesh" (Rom. 8:3) once veiled God in his glory, so too the resurrected Christ deigns, even chooses, to come to the world incognito. Here Luther's *theologia crucis* is woven into the fabric of Bonhoeffer's Christology.[35]

33. Ibid., 44.

34. Ibid. Clearly Bonhoeffer commits himself to the Lutheran doctrine of Christ's ubiquity. He cites Luther's statement "When he was on earth, he was far from us. Now that he is far, he is near to us."

35. In theses 19 and 20 of the *Heidelberg Disputation* (1518), Luther set forth the essential components of what has become known as his "theology of the cross" *(theologia crucis):*

Thesis 19: "The person who looks upon the invisible things of God, as they are seen in visible things, does not deserve to be called a theologian." Thesis 20: "But the person who looks on the visible rearward parts of God as seen in suffering and the cross does, however, deserve to be called a theologian."

With this seminal distinction Luther proposed nothing less than a revolution in theological method, for he was charting the territory for a way of thinking about God and knowing him quite alien to Medieval categories. Walther von Loewenich has likened Luther's *theologia crucis* to a key signature in a piece of music, which functions to govern the meter and mood of the entire score. Admittedly, Luther never raised his *theologia crucis* to the level of a formal criterion, at least not consciously, but it appears so systematically in his work that it might be said to undergird the entirety of his mature thought. Indeed, at one point Luther summed up his whole theology from this standpoint: *CRUX sola est nostra theologia* (WA 5.176.32–33.)

The person who looks upon the invisible things is a theologian of glory, who like Philip (John 14:8) circumvents Christ with his request "Show us the Father." By contrast, the true theologian looks upon the visible things of God as seen in the suffering and death of Christ. What distinguishes the true theologian from the false is the particular *place* where God is sought. Luther urges theologians to look neither behind nor beyond the death of Christ, but directly at it. The inner disposition of those who wish to know the truth of God must conform to God's own disposition as he emptied himself and endured a criminal's death. In other words, epistemologically speaking, the human approach to God must take its cue from God's approach to humanity. This is a hard word for God-seekers, who by nature would rather gaze upon God's glory and majesty. But theologians of the cross learn to content themselves with God in his crucified form, humbly clinging to the *backside* of God (*posteriora Dei*) precisely because it is the backside of *God.*

Theologians of the cross do not depict God as a stingy deity who delights in veiling himself and remaining aloof from human affairs; rather, they have learned that just as

Bonhoeffer now makes the hiddenness of Christ's presence the ful-crum on which the whole problem of Christology pivots. The central problem is not how to relate God on the one hand to the man Christ on the other; it is rather how to negotiate the veiled presence of the one God-Man. The *fact and identity* of his personal presence remains for Bonhoeffer a presupposition derived from the resurrection and ascension, but the *hiddenness* of that presence is a problem that requires careful examination.[36]

To put it another way, Bonhoeffer is less interested in philosophical problems pertaining to the incarnation—Chalcedon deals with the "that-ness," not the "how"—than in the *form* the incarnate Christ takes in the world. The problem, or scandal, is not the *humanness* of Christ's form. For the incarnation is to be understood in reference to the creation—a revelation of compatibility and noncontradiction between Creator and creature, "a true revelation of the Creator in the creature."[37] The *scandalon*, writes Bonhoeffer, "is found not in the incarnation of God, but in the doctrine of the humiliated God-Man," a theme Paul took up when he taught that Christ came in the "likeness of sinful flesh." How is this humiliation expressed?

> In this way, that Christ takes sinful flesh. The humiliation is necessitated by the world under the curse. The incarnation is related to the first creation; the humiliation is related to the fallen creation. In the humiliation, Christ, of his own free will, enters the world of sin and death. He enters it in such a way as to hide himself in it in weakness and not to be recognized as the God-Man. He does not enter in kingly robes of a *morphe theou*. His claim, which he as God-Man raises in this form, must provoke contradic-

---

God consented to show Moses his glory only from behind, and only with a protective shield, so too in the lowly death-ward movement of Christ he desires to protect us from the consuming fire of his glory. By veiling the Son's glory, God devised a way for us to survive an encounter with him. Yet a theology of the cross is about something far more than survival with God, as if we had only to put up with him and he with us. The *theologia crucis* implies that God has chosen, quite shrewdly, and perhaps consistently, to meet us in ways that contradict our expectations. Translation of theses 19 and 20 is taken from Alister McGrath's excellent study *Luther's Theology of the Cross: Martin Luther's Theological Breakthrough* (Oxford: Basil Blackwell, 1985), 148. For another scholarly treatment of Luther's *theologia crucis*, see Walther von Loewenich, *Luther's Theology of the Cross*, trans. Herbert J. A. Bouman (Minneapolis: Augsburg, 1976).

36. As Bonhoeffer's experience of the Holocaust unfolded, this problem grew ever more acute. This crucial element in his Christology explains his eventual direction in the *Ethik* and the late musings of the prison letters. In a very real sense, the impetus for nearly all his subsequent theological work lies in the hidden presence of Christ to the world. Christian ethics, for instance, will be articulated in terms of participation in this the hidden form of Christ so as to reveal him.

37. *Christ the Center*, 105.

tion and hostility. He goes incognito, as a beggar among beggars, as an outcast among outcasts, as despairing among the despairing, as dying among the dying. He also goes as sinner among sinners, yet how truly as the *peccator pessimus*.[38]

This humiliated One, who among humankind makes no spectacle of his deity, is yet the whole person of the God-man—this is the true scandal of Christ. To observers he appears no different from, perhaps even worse than, the common lot of sinners, taking up solidarity with them in matters of sin, shame, and death. The riddle of Christology lies in the fact that the king is a beggar, that Christ makes royal claims in such a veiled state as this. To observers they are at best ambiguous and at worst outrageous.

Moreover, as important as the resurrection and ascension of Christ are to Bonhoeffer's understanding of the *Christus praesens* as a point of entrance to Christology, as historical moments they do not signify an unveiling of the hidden Christ. Even the empty tomb proves itself ambiguous, because its historicity cannot be demonstrated.[39] The incognito endures as a structural element of Christ's person even in his contemporaneity. Whether in preaching, sacrament, or church—*or martyrdom*[40]—the resurrected Christ is always present precisely as the humiliated and rejected One.

The regularity of Christ's appearance incognito in space and time is a function of the ontological orientation of Bonhoeffer's Christology. Christology is at the same time ontology. Or, to say it differently, reality is describable in christological terms. Christ's personal structure impresses itself on reality so deeply that a description of Christ is virtually synonymous with a description of the real. Christology deals with the point of ontological union between God and the world. "Only in Christology," says Bonhoeffer, "is the question of transcendence put in the form of the question of existence."[41] The transcendence of God is understandable in the incarnation as nowhere else, a point André Dumas summarized

38. Ibid., 107.

39. Ibid., 112.

40. Stimulating to me is the thought that the ambiguity of Bonhoeffer's martyrdom might have its taproot in the incognito of Christ, not the sociopolitical landscape of the twentieth century. The indirectness between the martyr's confession and death may be a surface sign, or symptom, that Christ himself has withdrawn more deeply. It would mean that the more nuanced and sophisticated understanding of martyrdom I have been calling for is implicitly a call for a more nuanced and sophisticated Christology. Perhaps this could be sketched out with the aid of Eberhard Jüngel's essay "The Effectiveness of Christ Withdrawn." See Eberhard Jüngel, *Theological Essays*, ed. and trans. J. B. Webster (Edinburgh: T & T Clark, 1989), 214–31.

41. *Christ the Center*, 33.

skillfully when he wrote that Bonhoeffer's ontology "is an analysis of the creaturely existence *(Dasein)* of the present Christ."[42]

Though the christo-ontological approach was not new to Bonhoeffer in 1933,[43] it was nevertheless underdeveloped. This explains in part the difficulty of his cryptic descriptions of the synonymity of Christ and reality interspersed in *Christ the Center*. The other part of the difficulty is simply inherent in the kind of task Bonhoeffer has set for himself. For the most basic metaphysical judgments cannot submit themselves to clear demonstration without yielding their foundational status.[44] We find Bonhoeffer dangling out tantalizing statements such as "Space and time is the way of existence of the person of the risen one" and "It is the nature of the person of Christ to be in the center both spatially and temporally."[45] Yet what do these statements mean?

When Bonhoeffer attempts to clarify the meaning of these things in 1933 it amounts, in my estimate, only to a restatement of his premise. Clarification would come only gradually as the ethical implications of these theological problems worked their way to the surface. He does offer some guidance, however: the centrality of Christ does not mean that he is central to our personality, thoughts, and feelings. "His centrality is not psychological, but has the character of an ontological and theological statement."[46] Bonhoeffer is clear on yet another point. As ontological, Christ's centrality pervades the various modes of what theologians conveniently dub "general revelation"; Christ is the center of human existence, history, and nature. It would violate the integrity of what Bonhoeffer has said so far to construe this as influence or value, and so we must be willing to think quite audaciously of Christ's centrality in terms of his concrete (because it is spatial and temporal), personal presence *structurally internal to and constitutive of* human existence, history, and nature.

42. André Dumas, *Dietrich Bonhoeffer: Theologian of Reality*, trans. Robert McAfee Brown (New York: Macmillan, 1971), 114.

43. It emerged quite naturally from this thinking about Christ as a unity of act and being which dates to the time of his *Habilitationschrift*.

44. In other words, if one were successful in substantiating a metaphysical judgment by means of some other judgment, one would succeed, in effect, in relegating the substantiated statement to a lesser status than the substantiating one. In that case something even more foundational would have arisen. In the structure of thought some things have simply to be assumed if any progress is to be made. This is why ontology and metaphysics, at some level, must always be speculative. Therefore one should not use Bonhoeffer's own ambiguity against him at this decisive point but attempt to plot it against future developments in his thought.

45. *Christ the Center*, 60.

46. Ibid., 61.

The general truth that in Christ the Christian God orients himself toward the world is a given attribute of revelation and redemption.[47] Though surely not anthropocentric, this orientation contains nonetheless a remarkably personal dimension. For Bonhoeffer, the incognito of Christ makes it possible for him to come alongside us in a personal way. Indeed, Christ's orientation toward the world would be much too austere were it not for his hiddenness. As the hidden One, he plants himself deeply into the reality of the human, from which place he joins in the condition of cursed humanity, and through which he redeems it.

We come here to the critical matter of Christ's existence *pro me*, which is perhaps Bonhoeffer's most earnest attempt to articulate the significance of Christ's structural internality to the world. By assuming a *particular* instance of humanity, humbling it, calling it under his judgment, and gifting it with new life, God demonstrated his intent to be with humanity instead of without it, for it instead of against it. Christ is oriented to me—there for me—in the sense that he represents me but also there *for me* in the sense that he acts on my behalf. According to Bonhoeffer, it really is *my* humanity that he takes to himself in this way, and therefore *my* humanity is assimilated into the ontological structure of Christ. His orientation toward me has nothing to do with his usefulness to my human aspirations, even when they are most noble. That would be only another anthropocentric ploy to assimilate the Counter-Logos into the ontology of my sinful humanity. Rather he is for me in the sense that his desire is to include my humanity in his and thereby establish it anew. "He does not *have* the power of being for me, but he *is* the power."[48]

This, then, is how we should understand Bonhoeffer's use of the *pro me:* because the particular instance of human *being* that I am is taken into Christ's being, my humanity must no longer be considered in isolation from Christ's, nor his from mine. Christ *pro me* means there can no longer be any speech about the divine or the human *in abstracto.* If the structure of Christ is the structure of reality, and if Christ is the God-Man, then every general ontological question concerning human and divine deflects to the specific ontological question of Christ.[49] Christ's

47. Consider this late but representative text, taken from the 5 May 1944 letter to Bethge: "It is not with the beyond that we are concerned, but with this world as created and preserved, subjected to laws, reconciled, and restored. What is above this world is, in the gospel, intended to exist *for* this world; I mean that, not in the anthropocentric sense of liberal, mystic, pietistic, ethical theology, but in the biblical sense of the creation and of the incarnation, crucifixion and resurrection of Jesus Christ." *ATTF,* 504.

48. *Christ the Center,* 48.

49. I agree with Charles Marsh that this is a decisive point of difference between Bonhoeffer and Barth. As Marsh states it, for Bonhoeffer "God's aseity is interpreted by

existence *pro me* therefore epitomizes the ontological intentions of Bonhoeffer's Christology.

Discipleship

Upon his departure from Berlin, Bonhoeffer devoted himself for a time to parish work in London, after which he returned to Germany to assume a teaching role in one of the new seminaries of the Confessing Church. He now found himself in a vastly different context. At Finkenwalde, one of these new seminaries, his lofty academic style waned noticeably, but his rigor for a Christ-centered theology grew even stronger. In *Discipleship,* the primary work of the period, we find Bonhoeffer deepening his christological orientation, working through many of the same themes he had considered at Berlin. Several sections of this work are critical in our current quest to grasp Bonhoeffer's Christology—the sections titled "Single-Minded Obedience," "Discipleship and the Individual," and "Baptism." We will survey each of them briefly, but let me first call attention to the way Bonhoeffer introduces his book:

> In times of church renewal holy scripture naturally becomes richer in content for us. Behind the daily catchwords and battle cries needed in the church struggle, a more intense, questioning search arises for the one who is our sole concern, for Jesus himself. What did Jesus want to say to us? What does he want from us today? How does he help us to be faithful Christians today?[50]

Only rarely have Bonhoeffer's interpreters included *Discipleship* in their treatment of his Christology,[51] but these opening sentences of the book make it clear that Bonhoeffer *meant* the work to center upon Christ, and in a way that would prove ethically fruitful for his day.

God's promeity," while for Barth it appears to be the other way round. Bonhoeffer does not understand God's freedom from the far side so much as from the side of his free attachment to humanity in every historical aspect, which results in a much more positive treatment of the world and its value. Such a move is remarkable enough for one who was so influenced by Barth, but doubly remarkable when one considers the sense of foreboding evil that hung over Bonhoeffer's world. Bonhoeffer intentionally tied his concept of Christ *pro me* to Melanchthon and Luther (*Christ the Center*, 46–48), which to some extent may have inoculated him against what some would consider the excessively transcendent God of Reformed theology. For Marsh's discussion, see *Reclaiming Dietrich Bonhoeffer: The Promise of His Theology* (New York: Oxford University Press, 1994), 3–33.

50. *DBWE* 4:21.

51. One who does include it is Ernst Feil, *Theology of Bonhoeffer,* trans. Martin Rumscheidt (Philadelphia: Fortress, 1985), 76–78.

The either-or edge made visible in the genuine encounter with Christ that Bonhoeffer propounded in the Berlin lectures is ground razor-sharp in the section "Discipleship and the Individual," where he exegetes Jesus' words in Luke 14:26.[52] In this text Jesus is said to put his hearers in a place of extreme discomfort by asking them to break off their natural ties to life, whether family, nationality, or tradition. Discomfort is inherent in the call of Jesus, who intends to assist the individual by forcing her to come forth from the comfort of her social connections and make a decision. There is grace here, no doubt, for in erecting a barrier to her natural life Christ is showing himself to be an entirely sufficient source of the new life. And yet it is a severe induction to that life, for the individual experiences an inevitable loss. "No one can follow Christ," says Bonhoeffer, "without recognizing and affirming that the break *[Bruch]* is already complete."[53] But why would the God who devised the natural orders of life and deemed them "good" erect this barrier?

Christ has set up this barrier "by virtue of the incarnation," he says. Now Bonhoeffer has clarified for us the point that incarnation amounts to an affirmation of natural life, not its negation, so we should not take the barrier to imply contempt for natural life. What the barrier must signify is an ontological change in the *relationship* to natural life. Bonhoeffer elaborates:

> In becoming human, he put himself between me and the given circumstances of the world. I cannot go back. He is in the middle. He has deprived those whom he has called of immediate connection to those given realities. He wants to be the medium; everything should happen only through him. He stands not only between me and other people and things. *He is the mediator,* not only between God and human persons, but also between person and person, and between person and reality.[54]

Christ wants to be the Mediator *(Der Mittler)*. Or rather, he desires to be recognized and accepted as such, for Christ has already come between us and the world as a *fait accompli*. The relationship between the Christian and the world is now never an immediate one, but always and only a relationship mediated by the Christ who stands at the center.

Despite his obvious suspicions about natural theology, whose negative ramifications he had seen in the ideology of the National Socialists, Bonhoeffer cannot be accused here of abolishing the Christian's relationship to the natural world. His future course in the *Ethik* reveals just the

---

52. "Whoever comes to me and does not hate father and mother, wife and children, brothers and sisters, yes, and even life itself, cannot be my disciple."
53. *DBWE* 4:93.
54. Ibid.

opposite, for there Bonhoeffer's Christology became the transition point to a profoundly world-affirming ethic. Instead he is attempting to ground the self-world relationship christologically, so that the natural may be had on Christ's terms. Only where the breach with natural life is recognized and accepted in Christ can one cross the bridge back to genuine responsibility for it. What Christ divides off he then unites anew.

The disciple who bears responsibility for the world on Christ's terms, the same world that crucified Christ, must be prepared to suffer the consequences of the breach both openly and in secret. Externally it may take the form of a break from family and nation wherein one is called "to bear visibly the reproach of Christ, the *odium generis humani.*"[55] In this case, the physical death of martyrdom is a distinct possibility. Or the breach may be in secret, unknown to others, in which case one must always be ready to come into the open. The internality or externality of the breach depends on the will of Christ: "According to the will of Jesus, we are called one way or the other out of immediate relationships, and we must become single individuals, whether secretly or openly."[56] Here the dialectic between the secret and open break functions as the natural corollary of the veil of Christ's hiddenness in space and time that is at the same time a revelation. One's fidelity to Christ may lie shrouded in the ambiguity of historical events for a time, even a lifetime, and yet it has the *telos* of revelation.

Isolation vis-à-vis Christ is the severe mechanism by which Christ creates a new fellowship. "Everyone enters discipleship alone, but no one remains alone in discipleship."[57] Thus is the disciple compensated for her loss. Now every relationship passes through the Mediator *(Der Mittler)*. And yet, as Bonhoeffer stipulates,

---

55. Ibid., 96. "Hatred against humanity"—note here how closely Bonhoeffer's words approximate the guidelines for determining martyr status established by Pope Benedict XIV, viz., that those responsible for the martyr's execution operate *in odium fidei* ("in hatred of the faith"). For his faith, the martyr, like Christ, might be said to bear the hatred of humanity. As the editor's note in the new German edition of *Nachfolge* shows, Bonhoeffer's chosen phrase constitutes a type of wordplay. In the early Christian period Romans leveled the charge that the Christian religion hated the human race. The fate of Jesus and the martyrs shows it was the other way round. See *DBWE* (Gütersloh: Kaiser Verlag, 1994), 4:92.

56. Ibid., 98. Abraham is adduced as an example of one in whom the secret breach becomes open. He alone hears the call of God to offer his son Isaac, which he does not disclose to others. His willingness to sacrifice his son shows that he is ready to come into the open. When he returns from Mount Moriah with his son all is as before, and yet radically different. He has his son in a new way, for he now possesses him through the Mediator. The immediacy of the natural relationship has been broken, and Christ has stepped into the middle.

57. Ibid., 99.

". . . with persecutions": that is the grace of the community which follows its Lord under the cross. The promise for those who follow Christ is that they will become members of the community of the cross, they will be people of the mediator, people under the cross.

. . . As if to confirm the seriousness of his call to discipleship, and at the same time the impossibility of discipleship based on human strength, and to confirm the promise of belonging to him in times of persecution, Jesus then goes ahead to Jerusalem to the cross, and those following him are overcome with amazement and fear at the way he has called them.[58]

The disciple who has been severed from her natural relationship to the world is provided new access to it, but an access conditioned by the cross of Christ. Just as the resurrection and ascension of the crucified Christ did not lift his incognito but rather branded it upon all history, the incognito of suffering and weakness is made a defining property of the new life that is had through him.

In my earlier argument for Bonhoeffer as martyr I relied rightly and heavily on the *imitatio Christi* motif as a means of including Bonhoeffer in the church's martyr tradition. Now it is becoming clear that Bonhoeffer's own construal has more to do with incorporation than imitation. Laid against the backdrop of Bonhoeffer's ontological vision, *imitatio Christi* is actually a way of describing the taxonomical meld between Christ and his followers. In other words, "imitation" derives less from an act than from that ontological structure into which Christ's followers are baptized. With this lever the whole momentum of Christian ethics is shifted away from individual choices. Ethical choices will then be regarded, conceptually at least, as progressive manifestations of Christ's ontology in the realm of the human.

Bonhoeffer contends that the rite of baptism actualizes Christ's call into the structure of his own life. As a public and publicizing act, baptism displays the cancellation of all immediacy in respect to natural life. It does not accomplish the break, which again is a *fait accompli*, but it is a sign that the break has been actualized. Bonhoeffer writes:

> Baptism thus implies a *break*. Christ invades the realm of Satan, and lays hold of those who belong to him, thereby creating his church-community *[Gemeinde]*. Past and present are thus torn asunder. The old has passed away, everything has become new. The break does not come about by our breaking our chains out of an unquenchable thirst to see our life and all things ordered in a new and free way. Long ago, Christ himself has already brought about that break. In baptism this break now takes effect in my own life. I am deprived of my immediate relationship to the given realities

58. Ibid., 99.

of the world, since Christ the mediator and Lord has stepped in between me and the world. Those who are baptized no longer belong to the world, no longer serve the world, and are no longer subject to it. They belong to Christ alone, and relate to the world only through Christ.

The break with the world is absolute. It requires and causes our *death*. In baptism we die together with our old world. This death must be understood in the strictest sense as an event that is suffered. It is not as if we were asked to bring about this death ourselves through various kinds of sacrifice and renunciation. That would be an impossible attempt. Such a death would never be the death of the old self which Christ demands. The old self cannot kill itself. It cannot will its own death. We die in Christ alone; we die through Christ and with Christ. Christ is our death.[59]

Bonhoeffer inserted two small but significant footnotes on this page of text, each indicating that he had a martyr's death in mind as he wrote these words.[60] Though he consistently refused to make martyrdom a necessary feature of the ontological structure into which one is baptized, his references to it here show nevertheless that martyrdom should be considered its consummate manifestation.

Whether leading to martyrdom or not, baptism is a visible act of obedience by which one's faith is moved into the public sphere. This is in keeping with the experience of the original disciples, for whom "following Jesus was a public act."[61] In the rite of baptism, the secret breach is made known insofar as it brings one into the visible body of Christ.[62] Even as the one being baptized stands passively receiving Christ's death, she confesses to those around thereby her proximity to Christ. Specifically, she confesses that she is prepared to accept his death as her own, or that Christ has graciously included her in his death.

---

59. Ibid., 207–8.

60. The first note falls after the sentence closing with the words "and produces the death of the old man." It reads: "Even Jesus himself referred to his death as a baptism, and promised that his disciples would share this baptism of death (Mark 10:39; Luke 12: 50)." The second note falls after the last sentence quoted, and reads, "Schlatter also takes 1 Cor. 15:29 as a reference to the baptism of martyrdom."

61. Ibid., 210.

62. Any discussion of Christ's body that desires to remain faithful to the Reformation heritage must include the other sacrament of the Lord's Supper, and also preaching as essential *notae*. Bonhoeffer includes these as a matter of routine treatment. Yet it is worthwhile to note that only baptism is accorded an entire section of *Nachfolge*. Ostensibly he gives baptism a special place here because of its power to dramatize the believer's induction into the hidden christo-ontological center. The center space in which Christ resides is what it is only by virtue of his death, and can be accessed only through the kind of concrete participation in that death which baptism achieves. Indeed the rite of baptism carries such unique implications for the moral life that I have devoted special attention to it in this final phase of this study.

The manner of her dying may be unknowable in the performance of the rite—the specific path of discipleship unfolds only as one follows Christ—but the message of the rite is clear: her life is now a descending curve into the life of the Crucified One. For this reason, even as the baptized are brought to greater visibility before the public, they carry within them all the more their secret and hidden breach until such time as Christ reveals himself in his glory.[63] That is, they carry around his death as the hidden center of their life. Baptism is therefore a rite that accentuates the dialectic between life and death, between hiddenness and revelation. The Christ who penetrates the ontological center of life through the veil of death calls his followers there (and holds them there!) by the same means.

63. *DBWE* 4:251.

10

Finding Christ in the World

Advent is primarily about the coming of God, and only in a secondary way about our asking, seeking, waiting, and longing.

Maria Boulding

On the basis of what was accomplished in the previous chapter, it should now be possible to draw out the necessary connections between Christology and ethics in Bonhoeffer's thought. Implicitly these connections have already been forged, for over the span of his career *Christology* came to be regarded as a virtual synonym for *social ethics*. Our task now is to be more specific and nuanced about them. Perhaps we could say that Bonhoeffer's *Ethics* is his Christology in another key, a description of the modality of Christ's presentation to the world. Vestiges of both Luther and Barth are evident in Bonhoeffer's ethics,[1] but above all we should

---

1. The Barthian influence on Bonhoeffer's ethics comes through in a section titled *Ethik als Gebot*, in which ethics are said to be established on the grace of the electing God. Bethge confirms that at the time of this section's writing (1942–1943), Bonhoeffer was reading *Church Dogmatics* 2/2, the volume in which Barth unfolds his doctrine of election as nothing other than the gospel itself. We saw in the Berlin lectures Bonhoeffer's acceptance of Barth's presupposition that God's revealed Word forms the starting point for theological reflection. The ethical significance of this starting point lies in this: just as Barth's emphasis always falls on *God's* decision and not ours in the realm of election, so it always falls on God's decision and not ours in the realm of ethics. On a Barthian foundation ethics is constrained to occupy itself chiefly with the question "What is the will of God?" It is also worth noting that Bonhoeffer's insistence upon the "concrete" and his suspicions about an "ethics of conscience" line up well with Barth's own commitments, which emerge, among other places, in chapter 2 of Barth's *Ethics*, trans. Geoffrey Bromiley (Edinburgh: T & T Clark, 1981), esp. pp. 173–208.

Luther's influence is detectable in Bonhoeffer's treatment of the "divine mandates" (what Luther called "orders of creation").

see in it a bold new attempt to rework traditional ethical concepts. In this work, Bonhoeffer's christological articulation of reality *(Wirklichkeit)* applies the brake to traditional ethical systems and propels him in a provocative new direction.

The Christological Contour of Christian Ethics

Bonhoeffer strains to set out his vision in this key paragraph:

> Whoever wishes to take up the problem of a Christian ethic must be confronted at once with a demand which is quite without parallel. He must from the outset discard as irrelevant the two questions which alone impel him to concern himself with the problem of ethics, "How can I be good?" and "How can I do good?," and instead of these he must ask the utterly and totally different question "What is the will of God?" This requirement is so immensely far-reaching because it presupposes a decision with regard to the ultimate reality; it presupposes a decision of faith. If the ethical problem presents itself essentially in the form of enquiries about one's own being good and doing good, this means it has already been decided that it is the self and the world which is the ultimate reality. The aim of all ethical reflection is, then, that I myself shall be good and that the world shall become good through my action. But the problem of ethics at once assumes a new aspect if it becomes apparent that these realities, myself and the world, themselves lie embedded in a quite different ultimate reality, namely, the reality of God, the Creator, Reconciler and Redeemer. What is of ultimate importance is now no longer that I should become good, or that the condition of the world should be made better by my action, but that *the reality of God should show itself everywhere to be the ultimate reality.*[2]

In Christian ethics the matter of "ultimate importance," then, has nothing to do with the application of ethical principles aimed at individual or social good. Instead, it has everything to do with the manifestation of the reality of God as he has revealed himself in Jesus Christ. To resurrect my earlier vocabulary, *application* would signal the attempt to assimilate Christ into the structure of the world, whereas *manifestation* signals acceptance of the world on Christ's terms. In Bonhoeffer's ethics, the traditional tension between "Ought" and "Is" *(Sollen und Sein)* trans-

---

2. *Ethics*, 55 (emphasis mine). This paragraph is now considered to be the proper structural starting point for the *Ethik*. Previous compilations of this fragmented work had arranged "Christus, die Wirklichkeit und das Gute" (the section which it opens) in part 2. But in the newly reordered scholarly edition this paragraph rightly serves as the conceptual foundation.

mutes to the tension between reality *(Wirklichkeit)* and the realization of the real *(Wirklichwerden)*.[3] It may also manifest itself temporally as the tension between past revelation and the present moment, or, more abstrusely, between Christ and the Holy Spirit. Purveyors of Christian ethics are not required to jettison "the Good" as a theme, but they can retain it only insofar as they refer it to the *real*. That is, they must not permit "the Good" to function in abstraction from reality but must at all times remain anchored in the whole of created and redeemed life located in Jesus Christ.[4] To avoid abstraction—but also to stay true to *Christus praesens* in space and time—this matter of "ultimate importance" should be addressed *today*.

As Bonhoeffer sees it, the person who aspires to a Christian ethic must resist every bifurcation and ground herself in the comprehensive vision of reality we have been considering. Since Christ circumscribes reality, in him "we are offered the possibility of partaking in the reality of God and in the reality of the world, but not in the one without the other."[5] In Christ the reality of God realizes itself within the reality of the world. Thus every encounter with the world is an encounter with a reality that has already been "sustained, accepted and reconciled in the reality of God." For Bonhoeffer, the incarnation, death, and resurrection of Christ mean that God has penetrated the reality of the world, robbed it of its own existence, and enfolded it within his, not *de jure* but *de facto*. One can sum up the emerging task or "problem" of Christian ethics in a single question: how should life be conducted in a reality so configured?

Guided by this question, Bonhoeffer navigated polemically through what he felt to be the dangerous two-spheres *(zwei Räumen)* approach dominating his native Lutheran context. As he did so, he was careful to point out that the Two Kingdoms doctrine as it was understood in the churches of his day had moved away from Luther's intent. Indeed the term "Two Kingdoms" may itself suggest a Nazi misconstrual of Luther's intentions.[6] Luther had used the term "two-fold governance," by it proposing not an ontological theory but a practical guide for Christians, urging them to fulfill their secular responsibilities. God's authority

---

3. Ibid., 57 *(Ethik*, 34).

4. *Ethics*, 59. Cf. God's concrete value judgment that the creation as a whole was good (Gen. 1.31).

5. Ibid., 61.

6. Ulrich Duchrow, *Two Kingdoms: The Use and Misuse of a Lutheran Theological Concept* (Geneva: Lutheran World Federation, 1977), 9. A scholarly treatment of Luther's holistic intention and the historical digression from it can be found in an untranslated work by the same author, *Christenheit und Weltverantwortung: Traditionsgeschichte und systematische Struktur der Zweireichelehre* (Stuttgart: Ernst Klett, 1970).

was to be exercised in the temporal realm no less than the spiritual, for through it God wished to keep order, administer justice, and repress evil. Since the devil was active in both realms, it was necessary for the Christian also to be a good citizen and thereby check the tide of evil. For Luther, all of this was tied directly to the gospel. For he tethered the theory of God's twofold governance to his dialectical understanding of law and gospel as two words of God that function complementarily to achieve his ends. Though excessive chaos in the temporal sphere presents a problem to the church, generally the prevalence of sin in the temporal realm magnifies the true treasure of the gospel. The world's suffering under the curse is the alien work *(opus alienum)* by means of which God accomplishes his proper work *(opus proprium)*. The devil schemes to destroy both spheres while God asserts his sovereignty over both spheres. In this way Luther, unlike his twentieth-century followers, was able to maintain a complementary relationship between the secular and spiritual spheres.

Bonhoeffer is polemicizing against putative followers of Luther who have kept his terminology more or less intact but perverted his intent. In so doing, Bonhoeffer styles himself the true Lutheran, for as he points out, Luther's doctrine was itself a polemic against those who wished to detach from their worldly responsibilities.[7] By no means did Luther mean to imply that reality could be parceled into two entities that exist each in their own right, and then in turn employed as justification for noninvolvement in the world. The "spell" of this way of thinking must be broken, because it stands directly opposed to the thought of the Bible and the Reformation.

> Thus the theme of two spheres, which has repeatedly become the dominant factor in the history of the Church, is foreign to the New Testament. The New Testament is concerned solely with the manner in which the reality of Christ assumes reality in the present world, which it has already encompassed, seized and possessed. There are not two spheres, standing side by side, competing with each other and attacking each other's frontiers. If that were so, the frontier dispute would always be the decisive problem of history. But the whole reality of the world is already drawn into the Christ and bound together in Him, and the movement of history consists solely in divergence and convergence in relation to this center.[8]

The primary importance of Bonhoeffer's discussion concerning the two spheres devolves not on his appropriation of Luther but on the critical turn of argument it signifies. It may be too strong to say that ethics is

7. *Ethics*, 66.
8. Ibid., 64.

the motivation behind his christo-ontology, but clearly by the years 1940 to 1943, when Bonhoeffer was writing the *Ethics,* he had moved the ethical implications of his Christology into the foreground to provide an articulate rationale for involvement in the world precisely as a matter of Christian responsibility. Life in a Christ-configured reality is life immersed in the world.

We see then that the breach Christ effects and continues to effect between his followers and the world plunges them into it ever more deeply. In fact, any spirituality that withdraws from the world is tantamount to a denial of Christ. "One is denying the revelation of God in Jesus Christ," Bonhoeffer writes, "if one tries to be a 'Christian' without seeing and recognizing the world in Christ."[9] It is therefore imperative to be utterly clear about the breach Christ effects. By no stretch of the imagination is the follower of Christ cut loose from the world; instead, when Christ steps in as the Mediator *(Der Mittler)* he reroutes the natural, immediate bonds to the world through the center of his own person so as to give them more density and strength. To suppose that Christian ethics aims either at a personal righteousness that detaches from the world or at the world directly is the gravest of errors. In both cases, the solidarity between Christ and world is ignored. Christian ethics derives its impetus from the Christ at the center, and the criterion for ethical decision-making reduces to convergence or divergence from the will of God as revealed there.

"Ethics as formation" *(Ethik als Gestaltung),* the phrase hovering over Bonhoeffer's ethics, thus is a fitting description of his project so long as it is understood in the biblical sense of formation into Christ's likeness, as Bonhoeffer prescribed. "Christ remains the giver of forms," and therefore the formation of the world takes place not by human stratagems and programs but "by being drawn into the form of Jesus Christ."[10] "Ethics as formation" suggests that the world's formation shall take place in and through those whom Christ takes into his own form.[11] Followers of Christ do not possess a social strategy. Rather, they are possessed by Christ and thus made into agents of social transformation. Not in the usual sense, however. As ethical agents, they do not represent God and

9. Ibid.
10. Ibid., 18.
11. In this discussion I maneuver around a direct ecclesiological explication of Bonhoeffer's ethics. Some may consider this maneuver flawed, or even fatal, but I am of the opinion that whereas in Bonhoeffer's early work Christology was put in service of ecclesiology, from 1933 onward the opposite is true. The ecclesiological horizon never disappeared for him, that is true, but the christo-ontological one was, so to speak, established as the more comprehensive of the two. If Christ stands at the center, the church represents that piece of the world—that small band of followers—in which Christ is realizing his form.

his authority so much as they represent the world. Followers of Christ constitute fragments of space and time, segments of reality in which the de facto centrality of Christ is revealed. For Bonhoeffer, ethical action is therefore inseparable from the ontological becoming of the human. To be human is to be assimilated into the structure of Christ; to be assimilated into the structure of Christ is to participate in the conformation of the world with Christ. The lines of Bonhoeffer's anthropology, ethics, and Christology converge at a single point.

In an ethics of conformation, persons appear to be ethical objects before they are ethical subjects. Granted, it is not immediately obvious how such an ethic gives rise to action, let alone action that is free and responsible. But Bonhoeffer introduced this difficult concept only after considering the deficiencies of ethical theories that did not in his generation lead to responsible action. Narrating the recent past, he says the "ethical fanatics" supposed that the power and purity of their will could oppose evil successfully, yet like bulls they lost sight of the immensity of evil and rushed at the red cloth instead of the man who held it. Alas, they grew tired and got mired in unessential details. Some walked the "way of conscience," supposing that they could maintain some personal innocence. Yet evil comes to such a person "in countless respectable and seductive guises so that his conscience becomes timid and unsure of itself," and eventually "he is satisfied if instead of a clear conscience he has a salved one, and lies to his own conscience to avoid despair." Others supposed that Immanuel Kant's way, the "way of duty," held the best prospect. Yet "within the limits of duty there can never come the bold stroke of the deed which is done in one's own free responsibility, the only kind of deed which can strike at the heart of evil and overcome it." Persons of duty paid their obligations to the devil. Still others followed the ways of "reason" and "absolute freedom," but they shared a similar fate. Finally, there were those who fled the public realm into the safety of "private virtue." These retained their goodness, but at a price, for they played by the rules that evil itself dictated. They had to turn deaf, blind, and dumb to the sundry wrongs that surrounded them, and thus either were destroyed or became the most hypocritical of Pharisees.[12]

Such were the options in the ethical arsenal of Bonhoeffer's generation. In no way does Bonhoeffer scorn them; together they represent some of noblest achievements of humanity. Yet these approaches proved themselves benign in the face of horrendous evil. They were crafted in a time when "the established orders of life were still so stable as to leave

---

12. See *Ethics*, 3–8, for Bonhoeffer's full treatment of these standard ethical approaches. In this paragraph quotation marks denote Bonhoeffer's own classifications for the sake of clarity.

room for no more than minor sins of human weakness, sins which generally remained hidden, and when the criminal was removed as abnormal from the horrified or pitying gaze of society." Today, however,

> there are once more villains and saints, and they are not hidden from public view. Instead of the uniform greyness of the rainy day we now have the black storm-cloud and the brilliant lightning flash. The outlines stand out with exaggerated sharpness. Reality lays itself bare. Shakespeare's characters walk in our midst. But the villain and the saint have little or nothing to do with systematic ethical studies. They emerge from primeval depths and by their appearance they tear open the infernal or the divine abyss from which they come and enable us to see for a moment into mysteries of which we had never dreamed.[13]

Who is the wise man in such a time as this? Who will replace his "rusty sword" with a weapon appropriate to the task? The wise person is the one who sees reality as it is, reality rooted in God. This is simplicity and wisdom. The one who cultivates this vision liberates himself from the conundrums of ethical decision-making:

> Not fettered by principles, but bound by love for God, he has been set free from the problems and conflicts of ethical decision. They no longer oppress him. He belongs simply and solely to God and to the will of God. It is precisely because he looks only to God [the immediate relationship], without any sidelong glance at the world [the mediated relationship], that he is able to look at the reality of the world freely and without prejudice.[14]

The act that is free, and therefore the act that is responsible, and therefore the act that is ethical in the highest degree, originates in a realm beyond the ethical.[15] Yet not beyond the historical, for that would be an act that aims wide of concreteness. The free and responsible act springs from the reality of the concrete miracle of God and world reconciled in Christ.

While reducing all criteria for ethical decision-making to the one criterion of whether my action is in accord with reality simplifies ethics in one sense, in another sense it makes it more complex. If we grant that the problem of ethics is to participate in making known the chris-

---

13. Ibid., 3.

14. Ibid., 7 (bracketed explanations mine).

15. This idea was present in Bonhoeffer's thought at least as early as *Creation and Fall* (lectures given at Berlin in the winter semester 1932–1933), where, speaking of Adam's paradisal state, he says, "Adam knows neither what good nor what evil is and lives in the strictest sense *beyond good and evil;* that is, Adam lives out of the life that comes from God"(*DBWE* 3:87–88).

tological configuration of reality, and that such participation begins by an encounter with the Christ who is present, we still must deal with the confounding ambiguity of Christ himself. Behavior in accord with reality is behavior in accord with Christ, but what form does Christ wish to take in the world today, at *this* place and at *this* time? That is by no means a simple question, for in the course of Christ's earthly experience three distinct forms are visible, concretized for us in the pivotal moments of incarnation, crucifixion, and resurrection.[16] Even though these are three forms of the one Christ, nuanced differences between them translate into discrete modes of ethical action.

As Bonhoeffer understands it, incarnation means that God wills neither the destruction of humanity nor its deification. By it the Creator simply loves the creature and sanctions its creaturehood. The space and the freedom to be a genuine human being—that is what the incarnation gives. It wrests from humans every compulsion to become something other than what they are, and offers instead the possibility of contentment with what is. God in Christ is content to take humanity unto himself, to love it despite the wreckage of sin, and therefore followers of Christ will demonstrate an openness to the human condition *as it is*, not descending upon it with an air of superiority but receiving it as the object of God's love. An act that conforms to the Incarnate Christ is an act that loves the creation in general but also the human being in particular, for Christ became a real and particular human being.

Conformation with the Crucified Christ means that one stands as a human being under God's death sentence. Sin makes it necessary for the creature to die before God. And so "with his life he testifies that nothing can stand before God save only under God's sentence and grace." Daily and "humbly he bears the scars on his body and soul, the marks of the wounds which sin inflicts upon him."[17] Conformation with Christ the Crucified requires readiness to absorb the suffering of others into one's own being—for Christ suffered "the reality of the world in all its hardness"—and a commensurate acceptance of the world's fury so that when at last it exhausts itself, forgiveness might be offered and reconciliation accomplished.[18] It requires, too, the acceptance of guilt. God did not shun guilt but proved himself "willing to be guilty of our guilt." Suffering, rejection, wrath, and guilt are a school in Christian death. Their acceptance "serves to enable him to die with his own will and to accept God's judgement upon him." Bonhoeffer culls a saying from K. F.

---

16. *Ethics*, 20.
17. Ibid., 19.
18. Ibid., 9.

Hartmann to summarize his point here: "It is in suffering that the Master imprints upon our minds and hearts his own all-valid image."[19]

Last, to be conformed with Christ the Risen One is to be a new creature *amidst* the old, to have life amidst death and righteousness amidst sin. The new creature lives a life barely distinguishable from that of others and is quite unconcerned about distinguishing himself from them, for like Christ he wills to be found in solidarity with humanity,[20] sharing in God's sentence of judgment. The resurrected Christ is truly the glory of the new creature's life, but inasmuch as his presence remains hidden in space and time the creature's new life will also "remain hidden with Christ in God" (Col. 3:3). Again we note here Bonhoeffer's tenacity in channeling the benefits that accrue to humanity from Christ's resurrection back into the flow of earthly life. The movement from crucifixion to resurrection gives the appearance of Christ's withdrawal, or even a christological removal of God by human force.[21] Yet the removal is the very means by which Christ draws near again to the creation to be present within it.

None of these pivotal moments—incarnation, death, and resurrection—may be absolutized and isolated from the others.[22] That would violate the complementarity of the christological structure and throw the initiative for world-transformation back upon the ethical agent. An ethics derived in this way would be only a subtler lapse into just the kind of programmatic approach Bonhoeffer is trying to avoid. The ethical agent must understand that conformation is not the radical installation of Christ's form. Since Christ has already assumed form in this world,

19. Ibid., 19.

20. Bonhoeffer's prose at this point bears too strong a resemblance to the early and anonymous Christian document known as the *Epistle to Diognetus* (in *Ancient Christian Writers*, trans. James A. Kleist, vol. 6, ed. Johannes Quasten and Joseph C. Plumpe [New York: Paulist, 1948], 138–39) to be left to chance. In *Discipleship* (250–51) Bonhoeffer seems virtually to be paraphrasing lines of this letter, though he does not make his source explicit. Of particular interest is the way this early document portrays the subtleties of the Christian way of life, a life that is at once "extraordinary" and yet profoundly integrated into cultural norms and conventions. There Christians are described as indistinguishable in their language, dress, food, and custom, taking part in everything as citizens. And yet "they reside in their respective countries . . . as aliens." As a secret leaven they "hold the world together" and are its life in the same manner that the soul is the life of the body. If Bonhoeffer is in fact drawing from this source, we may take it as a clarification of his point that the new life of the resurrected Christ embeds itself deeply in the flow of history, and also as further indication of his bent toward a pre-Constantinian form of Christianity.

21. Cf. the provocative statement coming from the 16 July 1944 letter to Bethge (*ATTF*, 508): "God lets the divine self be pushed out of the world onto the cross. God is weak and powerless in the world, and that is precisely the way, the only way, in which God is with us and helps us."

22. *Ethics*, 89.

an ethics that seeks to raze the status quo amounts to a rejection of the conformation that has already occurred. On the other hand, there can be no easy acquiescence to the status quo, because Christ's form has not been fully realized. Responsible life before God must consider the delicate dialectics of resistance against and submission to the status quo under the perpetual question "Who is Christ for us today?" The answer to that question must be worked out carefully in conversation with Christ and with a critical eye on the present historical context. A Bonhoefferian ethics is neither passive nor simple. Nevertheless, a spacious freedom undergirds every ethical act upon the realization that Christ is in that act realizing his own form within the world.

In the preceding paragraphs I have given considerable attention to the structure of Bonhoeffer's ethics, and yet it is at best a sketch. A comprehensive treatment of Bonhoeffer's ethics is not, obviously, the goal of this chapter, and so I must resist the temptation to follow many of the important streams that fork off at this point. Our goal in traversing the *Ethics* is to follow through on the general ethical ramifications of his christo-ontological orientation so that we might then consider the thesis that his death by martyrdom encapsulates his theological work. At this point we have completed a survey of the general ethical ramifications as Bonhoeffer saw them.

While Bonhoeffer clearly did not want his ethics of conformation to become a theoretical system, by its very nature it seems to give little practical guidance for moral decision-making. The object of ethical action is perfectly clear: the world should be conformed to Christ. It is equally clear that ethical action is to be concrete and historical. But what are the ethical structures that regulate conformation? Can they be described at all? Is conformation left entirely to the caprice of God's will at every given moment? These questions are answerable only if we begin to bend the christo-ontological orientation back to the historical axis.

Penultimate and Ultimate: A Christological Revisitation of the Life-Death Dialectic

Over his brief career Bonhoeffer was an increasingly historical thinker: his *Discipleship* arose in part from the conviction that a pre-Constantinian form of Christianity was the antidote for the disease of National Socialism, his treatment of the Jewish question was tied to his analysis of Greco-Roman antiquity and its role in the decay of Western civilization, and in working through his Christology he refused, despite current trends, to retreat from the historical Jesus. It has become clear to me, notwithstanding their theological differences, that Bonhoeffer held true to the historical discipline he had learned from his teacher and Grunewald neighbor Adolf von Harnack.

Nowhere is that more obvious than in his discussion of the penultimate and ultimate. In *Ethics,* Bonhoeffer's distinction between ultimate and penultimate must be understood in the broader context of his attention to the historical. Within the categories of systematics, his attention to the historical can be enfolded into his growing commitment to the created order. Either way, Bonhoeffer recognized that we make ethical decisions under the oft-times ambiguous conditions of temporality, and he sought a theological structure that would prove capable to illumine such ambiguities and proffer guidance for those decisions. The ultimate-penultimate distinction is an eschatological one dealing with "last things" and "things before the last." Naturally, Bonhoeffer must give ontological priority to the ultimate, else he would have misnamed it, and so what is last is indeed of greater significance than what precedes it. The penultimate exists for the sake of the ultimate, not the other way round. And yet the ultimate needs the penultimate if it is to be made intelligible.

Now, while the two terms do not represent a static configuration of historical reality (ontological priority belongs to the ultimate) they nevertheless depict it dialectically. By means of his christological orientation, Bonhoeffer thus forces an eschatological distinction to function in the interests of temporality, or—again in the language of systematics—he maneuvers redemption in the interests of creation. Or, in terms of our life-death dialectic, he parlays God's final word—"Live!"—into the command "Die!"

Bonhoeffer introduced the penultimate-ultimate distinction by means of the article of justification:

The origin and the essence of all Christian life are comprised in the one process or event which the Reformation called justification of the sinner by grace alone. The nature of Christian life is disclosed not by what the man is in himself but by what he is in this event. The whole length and breadth of human life is here compressed into a single instant, a single point. The totality of life is encompassed in this event. What event is this? It is something final, something which cannot be grasped by the being or the action or the suffering of any man. The dark pit of human life, inwardly and outwardly barred, sinking ever more hopelessly and inescapably in the abyss, is torn open by main force, and the word of God breaks in. In the rescuing light man for the first time recognizes God and his neighbor. The labyrinth of life he has so far led falls in ruin. Man is free for God and his brothers. He becomes aware that there is a God who loves him;

that a brother is standing at his side . . . and that there is a future with the triune God.[23]

There are three things worth noting in this passage. First, in lifting up justification as the last word of God, Bonhoeffer wished to situate the penultimate-ultimate distinction within the larger dialectic of law and gospel. God makes the final determination of life in the word of justification, but since this gospel means life only when spoken in the context of his word of judgment which means death, justification, though ultimate, proves dependent on the penultimate. Second, justification brings an ethical awakening wherein the other, neighbor and brother, comes into sharp focus. Third, the qualitative significance of justification impinges upon time. In it the "length" of human life is compressed, and a "future" unfolds. Bonhoeffer returned to this point just a few paragraphs later:

> The justifying word of God is also a final word in the sense of time. It is always preceded by something penultimate, some action, suffering, movement, volition, defeat, uprising, entreaty or hope, that is to say, in a quite genuine sense *by a span of time, at the end of which it stands.*[24]

A Christian ethics based upon God's final word of justification turns its attention to time and thus manifests its concern for the ultimate in devotion to the penultimate. This is only fitting, because historical time has itself been taken into the penultimate-ultimate structure of law and gospel. Historical time is God's preparation for the ultimate, and therefore it is a subordinate reality someday to be annulled. But insofar as it is God's preparation it is intrinsic to the gospel itself. Bonhoeffer continues:

> Luther had to pass through the monastery, and Paul through his bigoted zeal for the law; even the thief had to go through guilt to the cross; for only thus could they hear the last word. A way had to be trodden; the whole length of the way of the things before the last had to be traversed; each one had to sink to his knees under the burden of these things, and yet the last word was then not the crowning but the complete breaking off of the penultimate. In the presence of the last word the situation of Luther and Paul was in no way different from that of the thief on the cross. A way must be traversed, even though, in fact, there is no way that leads to this goal; this way must be pursued to the end, that is to say, to the point where God sets an end to it.[25]

23. Ibid., 79.
24. Ibid., 83 (emphasis mine)
25. Ibid.

Despite the penultimate's derived value, Bonhoeffer portrays it as the way to the ultimate, and for that reason it cannot be dispensed with.

So long as God permits history to continue, what the penultimate needs is *preservation*. Preservation of the penultimate is a preparation for the ultimate. "Preparation," says Bonhoeffer, "is the purpose of everything that has been said about the things before the last."[26] Preparation is precisely what the great Advent text calls for, and Bonhoeffer makes prolific use of it: "Prepare the way of the Lord, make his paths straight. Every valley shall be filled, and every mountain and hill shall be made low, and the crooked shall be made straight, and the rough ways made smooth; and all flesh shall see the salvation of God" (Luke 3:4–6). Such preparation is not merely an inward process but "a formative activity on the very greatest visible scale" in which all that has been abased and subjected to human sin is now to be raised up. On the one hand, "there is a depth of human bondage, of human poverty, of human ignorance, which impedes the merciful coming of Christ," and on the other there is "a measure of power, of wealth, of knowledge, which is an impediment to Christ and to His mercy."[27]

Not wishing to revert to law, Bonhoeffer is careful to stress that one can neither hinder nor compel Christ's coming in any final sense. Christ makes a way for his own coming. Even so, there are conditions that impede the reception of that grace, conditions that make faith extremely difficult, and therefore "this does not release us from our obligation to prepare the way for the coming of grace, and to remove whatever obstructs it and makes it difficult."[28] To the contrary, preparation for Christ is a great ethical responsibility *(Verantwortung):* "The hungry man needs bread and the homeless man needs a roof; the dispossessed need justice and the lonely need fellowship; the undisciplined need order and the slave needs freedom."[29]

Followers of Christ do not take up these concerns as a matter of "earthly reform," though visible reform may result, and they certainly do not take them up as a prerequisite for Christ's final coming. Instead they take them up as acts of humiliation, for in humiliation these physical matters are simultaneously spiritual ones. In Bonhoeffer's words, "The visible actions which must be performed in order to prepare men for the *reception* of Jesus Christ must be acts of humili-

26. Ibid., 93.
27. Ibid.
28. Ibid., 94.
29. Ibid., 95.

ation before the coming of the Lord, that is to say, they must be acts
of *repentance.*"[30]

Repentance, for its part, implies guilt. Humble solidarity with others
in need, sharing in the acceptance of guilt—in Bonhoeffer's judgment
these are the things that fortify the penultimate and thereby protect
the ultimate. Congruent with incarnation, this is action that loves
the creation. Congruent with crucifixion, this is suffering action in
which guilt and its consequences are borne, if need be, unto death.
Congruent with resurrection, this is action performed at the dawn of
that new life within the old. It is action that, in a single movement,
humbles the haughty and raises the low, that is to say, it is action that
removes the impeding obstacles of human pride and power on the
one hand and human degradation on the other. It is action that carves
out a bit of space and time to make, as it were, an indentation in the
old order of being, which Christ fills with his own being. Through
the categories of penultimate and ultimate Bonhoeffer found a way
to anchor his ethics of conformation in temporality.

Immersed in the penultimate realities of suffering and death, he also
found there a meaning for his own life:

> In these turbulent times we repeatedly lose sight of what really makes
> life worth living. We think that, because this or that person is living, it
> makes sense for us to live too. But the truth is that if this earth was good
> enough for the man Jesus Christ, if such a man as Jesus lived, then, and
> only then, has life a meaning for us. If Jesus had not lived, then our life
> would be meaningless.[31]

More important than Paul and Luther, Jesus had to trudge through these
penultimate realities. At their darkest, these realities came to him as
the "cup of death." He asked that it might pass. His prayer was heard
and answered, albeit unexpectedly. For the cup would pass, "but only
by his drinking it." For "in order to overcome the suffering of the world
Jesus must drink it to the dregs."[32] It was God's will that Jesus serve the
ultimate by tending to penultimate things.

The ethical thrust toward the penultimate can be seen in a portion
of "After Ten Years," an essay written in the thick of the conspiracy in
which Bonhoeffer speaks for himself and the fellow resistors:

30. Ibid., 96 (emphases mine). A concrete turning, or action, is what Bonhoeffer (and
the New Testament) means by μετάνοια. Like the liberation theologians, Bonhoeffer here
interprets John the Baptist's call to repentance as a call to visible change.

31. 21 August 1944 letter to Bethge (*ATTF,* 513).

32. *DBWE* 4:90.

There remains an experience of incomparable value. We have for once learnt to see the great events of world history from below, from the perspective of the outcast, the suspects, the maltreated, the powerless, the oppressed, the reviled—in short, from the perspective of those who suffer. . . . We have to learn that personal suffering is a more effective key, a more rewarding principle for exploring the world in thought and action, than personal good fortune. This perspective from below must not become the partisan possession of those who are eternally dissatisfied; rather, we must do justice to life in all its dimensions from a higher satisfaction, whose foundation is beyond any talk of "from below" and "from above." This is the way in which we must affirm it.[33]

In Bonhoeffer's case, the view from below is taken up as a matter of concrete responsibility for penultimate things. As with Jesus, shouldering that responsibility requires me, at the same time that I say yes to my life and the lives of others, to say no to my own life.[34] Only when this yes-and-no is assimilated into my life will my action be a response to reality as given in Jesus Christ.

A Profile of Bonhoeffer's Earnestness Concerning Death

With these last insights regarding temporality behind us, we are now poised to channel the various tributaries of this chapter into a main argument. I want to return here to the brief but crucial period just prior to the Christology lectures to examine more carefully Bonhoeffer's personal-theological disposition, for it was in that period, I believe, that he internalized the prospect of a martyr's death.

Two lengthy quotations dated to 1932 are well worth our attention. They are fragments that Bethge included in his biography ostensibly as evidence pointing to Bonhoeffer's inner motivations for becoming a theologian. Written in the third person, they represent Bonhoeffer's distant recollections of childhood. I reproduce them here in the fullest form, just as they exist in Bethge's work. In the year of their composition, according to Bethge, Bonhoeffer was occupied with concerns about his "origins," both theological and personal. Although cryptic, these texts open an autobiographical window to Bonhoeffer's personal struggles

---

33. From Bonhoeffer's essay "After Ten Years," in *Dietrich Bonhoeffer: Witness to Jesus Christ*, ed. John de Gruchy (Minneapolis: Fortress, 1991), 268.

34. "We 'live' when, in our encounter with men and with God, the 'yes' and the 'no' are combined in a unity of contradiction, in self-less assertion, in self-assertion in the sacrifice of ourselves to God and men." And again, "Wherever the divine 'yes' and 'no' become one in man, there there is responsible living." See *Ethics*, 192–94.

concerning death, pride, humility, and the questionable earnestness of his leap into the scorned profession he had chosen. Given the fact of his martyrdom, I think we may read them teleologically, that is, not merely as reflections upon his past but as projections of his life:

> He liked thinking about death. Even in his boyhood he had liked imagining himself on his death-bed, surrounded by all those who loved him, speaking his last words to them. Secretly he had often thought about what he would say at that moment. To him death was neither grievous nor alien. He would have liked to die young, to die a fine devout death. He would have liked them all to see and understand that to a believer in God dying was not hard, but was a glorious thing. In the evening, when he went to bed over-tired, he sometimes thought that it was going to happen. A slight sense of dizziness often alarmed him so much that he furiously bit his tongue, to make sure he was alive and felt pain. Then in his innocence he cried out to God, asking to be granted a deferment. These experiences dismayed him to some extent. For obviously he did not want to die, he was a coward; his theatrical ideas disgusted him. And yet in moments of strength he often prayed that God might after all release him, for he was ready to die, it was only his own animal nature that again and again made him contemptible in his own eyes, that led him astray from himself.
>
> Then one day he had a grotesque idea. He believed himself to be suffering from the only incurable illness that existed, namely a crazy and irremediable fear of death. The thought that he would really have to die one day had such a grip on him that he faced the unalterable prospect with speechless fear. And there was no one who could free him from this illness, because in reality it was no illness, but the most natural and obvious thing in the world, because it was the most inevitable. He saw himself going from one person to another, pleading and appealing for help. Doctors shook their heads and could do nothing for him. *His illness was that he saw reality for what it was*, it was incurable. He could tolerate the thought for only a few moments. *From that day on he buried inside himself something about which for a long time he did not speak or think again.* His favourite subject for discussion and for his imagination to dwell on had suddenly acquired a bitter taste. He spoke no more about a fine, devout death, and forgot about it.[35]

Except he did not forget about it. It is no accident that here in 1932, shortly after the "momentous change" that occurred in him, he is recalling his earlier suppressions of death and bringing them out for review. Along the personal path of costly discipleship he now treads, he can no longer suppress death. Death is what Christ demands of his disciples, and therefore it is incumbent upon them to assimilate it consciously

---

35. *DB*, 38–39 (emphases mine).

into their life of faith. Bonhoeffer had buried within himself something that "for a long time he did not speak or think [about] again," but in the piece just quoted he *is* thinking and speaking about it again.

And his thinking and speaking does not limit itself to autobiographical fragments like this one. In fact, his theological work from this time on becomes his venue of choice for thinking and speaking about death. It is not necessary for our purposes to divine the source of Bonhoeffer's childhood preoccupation with death, which may or may not link up directly with theological issues. Nor can we say for sure that this auto-biographical review relates to his "conversion" in any direct way. There are many issues of a psychological nature here that I choose to ignore as a matter of both personal competence and expediency.[36] What I must not ignore, however, is that Bonhoeffer had in an earlier period buried something that by 1932 is being exhumed: his personal confrontation with that unnerving reality for which there is no cure.

We can now place this review of death against the backdrop of his newly begun career as a theologian. It was a career he undertook, apparently, on questionable motives:

> One day in the first form, when the master asked him what he wanted to study, he quietly answered theology, and flushed. The word slipped out so quickly that he did not even stand up. Having the teacher's gaze and that of the whole class directed at him personally and not at his work, and being suddenly called upon to speak out like this, gave him such conflicting feelings of vanity and humility that the shock led to an infringement of ordinary class behaviour, an appropriate expression of the consternation caused by the question and the answer. The master obviously thought so too, for he rested his gaze upon him only for a moment longer than usual and then quickly and amiably released him. He was nearly as disconcerted

---

36. Kenneth E. Morris, *Bonhoeffer's Ethic of Discipleship: A Study in Social Psychology, Political Thought, and Religion* (University Park: Pennsylvania State University Press, 1986), has dealt at length with these two texts from a psychological perspective to suggest a profile of Bonhoeffer as a man whose ideas on discipleship emerged from the complex matrix of his family, in which, Morris argues, Dietrich's alignment with his mother Paula's religious sensibilities over and against the hard-nosed realism of his father and brothers created a conflict that he internalized. It worked itself out in Bonhoeffer's simultaneous resistance against and submission to authoritarian figures. Closest to home this tension character-ized the relationship to his father, but it can also be seen, says Morris, in his dealings with Barth and Harnack. The theological "path of discipleship" (beginning according to Morris in 1932) was an attempt to work out this inner conflict.

I believe there is a great deal of truth in Morris's intriguing thesis. His work is master-fully done. And I admire him as an interpreter who has in sustained fashion taken up a standpoint within the narrative, even attempting to make sense of the death motif in Bonhoeffer in his psychological interpretation. And yet I think there is a way of reading the Bonhoeffer narrative from within on a *theological* basis.

as his pupil. "In that case you have more surprises to come," he said, speaking just as quietly.

Actually the question "how long?" had been on his lips, but, as if that would have touched on the secret of his own early and passionately begun and then quickly dropped study of theology—and also because he felt displeased with himself at having nothing better to say to a boy whom he had known and liked for a long time—he grew embarrassed, cleared his throat, and went back to the Greek text which was the subject of the lesson.

The boy absorbed that brief moment deep into himself. Something extraordinary had happened, and he enjoyed it and felt ashamed at the same time, Now they all knew, he had told them. *Now he was faced with the riddle of his life.* Solemnly he stood there in the presence of his God, in the presence of his class. He was the centre of attention. Did he look as he had wanted to look, serious and determined? He was filled with an unusual sense of well-being at the thought, though he immediately drove it away, realizing the grandeur of his confession and his task. Nor did it escape him at that moment that he had caused the master a certain embarrassment, though at the time he had looked at him with pleasure and approval. The moment swelled into pleasure, the class-room expanded into the infinite. There he stood in the midst of the world as the herald and teacher of his knowledge and his ideals, they all had now to listen to him in silence, and the blessing of the Eternal rested on his words and on his head. And again he felt ashamed. For he knew about his pitiful vanity. How often he had tried to master it. But it always crept back again, and it spoilt the pleasure of this moment. Oh, how well he knew himself at the age of seventeen. He knew all about himself and his weaknesses. And he also knew that he knew himself well. And through the corner of that piece of self-knowledge his deep vanity again forced an entry into the way of his soul and alarmed him.

It had made an impression on him when he had read in Schiller that man needed only to rid himself of a few small weaknesses to be like the gods. Since then he had been on the watch. He would emerge from this struggle like a hero, he said to himself. He had just made a solemn vow to do so. The path that he had known he must follow since the age of fourteen was clearly marked out for him. But supposing he failed? Supposing the struggle proved vain? Supposing he was not strong enough to see it through?

The words "You have more surprises coming" suddenly rang in his ears; surprises about what, what could happen, what did this voice mean? What was the meaning of the curious, mistrustful, bored, disappointed, mocking eyes of his class-mates? Didn't they think him capable of it, did they not believe in the sincerity of his intentions, did they know something about him that he did not know himself?

Why are you all looking at me like that? Why are you embarrassed, sir, what sort of incomprehensible drivel are you mumbling? Look away from me, for heaven's sake, denounce me as a mendacious, conceited person who does not believe what he says, but don't keep so considerately silent, as if you understood me. Laugh aloud at me, make noise, noise, don't be so abominably dumb—it's intolerable. There is the throng, he stands in the midst of it and speaks, speaks, fervently, passionately, his features . . . his dark blonde hair, his ideal hopes—he corrects himself—a leaden silence lies over the throng, a dreadful, silent mockery. No, it cannot be, he is not the man they take him to be, he really is in earnest. They have no right to scorn me, they are unjust to me, unjust . . . all of you . . . He prays. . . . *God, say yourself whether I am in earnest about you.* Destroy me now if I am lying, or punish them all; they are my enemies, and yours, they do not believe me, I know myself that I am not good. But I know it myself—and you, God, know it too. I do not need the others. . . . I, I . . . I shall triumph. . . . Do you see how I triumph, how they retreat, their consternation. . . . I am with you, I am strong. . . . God, I am with you.

Do you hear me? Or do you not? To whom am I speaking? To myself, to you, or to those others here? Who is that speaking? My faith? My vanity. . . . *God, I want to study theology. Yes, I have said so, and they all heard it. There is no more retreat.* I wish to, I wish to . . . but if . . .

And just as the commotion turns to something new, all he hears is the teacher's voice from a distance—no one else could have spoken in the meantime—"Aren't you feeling well? You don't look well." He pulls himself together, stands up, and as usual translates the difficult Greek text without error.[37]

This soliloquy may well be a fictionalized version of Dietrich's family's reaction when he announced his ecclesiastical intentions to them. The form master's reaction of embarrassment tinged with pleasure well fits with his father's hesitancy. Karl Bonhoeffer later indicated that when he first heard of Dietrich's intention he thought "a quiet, uneventful, minister's life . . . would really almost be a pity" for his son, and his older brothers in particular did not take him seriously, making sport of his choice.[38]

Whether Bonhoeffer is now fictionalizing this event is aside from the main point. Somewhere there gathers an audience, detractors perhaps, who sit in judgment of his authenticity. Just as in the first quotation he was the center of attention on his deathbed with all looking on, here once again he is on stage "in a class-room expanded into the infinite." He is "in the midst of the world as herald and teacher," and his detractors must now "listen to him in silence." At this moment of pleasure, he is pierced by his pride and grows more somber. Perhaps the skeptics are right about him after all, for it appears the origin of his career is besmirched by a weedlike vanity that he cannot choke off. And yet, as

37. Ibid., 40–41 (emphases mine).
38. Ibid., 37.

if the boyish announcement had bound him in an oath, he longs to become earnest about his choice.

It is no coincidence that at the same time Bonhoeffer is exhuming his fear of death he is also revisiting the matter of his earnestness as a theologian. It is impossible to know the specific stimulus for these fragments, but in them I believe Bonhoeffer is now narrating his own past from a decidedly new vantage point. What was buried has now been dug up; the riddle of his theological origins is being resolved.

These interrelated reflections intersect at the center of our discussion on death and martyrdom. When Bonhoeffer met up with the demands of the unassimilable Christ (either "man must die or he must put Jesus to death") of the Sermon on the Mount, he also came to grips with his own death in a way he had never done before, a way that became ethically fruitful for his life. In Heideggerian terms, we might say that whereas before he experienced "anxiety" over the certainty of his own death and "could tolerate the thought for only a few moments," that is, could not maintain "resoluteness," in 1932 he is now no longer shrinking back from the reality of death. Authenticity, or what he here calls "earnestness," is the result. In other words, the exhumation of death in the first fragment is directly related to a new sense of earnestness about his profession in the second. Bonhoeffer is proving the truth of Kierkegaard's statement that death is a "teacher of earnestness" on a consciously Christian basis. However, unlike Heidegger's (or even Kierkegaard's) existential approach to death, Bonhoeffer's resoluteness, though existentially every bit as acute as theirs, is a cruciform disposition of faithful submission to Christ.

Aside from this new birth of earnestness, Bonhoeffer's imagined audience is interesting in its own right, for it raises the prospect that his thoughts and deeds are from this time forward a kind of performance before a gallery of spectators. I am aware that the word *performance* conjures either the notion of pharisaical ostentation or an element of disingenuousness to one's actions. Considering Bonhoeffer a "performer" in that sense would be using his admission of vanity against him. It would also run quite askew from the kind of constructive task in which I am engaged. There are other, more fruitful ways of thinking about performance whose explorations I cannot undertake. Let me here simply call attention to the fact that in its formative period martyrdom was an eminently public event. It is no stretch to call the actions of the martyrs in the amphitheaters of Rome a Christian performance. They died literally before a gallery of spectators. That does not mean, of course, that their entire life was lived as a public spectacle—quite to the contrary in fact. But at a critical juncture in their life they were forced out of the quietness of their secret discipline *(arcana disciplina)* into the devouringly eager gaze of the public.

In Nazi Germany the situation was reversed, for in many respects Bonhoeffer was forced out of complicity with public ideals into the secrecy of subterfuge. On the morning of his hanging there were scarcely any witnesses. And yet, ironically, Bonhoeffer has become one of the most discussed, most "witnessed" martyrs of his century. And the gallery continues to grow. Despite the paucity of onlookers at the moment of his expiration, it seems that powers latent within martyrdom itself have secured for him a public profile. This, of course, relates directly to my thesis that the martyr's death accentuates his *life*. Bonhoeffer's life is what this so-called gallery assembles to see, a life whose final phase was indeed lived in the high secrecy of political resistance, quite out of public view, and with little open confession to mark the way. In that way his unadorned death was a fitting end. But through the lens of martyrdom this phase can now be seen as a "performance" of Bonhoeffer's theology in the political sphere. Popular sentiments in favor of Bonhoeffer's martyrdom are a vote from the gallery that this phase of apparent secrecy was in truth a "coming out" of his faith.

When we weigh together the facts of Bonhoeffer's childhood fascination with death, his temporary repression of it, his subsequent personal assimilation of it in the period of his "conversion," and its appropriation in his professional work with the fact of his martyr's death, the conclusion that his life was lived in anticipation of this end seems inescapable. What that means, however, is not altogether clear. Some will construe Bonhoeffer's death as the self-fulfilled prophecy of a man with a "death wish," scripted, that is, from the human side. Others will say God marked him for martyrdom. I think the proper construal of his martyr's death is one that takes a foothold in his own theology and ethics. Accordingly, I submit that his natural curiosity about and preoccupation with death (even to the point of psychological impediment) was *redeemed* by the new understanding of reality *(Wirklichkeit)* that he acquired. When he encountered the living Christ in the early 1930s, he found christological footing for his existential dealings with death, at which point his death ruminations were not overcome but subsumed in a higher end.

What Bonhoeffer discovered, perhaps to his own surprise, was that his incessant fascination with death was actually luring him closer to the reality he would eventually describe christologically, a reality governed by Christ's death. Sensitivity to death was sensitivity to reality; nearness to death was nearness to reality. All he needed to ascertain was the christological texture of that reality. When he did, the enduring spatiotemporal presence of the Crucified Christ and its ramifications became a benevolent cradle in which Bonhoeffer could come to peace concerning his own death. Preaching to his London congregation on

"Death Sunday" (November 1933), he was drawing already from his own experience of transformation:

> Death is hell and night and coldness if our faith does not transform it. That we can transform death is truly miraculous. When our faith in God touches it, the grim reaper who frightens us turns into a friend and messenger of God; then *death turns into Christ himself.* Yes, those are deeply hidden things. But we are permitted to know them.[39]

No doubt, the miracle that "death turns into Christ himself" marks a growth of Bonhoeffer's personal courage vis-à-vis death, a courage he hoped to nourish in his listeners. But coming on the heels of the Berlin lectures this is a theological miracle as well, for when the devastating projectile of death as collapse enters the gravitational field of Christ it "turns into Christ himself." That is to say, the projectile swerves toward Christ, who then absorbs its blow in his own death, ontologically reconstitutes it, and uses it henceforth as a means of bending the world toward his own aims.

Two years later Bonhoeffer's Finkenwalde sermon "Learning to Die" carried the thought forward to its conclusion. Clearly not all who die do so blessedly. A blessed death awaits only those "which die in the Lord"—those who "learned how to die in time" and "clung to Jesus up to the last hour, whether amidst the sufferings of the first martyrs, or in the martyrdom of a silent loneliness." Nearing the end of the sermon, Bonhoeffer rushes the point:

> To die in Christ—that this be granted us, that our last hour not be a weak hour, that we die as confessors of Christ, whether young or old, whether quickly or after long suffering, whether seized and laid hold of by the lord of Babylon or quietly and gently—that is our prayer today, that our last word might only be: Christ.[40]

Death is an encounter with Christ, and thus death and Christ are worked here into virtual synonymity.

But Bonhoeffer did more than make peace with death. Eventually he developed that inner freedom and willingness toward it, and even eagerness, so characteristic of the early martyrs, without breaking the necessary tension of willing-but-not-too-willing. Surrounded by the stark realities of war and constant death, in January 1943 he acknowledged that "fundamentally we feel that we belong to death already," but quickly added, "It would probably not be true to say that we welcome death

---

39. *ATTF,* 221–22. Emphasis added.
40. Sermon prepared for Memorial Day, 24 November 1935 (*ATTF,* 267–68).

... nor do we try to romanticize death ... still less do we suppose that danger is the meaning of life." Rather, "we still love life." And it is from this situation that

> we should like death to come to us, not accidentally and suddenly through some trivial cause, but in the fullness of life and with everything at stake. It is we ourselves, and not outward circumstances, who make death what it can be, a death freely and voluntarily accepted.[41]

Bonhoeffer's Martyrdom as Conformation

I noted early in the study that the prevailing structure of twentieth-century martyrdom serves to broaden our understanding of martyrdom generally. We saw that an especially prominent feature of contemporary martyrs is their calculated solidarity with victims of human injustice. When Bonhoeffer bent his attention toward the penultimate, he epitomized that movement. He believed the earth had a right to his labor, saying on one occasion, "The earth remains our mother, just as God remains our Father, and our mother will only lay in the Father's arms him who remains true to her,"[42] and on another, "This world must not be prematurely written off."[43] No person, he judged, had the right to bypass earth for heaven. Accordingly, he freely assumed responsibility for the course of history,[44] as a matter of class and family values, yes, for these surely played their part, but also keenly as a matter of Christian conviction, for the departure point of *Christus praesens* can find its ethical efficacy only on the plane of human history. He became, then, a concrete guardian of both the neighboring Jew and that vast cultural complex he had inherited. He understood quite clearly that in his tumultuous time guardianship would involve guilt-bearing and physical death. But these were precisely the means by which Christ furthered his conformation of the world. Jesus freely assumed the collective guilt of his race and freely bore it unto death.

---

41. "After Ten Years," in *LPP*, 16.

42. Bonhoeffer, *No Rusty Swords: Letters, Lectures, and Notes 1928–1936 from the Collected Works*, ed. Edwin H. Robertson, original trans. Edwin H. Robertson and John Bowden, rev. John Bowden with Eberhard Bethge (London: Fount, 1970), 43.

43. *ATTF*, 508.

44. "We ... must take our share of responsibility for the moulding of history in every situation and at every moment, whether we are the victors or the vanquished. One who will not allow any occurrence whatever to deprive him of his responsibility for the course of history—because he knows that it has been laid upon him by God—will thereafter achieve a more fruitful relation to the events of history than that of barren criticism and equally barren opportunism" (*LPP*, 7).

Against this horizon, Bonhoeffer could project himself convincingly as a martyrological instrument of conformation, freely assuming responsibility for others and every stain of guilt that may accompany the responsible act. It is in this sense that we are to understand his prediction that the blood of modern martyrs will not be so innocent as those in earlier times. He may not have known it at the time, but in conjunction with his own martyrdom that statement marked a quantum leap forward in the evolution of the Christian concept of martyrdom. Martyrdom fits within the structure of responsible life before God, for it is a way of loving the earth, the extreme form of care extended to others. By it a fissure is opened in the earth-crust of fallen life which the ontological core of Christ then expands to fill. Paradoxically, the martyr's own achievements—freedom toward death, love of neighbor, fulfillment of her humanity—are consumed as a sacrifice in the molten fire of Christ's advance. The achievement is only participation in Christ's conformation of the world, the achievement of offering by one's final submission to God of a little time and space wherein what is ordinarily hidden from view can be seen at the surface: that Jesus Christ is Lord of all.

11

Journey to Finkenwalde

The monk is one who is separated from all, yet is united to all.

Evagrius Ponticos

My purpose in this chapter is to unfold a set of ideas that make it possible to interpret Bonhoeffer's experience at Finkenwalde in a way consistent with martyrdom. Though my interpretation lies embedded in the text, I do not give a focused treatment of Finkenwalde until the next chapter. My immediate focus is upon the conceptual tools my interpretation requires.

Bonhoeffer's effort to mold a Christian community at the preacher's seminary in Finkenwalde was his most fulfilling work as a church leader. We cannot overlook it. Yet what role could Finkenwalde play in Bonhoeffer's journey to martyrdom? The answer is somewhat complex. To help, I call upon the assistance of Ronald Green and his book *Religion and Moral Reason*. Green's model contains the power to illumine the inherently moral aspects of a religious community and provides a theoretical basis for plausible explanations of what Bonhoeffer's "experiment" might have accomplished both for him and for other members of the community. Before introducing Green's work, however, I try to script Bonhoeffer's experience in community by discussing the broader issue of ethics and rationality and why it has a bearing on our theme.

Ethics and Rationality

It is reasonably certain that Bonhoeffer's belief (his theology in general and his Christology in particular) and his death by martyrdom—a

death that I have been calling an *ethical* act performed in freedom—
hang together. This fact, however, piques curiosity for other things.
The chief stimulus for this theological-ethical study, as opposed, say,
to one confined more strictly to theology, lies in my sustained interest
in the taxonomy of the theological-ethical relation itself. It is one thing
to recognize or ascribe continuity of belief and behavior; it is quite
another to understand it from the inside. If, from the perspective of his
martyrdom, we conclude that Bonhoeffer's theology looks like a theology
of death that he lived out concretely, then we have only stumbled to the
threshold of the more serious question of *how*, or *by what means*, his
theology engendered the particular set of behaviors that precipitated
a martyr's end. Or, even more critically, dare we attribute that much
formative power to his theology at all?

We should remember that Bonhoeffer was not the only Holocaust
theologian who understood Christ's call to assume responsibility for those
under persecution. Pierre-Marie Theas, a French bishop, for example,
could appeal to a theology of creation to establish responsibility for all
people as brothers, as could theologians in the Confessional Synod of
the Old Prussian Union. Still others could read Galatians 3:28—a text
that "proved to be extraordinarily productive in motivating Christians
to resist Nazi racism and support Jews"—as an assertion that ethnic
and national distinctions are abolished by Christ and easily draw out
the ethical implications.[1] From a Christian point of view, there was no
shortage of rational apparatus to guide ethical decisions, and yet the
overwhelming majority of those with Christian upbringing and moral
instruction became "bystanders."[2] Looking back, Bonhoeffer was a
rarity among theologians of his day, even Christians of his day, the
vast majority of whom, though adherents of the same religion founded
upon the Christ of the cross, either shrank back from any concrete
action whatsoever or found other "ethical" paths, some of them most
admirable, through the tyrannical mayhem.

For example, Eberhard Arnold, founder of the Bruderhof, recognized
as early as Bonhoeffer the disastrous moral consequences of National
Socialism. But Arnold's response was to "look away from the dangers,
focus on the mystery of *Gemeinde*, and draw strength from the spiritual
powers that help the believers to withstand persecution and face the
enemy." On the surface, Arnold's Bruderhof does not appear substantively

---

1. David P. Gushee, *The Righteous Gentiles of the Holocaust: A Theological Interpretation*
(Minneapolis: Fortress, 1994), 132–36.

2. In Holocaust literature this term has acquired a somewhat technical meaning, denot-
ing in particular a distasteful neutrality that is flanked on the one side by "perpetrators"
and the other by "rescuers." According to Gushee, fewer than 1 percent of Gentiles actually
assisted Jews (ibid., 67).

different from Bonhoeffer's Finkenwalde. But put in the larger context of the church struggle *(Kirchenkampf)* and the avowed sociopolitical impetus of Bonhoeffer's thought, the aim for Finkenwalde went beyond helping believers to withstand persecution. As Bonhoeffer had put it in a 1931 letter to Helmut Rössler, it was the church's invisibility in the West that was so damaging to its mission.

Much more attention needs to be paid to the similarities and differences between Arnold's and Bonhoeffer's vision for Christian community. Hardy Arnold (Eberhard's son), who twice had lengthy conversations with Bonhoeffer in 1934, had invited Bonhoeffer to visit the Rhoen Bruderhof to see how a community based on the Sermon on the Mount might work itself out in practice. Of these conversations Hardy remarked, "Bonhoeffer impressed me enough to make me phone my father, and he too considered the encounter important. . . . My father warmly supported my invitation to Bonhoeffer." Bonhoeffer was never able to visit, but his interest in the Bruderhof ostensibly led him to purchase from the Liechtenstein Bruderhof a fifteen-volume series *Source Books of Christian Witnesses throughout the Centuries.* To the present, various Bruderhof communities in Europe, Canada, and the United States have remained cautiously interested in Bonhoeffer. The caution stems from the Bruderhof's strict rejection of all violent means regardless of external factors. Hans Meier provided the dominant interpretation when he concluded, "It seems that the increasingly obvious criminality of Hitler's government and the diminishing resistance against this criminality by the Confessing Church drove Bonhoeffer into a kind of human despair. In this despair he was ripe for the temptation to manipulate history via the device of assassination."[3]

Unable to endure the tension between the period of Bonhoeffer's Finkewalde community and the final period of his life, Meier severs Bonhoeffer's political activities from Bonhoeffer's experience of community. For Meier and the Bruderhof, perhaps one could go so far as to say that Bonhoeffer succumbed to temptation precisely because he *lost* his community. To the contrary, I would like to interpret Bonhoeffer's political action and martyrdom as an ethical engagement made possible by community.

---

3. For an understanding of Arnold's strategy, see Markus Baum, *Against the Wind: Eberhard Arnold and the Bruderhof,* trans. Bruderhof Communities (Farmington, Penn.: Plough, 1998), 215. For Bonhoeffer's letter to Rössler, see *GS* 1:61. For Hardy Arnold's interaction with Bonhoeffer, see "Conversations with Dietrich Bonhoeffer," *The Plough,* no. 6 (September 1984): 4–6. For Hans Meier's critique, see "Bonhoeffer's Later Beliefs," *The Plough,* no. 6 (September 1984): 7–8.

I have shown already how from Bonhoeffer's Christology there evolved a world-affirming ethic based upon the cross. Pivotal to this movement was the notion of a breach *(Bruch),* actualized in baptism, by which Christ tears the disciple away from her natural association with the world. *Discipleship,* of course, is the work in which Bonhoeffer developed this idea of a breach with the world especially clearly, and it is the crowning literary achievement of the Finkenwalde period. But it is also the work in which Bonhoeffer made the breach the disciple's passage to a new, mediated relationship to the world, the full expression of which is found in the *Ethics.* Bonhoeffer made every conceivable track of connection with the world run through Christ, like a roundhouse for switching locomotives. Bonhoeffer's breach is notably two-sided: it is both a departure from the world and arrival to it, death to the world and life for its sake.

It is no coincidence that Bonhoeffer would develop this idea in the Finkenwalde period. For it was a time when for the sake of a surer engagement with the world, "retreat" from it was necessary, a time when for the sake of a better social ethic, the sociality of the Christian community required special emphasis. That is, the form of life cultivated at Finkenwalde plays, by design, a mediating, indeed catalytic role on the road of Christian discipleship. Having experienced a breach with the reigning powers in the larger social, political, and even religious world, this tiny community located in the riches of Christian fellowship a means by which to engage that same world differently. Finkenwalde made a passage between theology and ethics.

Congruity between theology and ethics has long been a spiritual concern. Centuries ago Gregory the Great, speaking from his own reluctance to assume the office of bishop of Rome, warned of the need:

> There are some who investigate spiritual precepts with shrewd diligence, but in the life they live trample on what they have penetrated by their understanding. They hasten to teach what they have learned, not by practice, but by study, and belie in their conduct what they teach by words.[4]

"Practice what you preach" goes the adage, and for good reasons. In the eyes of the renowned Gregory, failure to do so would bring scandal upon the gospel and jeopardize the souls of the faithful.

Though the gospel may be imperiled, and that is a serious matter, there are yet other related reasons to care about the congruity of life

---

4. From Gregory the Great, *Pastoral Care,* trans. Henry Davis, in *Ancient Christian Writers,* vol. 11, ed. Johannes Quasten and Joseph C. Plumpe (New York and Ramsey, N.J.: Newman, 1978), 23–24.

and faith, among them the integrity of the self that is seen by others, which opens upon the domain of social reputation. Most people seem to want a good reputation, and the prospect of a poor one constrains certain behaviors to which they might otherwise be given. But there is yet another reason to care about the congruity of faith and practice. Is it not a reflection on one's belief system itself? And does it not therefore link up with our most basic visions of reality and rational order? In the extreme case, to belie in conduct what is taught in word is tantamount to disowning one's beliefs. Granted, people regularly say things later called into question by their actions. Not every deviation is a disowning. Most times, in fact, we manage to shrug off such inconsistencies and classify them as behavioral lapses. Who is perfect, after all? On occasion we all fail to live by our beliefs. But when a person's behavior is consistently inconsistent with their beliefs, we may revert to a more negative conclusion: such people do not really believe what they say. It might be suggested, then, that whether people really believe what they say they believe can often be gauged by the congruity or incongruity of their life. In the final analysis, behavior may in fact be a more reliable indicator of belief than what people say they believe.

This means, interestingly, that one of the criteria we typically use to judge moral character—is a person faithful or unfaithful to his or her word?—might in some cases be insufficient. A life that consistently deviates from the beliefs said to undergird it may not really be founded on those beliefs at all. In common parlance we may call such a person inconsistent, deceitful, or even a liar, but possibly she is manifesting precisely the opposite: either consistency with a set of beliefs not disclosed to the broader social community or, perhaps, the consistent outcome of an incoherent set of beliefs. A habitual liar, for example, may lie and stay true to his own construal of reality. While behavior is exceedingly complex and therefore cannot be said to arise directly from belief, neither does it arise ex nihilo.

Of course behavior reveals more than its undergirding belief structure. Something significant is revealed no doubt about the *self*. Consider the intense personal crisis that comes when one articulates and assents to a set of beliefs yet cannot follow through on the moral implications. Say one subscribes to the Judeo-Christian belief stipulating that sex outside of marriage is sin, and nevertheless engages in such behavior. That person may respond in a number of ways, among them diversion, outright denial, and an alteration of beliefs regarding sexual behavior. But if one is honest, will it not be the self, more than belief, that is called into question? Sometimes the anxiety produced by the asymmetry of belief and behavior can be agonizing even to the point of neurosis. If ethics does indeed have a rational basis, then beneath this crisis of self there may yet be a crisis of belief, but explaining it merely as such is much too simplistic. "Believing" is a function of the self. Only by a process of abstraction can beliefs be considered in isolation from the person or persons who hold them. At the same time, however, we must note that beliefs are not usually assembled at random. They are systematized or brought into constellations for the sake of rational coherence and guidance in practical matters pertaining to everyday life. The sheer universality of belief systems—basic orientations to reality—across human cultures witnesses to the innate human requirement that life be rationally ordered. Thus even while it is surely the self that is called into question in our example, it is a self socially, culturally, and religiously constituted, that is, a self situated in a larger system of beliefs. Ultimately, therefore, every crisis of behavior must impinge upon the question of belief.

Perhaps all of this is but a roundabout way of stating a maxim so basic that we could not imagine reality to be otherwise. Belief and behavior bear an intrinsic relation to one another. Beliefs have ethical consequences; ethical decisions have structural mooring. Just *how* they are related is no doubt an extremely complex issue, but to deny the relation is virtually to drain ethics of all rationality. Outside of this relation one might still talk about choices, but they would be simply choices, nothing more and nothing less, neither "ethical" nor "unethical."

Ethical choices by nature are supported on the larger scaffold of reason. There is considerable debate whether religion is essential to this rational scaffold. At the practical level, after all, nearly all human behavior can be explained sociologically, though it is doubtful whether questions of ultimate significance—questions pertaining to the *meaning* of human behavior in the greater scheme of the cosmos—can be answered satisfactorily by sociological description. Whatever might be said about the necessity of religion to the rational scaffold of ethics, this much seems clear: religion is at least one powerful and elaborate (probably the most powerful and most elaborate) rational support structure for ethics. Without *some* rational basis, religious or otherwise, it is difficult to see how there could be any discourse about morality at all. Belief systems and patterns of behavior are necessarily related.

But again, what is the taxonomy of this relation? As Ronald Grimes has observed, "There is a well-worn track being cut from narrative [belief] to ethics [behavior]," so much so that "ethics seems to be the Rome to which all roads lead."[5] Recent decades have witnessed a virtual explosion of narrative theologies, on the assumption that narrative or

5. Ronald Grimes, "Of Words the Speaker, of Deeds the Doer," *Journal of Religion* 66, no. 1 (January 1986): 6.

belief somehow constitutes the human being. I myself argued in this
vein earlier when, using Heidegger and Rahner, I attempted to construe
Bonhoeffer's life as a continuous whole. But the time has come to ask
whether there might be other ways of construing the self that acts.
Grimes wonders whether the road from narrative to ethics might in
fact pass through ritual. What is missing from the narrative-to-ethics
way of doing theology is a "subjunctive" mode, he says. Ritual offers
the human being a "liminal zone" wherein, cut off from the nonritual
world, he may engage in a "fuller exploration of unconscious motives"
than image-to-action models usually allow. Rituals provide opportunities for "trial runs," and thus they illumine more clearly our proneness
to self-deception concerning the degree to which we have embodied
our ethics.[6]

Grimes is targeting figures like James William McLendon Jr. and
Stanley Hauerwas, who, he judges, have overdetermined ethics from
the narrative side. An ethicist like Hauerwas, for example, stresses the
narrative of Scripture as the story that frames Christian life, and then
draws the connection between the church's faithful remembrance of
its shaping stories and ethical outcomes. Here "ethics, as an academic
discipline, is simply the task of assembling reminders that enable us to
speak and to live the language of the gospel."[7] In an ostensibly natural
manner, moral behavior springs from a way of seeing reality—"we must
get our vision right before we can get our actions right."[8] One certainly
would not call Hauerwas's approach antirational, but it does seem prera-
tional at least. Learning ethical behavior is said to be much like language
learning, wherein the grammar, or rules, are memorized only after one
learns to speak. Being immersed in a Christian community—a tradition
of seeing whose primary story is the gospel—is ethically formative.

And yet, as everyone knows, coming into regular contact with the
Christian story or myth does not lead inexorably to moral action. Nor
does it automatically produce moral character. This is why Grimes's
question ought to be taken seriously. Might ritual, especially liturgical
ritual, effect changes in our behavior? If so, might we then be obliged
to devote more attention to ritual as a segue to ethics? Grimes has
called liturgy "the rituals in whose work we rest," by which he means
to suggest that while liturgy is "work," it is a work performed so that
we might be "acted upon." That is, liturgy is work that aims symbolically to cultivate "deep receptivity": we tap into the way things flow or

---

6. Ibid., 8.
7. Stanley Hauerwas and William H. Willimon, *Resident Aliens* (Nashville: Abingdon, 1989), 89.
8. Ibid., 102.

connect with the order of reason such that a result is produced in us.[9] In this mode, rituals do not communicate narrative content so much as they transform our lives. They *accomplish* something. Of course, as a survey of any community will show, mere repetition of behaviors is no better a guarantee for moral action than storytelling. In the final analysis, ethics cannot be reduced either to pure cognitive content or pure prereflective behavior, but must be entered upon by moving both concepts into a larger, paradigmatic endeavor.

Of particular interest for our project is the twin relevance of myth and ritual for social ethics. Perhaps as a hangover from the nineteenth-century opinion, ethicists have frequently paid more attention to the relationship between myth and behavior than to that between ritual and behavior—somewhat ironically, because ritual, though not "ethical" in the formal sense, is clearly a kind of human behavior. That is why the work of Ronald Green proves interesting and valuable here. His efforts represent an intentional weaving together of narrative, ritual, and ethical elements. Theology, ritual, and ethics do not always go together, but they appear so often together that their deep interconnection is virtually certain. Perhaps all this would have little relevance for Bonhoeffer were it not for the fact that he poured his energies into a community whose very existence was founded on his christological rendering of reality, whose internal life was ritualized to a fairly high degree, and whose aims he propounded in ethical terms.

So far I have stressed Bonhoeffer's theology as an integral part of his martyrdom, even to the point of having martyrdom as its *telos*. There are many reasons for supposing that his theology forms the rational scaffold of his behavior. As important as Bonhoeffer's theology is, I am aware also that theology alone may be ill-suited to explain fully his personal path. Concrete caregiving to the earth and its history, assumption of responsibility toward the penultimate, and personal sacrifice to the conforming action of Christ are all appropriate ethical descriptions of Bonhoeffer's belief system, and they would remain so even if in the crucible of moral conflict Bonhoeffer had shown cowardice and lapsed from his own beliefs. It is noteworthy that on numerous occasions Bonhoeffer doubted his moral courage and feared he might turn traitor to his beliefs as many others had done. In our frailty, we can imagine with Bonhoeffer a situation in which our most rationally founded ethical theories—even if they are ones of deathward self-sacrifice grounded in reality itself!—could be temporarily suspended in the instinctual urge for self-preservation. Of course, such suspension may be either a bridge to apostasy or a call to repentance and renewed commitment, the first

9. Ronald Grimes, "Modes of Ritual Necessity," *Worship* 53 (March 1979): 134–35.

marking a reneging on belief and the second ratifying it, albeit in a less than perfect way.[10] Suspending need not mean severing. But the point comes to this: while one's behavior can be retrospectively inferred from one's belief structure, judged to be rooted in it and nurtured and preserved by it, it cannot with certainty be predicted from within the temporal flow of events. And so we ask, how and by what means did Bonhoeffer (and by implication those like him) maintain fidelity to his beliefs at a time when others did not? Obviously moral decision-making is a phenomenon no less complex than human beings themselves, so I do not here expect to parse it with finality.

The "Moral Point of View"

In *Religion and Moral Reason,* Ronald Green argues persuasively that there exists a universal structure, a "deep structure" of moral decision-making. This structure expresses itself differently in the world's religions, sometimes in strikingly variant ways, but the observable differences are not believed to be fundamental. They remain at all times variations on the one moral theme. Green's universal thrust is critical to his project, which he sees as an appropriation of Kant's "categorical imperative": Act only on that maxim whereby you can at the same time will that it should become a universal law. Green is not specific about it, but Kant, it will be remembered, added a qualifier to the categorical imperative. It is not the mere willing that my action be universally adopted that guides decision-making, but a *willing without contradiction,* such that I could reasonably and consistently project my action universally without in some way involving myself in a contradiction.[11] If that is forgotten, Kant's categorical imperative can be easily construed in more utilitarian terms, where ethical decisions are taken in view of the greatest possible degree of happiness that may result from the available options (though in fairness, one should add that a utilitarian like John Stuart Mill was quite careful not to let ethics degenerate to the issue of *personal* happi-

10. One thinks, for example, of the Stuttgart Declaration (October 1945), by which the German church expressed its guilt and moral lapse—"we accuse ourselves that we didn't witness more courageously, pray more faithfully, believe more joyously, [and] love more ardently"—and simultaneously rededicated itself to a "new beginning." Franklin Hamlin Littell, *The German Phoenix: Men and Movements in the Church in Germany* (Garden City, N.Y.: Doubleday, 1960), 189–90.

11. Kant rules out the wish, for example, that one might will the universality of a law that says "Break promises when it is expedient to do so," for it contradicts the very notion of a promise. See Frederick Copleston, *A History of Philosophy,* vol. 6, *Wolff to Kant* (Garden City, N.Y.: Image, 1985), 324–26.

ness), a construal that Green takes to be a corruption of Kant's original intent.[12] Kant's intent was not to offer a mere rule of "generalization" or "universalization" so much as to develop what might be called "the moral point of view."[13] Green describes the moral point of view as one of "radical impartiality" or "omnipartiality." These terms suggest that while there is room in moral reason for personal interests, first and foremost is "the requirement that we assess our conduct not just from the egocentric perspective of our own situation but also from the standpoint of others we might affect."[14] To say it in Kantian terms, as we project our action universally, we must not will *selfishly* that it would become law, but we must be capable of imagining others to will it too. Omnipartiality is the moral point of view in which *everyone's* interests are considered.

This "moral point of view" characterized by omnipartiality is a basic element of reason's "deep structure." It touches upon one of the salient features of the ethical life: in an ordered social existence one's personal happiness must be subordinated to a larger whole. But in so doing it touches also upon the troublesome paradox of the ethical life: "self-denial and self-restraint are conditions of human happiness and self-fulfillment," which means that while the impartial application of reason generally serves my self-interests, say, for the security of a predictable social order, or the prospective security of knowing that at some future point my interests will be taken into account by others and so on, there are yet times when impartiality is seriously disadvantageous to my interests.[15] There may be times when impartiality places my family or myself in grave peril. What then?

This was the situation faced by Bonhoeffer and nearly all those who resisted the racism of the National Socialists. For at the forefront of the Nazi agenda was "the destruction of the entire web of relationships that existed between Jews and Gentiles—as friends, schoolmates, colleagues, neighbors, fellow citizens, and, most fundamentally, as human beings—and [they] used the full power of the state to accomplish this goal."[16] To achieve public compliance, serious threats were made to all who refused to disavow their connections to Jews. For example, *Rassenschände* (the Nazi classification of those who defied the stipulation of the Nuremberg Laws that no person of Aryan descent was to have sexual relations with Jews) and *Judenfreundlichkeit* (friendship to Jews)

---

12. Ronald M. Green, *Religion and Moral Reason* (New York: Oxford University Press, 1988), 5.

13. Ibid., 6.

14. Ibid.

15. Ibid., 4, 18.

16. Gushee, *Righteous Gentiles*, 5.

became criminal offenses punishable by sentence in a concentration camp, and on occasion death.[17] In such a time as this, maintaining an omnipartial point of view became a matter of political and ideological insubordination, with devastating personal consequences.

Under certain conditions, then, sticking to the omnipartial point of view seems excruciatingly difficult. This is why, says Green, "religions devote so much effort to encouraging their adherents to think and act from the moral point of view."[18] At the heart of the matter it is not always obvious why one ought to be moral at all. Green even goes so far as to say that under certain conditions the moral point of view simply is not "rationally compelling." The paradox, then, suggests that many of the conundrums of moral decision-making arise not from a failure to think things through but from a cleavage in reason itself:

> What we have here, in effect, is a conflict between two equally important and equally viable exercises of reason. On the one hand, there is what is termed "prudential" reason: self-serving rationality exercised in the name of personal happiness. On the other hand, there is moral reason, which involves the same self-serving rational choice but now exercised from an impartial point of view. The great similarity between these forms of reason and their common practical goal of human welfare makes it easy to confuse them.[19]

It is possible for people to find themselves in a moral dilemma in which each of two alternatives, personal-familial welfare and common welfare, is rationally grounded. That is to say, one can be immoral and rational at the same time. In "ordinary" ethical conflicts the advice is frequently given that we should try to think more objectively, more impartially, because impartiality is valued as a means of solving conflict. Hence the reliance upon mediators, more neutral parties who have a firmer grasp on the total situation. But as Green points out, in the extreme conflict between prudential and moral reason, this means of acquiring rational order for our decisions breaks down.[20] Opting for either prudential or moral reason will in the extreme case mean sacrificing one form of reason to the other. This dilemma does not imply ethical relativism. For the moral point of view remains as a standard and thus renders difficult any attempt to justify the triumph of prudential reason. But that is beside the point. The real question in such a dilemma is, why

17. Sarah Gordon, *Hitler, Germans, and the "Jewish Question"* (Princeton, N.J.: Princeton University Press, 1984), 212, 265.
18. Green, *Religion and Moral Reason*, 12.
19. Ibid., 13.
20. Ibid., 14.

should one be moral at all when it is going to cause severe personal harm? What reasons can be adduced for the moral point of view when reason itself is divided?

This brings us to the second element of the "deep structure": religion's insistence on the reality of moral retribution.[21] While admitting that religion possesses nonrational aspects, Green nevertheless understands it to be a "rational enterprise . . . reason's effort to resolve its own dispute and to make possible coherent rational choice."[22] As a "rational enterprise," religion cannot ignore the discrepancy between prudence and morality. It must explain it. Typically it does so by insisting that the discrepancy is only apparent, and in turn encourages its adherents to make their choices in view of an ultimate horizon where, it might be said, self-interest merges with the interests of others.

> Although the individual may appear to run terrible risks in choosing to be moral, these risks are not the last word on the matter. Beyond sacrifice lie possibilities of fulfillment directly proportional to moral effort. Moral retribution is certain. The righteous are rewarded. Those who risk their lives shall gain them.[23]

To speak theistically for a moment, one could, I think, reproduce Green's point in the simple phrase "God watches and remembers." Just as no sparrow falls without God's notice, no act done in impartiality will be forgotten. Religion encourages us to consider that moral choices are made in full view of God, even when by every appearance God seems absent. The person who desires to act morally and rationally at the same time needs the encouragement of a God who watches and remembers, and the prospect that *at some point* moral retribution will be meted out.

Perhaps this need lay beneath the popularity of the song recorded some years ago by Bette Midler, which supported the idea of a moral point of view in the refrain "God is watching us from a distance." More germane to our topic, one sees it too in the martyrological literature. Cyprian of Carthage, speaking to those facing moral decisions during the horrors of persecution, pleads for fidelity: "If the battle shall call you out . . . engage bravely, fight with constancy, as knowing that you are fighting under the eyes of a present Lord."[24] Cyprian was only giving expression to the common conviction that even if their cases could

21. Ibid., 12.
22. Ibid., 15.
23. Ibid., 15.
24. Cyprian of Carthage, *Letters* 8 *Ante-Nicene Fathers*, vol. 5, *Fathers of the Third Century: Hippolytus, Cyprian, Caius, Noration, Appendix*, ed. Alexander Roberts and James Donaldson (Peabody, Mass.: Hendrickson, 1994), 289.

not be vindicated before earthly rulers, would-be martyrs should take comfort in a God who would one day vindicate them and serve justice to their persecutors.

Obviously moral retribution implies punishment for the unrighteous too. In certain streams of the Christian religion the prospect of God's wrath and the threat of everlasting torment in hell are used regularly as moral incentives, often functioning simultaneously as incentives for evangelism, which is made into a kind of cornerstone of moral life. This emphasis raises rational problems of another kind, but it needs to be said that moral retribution can be an incentive from either side.

In the early stages of a religion's development, hopes are kindled for a swift, this-worldly retribution. But as dashed hopes of its adherents accumulate, religion must offer an increasingly sophisticated explanation of the suffering of those who choose morally. Gradually the emphasis shifts away from the question of how the righteous are to receive their reward. Instead sin is brought more clearly into focus, and with it the aspiration for transcendence.[25] Green expands: "This means that as religious thought develops, the insistence on retribution, though never relinquished, becomes supplemented by teachings that point the way beyond the world of moral reward and punishment."[26]

The question of a "way beyond" may emerge amid personal suffering brought on by the sin of others, but it may also emerge from a close inspection of one's own moral life. Rigorous application of the moral point of view requires every moral choice to be made from the stand-point of impartiality. And yet in the freedom of moral decision-making people occasionally fail. When the fixity of the moral point of view is combined with the de facto experience of sin, the third element of the "deep structure" emerges: "an awareness of the depth and intractability of human wrongdoing, and the need for suspension of moral self-judg-ment."[27] If the moral point of view is to prevail amid moral failures, that is, if people are to continue to commit themselves to impartiality without succumbing to despair over their own lapses, then religion must set before its adherents a series of "transmoral" beliefs that suspend moral retribution when it is needed, offering possibilities of forgiveness, repentance, grace, and so forth. The God who watches is able to provide a reprieve for those who deviate from the moral point of view.

This time it is Green who speaks theistically: "In theistic traditions, this idea underlies the important themes of divine grace and forgiveness. Although God upholds morality, he is not ultimately constrained by it,

25. Green, *Religion and Moral Reason*, 17.
26. Ibid.
27. Ibid., 19.

and he is able to suspend punishment and redeem sinners."[28] Since God, dwelling in a realm beyond good and evil, is the very precondition for the moral point of view, he may reinforce it by granting forgiveness and redirecting one toward the goal with renewed moral verve.[29]

God's grace may be a solution to the problem of moral failures, but it opens other insuperable problems for religious thought, among them the possibility that one may bank on this realm beyond morality and undertake, in a more or less calculated manner, an immoral action that might later be forgiven. In Bonhoefferian terms, we might call this a version of cheap grace. At one level the prospect of grace and forgiveness appears to work against the moral point of view, yet religions consistently and emphatically reject the antinomian impulse and strive instead to utilize the transmoral realm to facilitate moral resolve.[30]

While Green understands well the antinomian threat, he does not explore in sufficient depth the extent to which one's capacity to anticipate the transmoral affects moral decision-making. Obviously the transmoral may be used to rescue one from despair in the wake of moral failure, but as part of the religion's structure it may also serve to free one from the burden of moral decisions themselves and equip one for action that might otherwise be unthinkable. What if, for instance, from within the moral code of a religion like Christianity, an action was simultaneously a moral violation and yet undertaken from the standpoint of impartiality? And what if in the complexity of that situation one simply could not account for all the possible consequences of an action? What if, in other words, one had to risk the immoral in service of the moral point of view? Or again, what if, as Kierkegaard tried to articulate in his panegyric on Abraham, the God who established the moral order *himself* delivered a command to break it?[31] Would that not demand a "teleological suspension of the ethical" and constitute an immoral venture of faith? In most cases, banking ahead of time on God's forgiveness would be a reversion to "cheap grace," but one can imagine situations where *that fact alone* could free one for bold and necessary action.

When Bonhoeffer made his prediction that the martyrs of his day would be stained with guilt, he was revealing his belief that under Hitler morality had become almost hopelessly inverted. On the one hand he

---

28. Ibid., 20.

29. On several occasions Jesus suspends moral judgment in the face of sin and gives the offender the admonition to go and sin no more (e.g., John 5:14; 8:11).

30. Ibid., 21. Green adduces the classical example of Paul, who, upon expounding the riches of grace, had then to reject the possibility of sinning so that grace could abound (Rom. 6:1).

31. Søren Kierkegaard, *Fear and Trembling*, trans. Walter Lowrie (Princeton, N.J.: Princeton University Press, 1968).

understood his conspiratorial activities, especially the plot on Hitler's life, as a sin that could not be justified on the basis of Christian morality. On the other hand he was sustained in his action precisely by fixing his vision on the transmoral realm.[32] In times when ethical choices move not between the poles of good and evil but between greater and lesser evils, assimilation of the transmoral realm makes certain ambiguous moral actions possible and their consequences bearable. Bonhoeffer looked to the transmoral not to soothe his conscience, that is, not to find justification for his sin—to justify the sin is what one might expect from a seeker of "cheap grace"—but to sustain him in impartiality *irrespective* of an easy conscience.[33] A stanza from his poem "Stations on the Way to Freedom" makes the point most clearly:

> O Wondrous transformation! Your hands, strong and active, are bound.
> Powerless, alone, full clearly knowing your action has ended,
> from your lips there yet comes the cry of relief,
> that, calmly and trustingly, you surrender your struggle to more
>   powerful hands.
> And contented in heart you rest now in peace.
> For in one blessed moment the soul of freedom you touched,
> to entrust it to God that God might fulfill it in glory.[34]

As these lines suggest, one must embrace fully the risks of morally ambiguous action and place all consequences into "more powerful hands." Else there can be no true freedom.

In deference to Green, I should say that the freedom of the transmoral domain is surely not unbridled, antinomian freedom. Rather it is a freedom available only to those who have already morally disciplined themselves and learned to subordinate their self-interests to the demands of omni-partiality.[35] It is a freedom that latches on to the realm beyond good and evil for the sake of others, a freedom that recognizes not only the wrongs

---

32. At various points in the *Ethics* Bonhoeffer resists the distinction between good and evil because it stops short of reality. According to him, Jesus' confrontations with the Pharisees revealed that while men want to know the difference between good and evil, God wants attention to be focused on the more important matter of his will. In Jesus Christ there is an overcoming of the knowledge of good and evil, which is at the same time a migration to freedom (*Ethics*, 151–61).

33. Consider the following line from the *Ethics* (214): "It is precisely in the responsible acceptance of guilt that a conscience which is bound solely to Christ will best prove its innocence."

34. *ATTF,* 516–17.

35. The stanza quoted above bears the heading "Suffering" (Leiden). It is one of four headings (stations) on the way to freedom. The others are, interestingly, "Discipline" (Zucht), "Action" (Tat), and "Death" (Tod).

of others but the wrong that lies within and therefore assumes a share of responsibility for the ambiguity of the present ethical situation.

This stanza from Bonhoeffer's poem—indeed the entire poem—is helpful to our understanding of his martyrdom as ethical act. For his martyrdom, together with all the acts that propelled him toward it, was performed against the horizon of God's judgment. I do not mean God's "wrathful judgment" but simply the judgment by which God, as God, makes the final determination of a life, in the words of the poem, "that God might fulfill it in glory."

Bonhoeffer closes the poem with these words: "Freedom, so long have we sought you in discipline, action and suffering. Dying, we now behold you indeed in the face of our God." Written the day following the failure of the 20 July 1944 plot on Hitler's life, these words perfectly situate Bonhoeffer's moral striving against the looming prospect of imminent death. In them we see a man whose vision has been lifted to the transmoral as the omega point of his moral struggle, a guilt-bearing sinner prepared to die with his full weight leaning upon God.

Green's paradigm has much to commend it. Chief among its attractions is the way it brings the entire construal of reality to bear upon ethical choices. It is not substantially different from saying that people act according to what they hold to be true, or according to a *Weltanschauung*, except that he has deftly shown religion to be an essential feature of the "rational scaffold." As we follow Green a step further, however, we will see that religion is more than an assemblage of rationally ordered beliefs to guide behavior. True though that is, it does not do justice to the full range of its functions. In addition to providing a coherent framework for morality, religion finds ways to vivify and inculcate the moral point of view among its followers. One of the ways religion does this is through ritual.

Ritual and Community

The role of ritual as a moral teacher was either barely noticed by earlier theorists or simply subsumed in their larger quest to understand ritual's role in expressing group values and social structures.[36] Victor Turner, in his book *The Ritual Process*, was the first to develop the pedagogical aspects of ritual. For this reason, aside from Immanuel Kant, Victor Turner is probably the most important figure on Green's conceptual horizon.[37] Yet inasmuch as Turner has "only an inchoate no-

36. Green, *Religion and Moral Reason*, 134.
37. In the paragraphs to follow the reader should assume Green's reliance upon Victor Turner (who at important points drew upon the work of Arnold van Gennep).

tion of the moral-reasoning process, he is unable to locate ritual within the larger context of rationality."[38] When Turner's weakness joins with Kant's strength, Green's project assumes its final shape. He will take the insights of Turner and consider them in the rational context of religion's "deep structure."

Green suggests that we see rituals as "liminal" moments in human community,[39] moments of transition from one state of life to another, or rites of passage. These transitions are not accomplished all at once but happen progressively in three distinct stages, each marked by appropriate rites. *Separation* from the old life constitutes the first stage and is accomplished by rites of detachment. Next there is the stage of *liminality* proper, a "betwixt and between" stage where persons are neither bound by past cultural norms nor established in the new ones. Taboo foods may be eaten, and strictures regarding sexual practices may be lifted temporarily, but initiands are also subjected to ritual afflictions, and a series of humiliations may have to be endured. The shared experience of deprivation and suffering is key, because the liminal phase aims to produce an "intense comradeship and equality" that will be etched permanently on the initiand's experience. But it lasts no longer than is necessary, and the process moves as a matter of course toward the key rite of *aggregation* or *reincorporation,* which inducts the initiands into the new social order, whose defining feature is *communitas.*

Communitas is an elaborate concept with a wide array of meanings. It can be used to refer to the most elemental social bonds, in which case it is actually a precondition for the ordering of society. But it can also be applied in a more restrictive sense (the one in which Green is most interested) to the nature of the interpersonal bonds that connect a sub-society and distinguish it from the larger society. In this second sense,

> where the status system is characterized by social heterogeneity and often proudly maintained differences in rank or authority, *communitas* is characterized by homogeneity, social equality, and humility; where ordinary society stresses the physical accoutrements of ordered existence, such as distinctions of clothing and private property, *communitas* effaces these distinctions and stresses common sharing of simple necessities; where the status system places a premium on the avoidance of pain and suffering and the provision of creature comforts to some, *communitas* involves the voluntary acceptance of hardship and suffering by all.[40]

38. Ibid., 135.

39. *Liminal* is derived from the Latin *limen,* whose meanings include "threshold, lintel, doorway, entrance."

40. Green, *Religion and Moral Reason,* 136.

Above all else, *communitas* includes an understanding of the basic humanity one shares with others, an "essential and generic human bond" that is the very basis of social cohesion.

The ritual moment mediates the human bond, by virtue of both its internal discipline and its results. Thus the tremendous moral ramifications of rituals: they put one in touch with that omnipartiality so essential to the moral point of view. Through its rituals, a religion actually can inscribe the moral point of view upon its adherents. Green elaborates:

> In this process of moral tutelage, the ritual humiliations and ascesis of liminal moments play an important part. Voluntarily undertaken, they symbolize and enact the essential relinquishment of possession, comfort, or advantage that marks adoption of the moral point of view. For the privileged "winners" in society's unavoidable process of social differentiation, respecting the moral principles that underlie a cooperative order—thinking or acting morally—is always to some extent a sacrifice. It may also, at any moment, require accepting a new and immediate vulnerability to hardship or suffering. In ritual humiliations, this negative dimension of moral commitment is displayed, even as it is immediately fused with the positive solidarity of *communitas*. Ritual thus communicates the easily forgotten lesson that self-renunciation on everyone's part through moral commitment is the necessary precondition of moral flourishing. In addition, the experience of suffering has direct pedagogical value. As the quest for luxury and ostentation gives way to an appreciation of simple necessities, as finely wrought pleasures are replaced by a welcomed relief from induced hardship, ritual participants are afforded a clearer apprehension of the genuine order of human priorities. They are made, above all, to see and value those generic human goods whose protection must be the first talk of any just society.
>
> Ritual moments are thus a pedagogy in ethics.[41]

To bring the moral ramifications of ritual and *communitas* into brighter light, Green turns to the Christian rite of baptism as it was practiced according to the *Apostolic Tradition* of Hippolytus.[42] In this early period, baptism was understood as a voluntarily assumed rite of initiation into the Christian community. For our purposes, one's incorporation into the church should be considered entrance into an alternatively ordered social group. As Christian baptism evolved, it became an elaborate ritual with numerous phases lasting up to three years, culminating in Holy Week. Much of the preparatory ritual was aimed at separating new converts from their old ways of life. We see

41. Ibid., 143.
42. I will draw from my own knowledge of this document, for there are pertinent symbolic details that Green omits in his account.

this in the instructional section placed just prior to the formal liturgy of baptism, where various questions are addressed concerning the viability of the "professions and trades" of incoming catechumens, many of which are considered dangerous and still others downright impossible for Christians because of their symbolic participation in the values of the larger culture. At various points the catechumens pray by themselves "apart from the believers," are prevented from giving the kiss of peace, and are interrogated as to the sobriety of their lives and their moral earnestness. Periodically they are removed from the believers to be exorcised (an attempt to disengage the spirits ruling their previous lives). As the liminal moment of their baptism approaches, they meet with more rituals, including fasting, prayer vigils, additional exorcisms, anointings with oil accompanied by the bishop's breath in their face, and continued catechesis.

Then, on Easter Sunday, the baptismal is prepared and the initiands remove their clothing, a symbol of humility that leaves something very close to a "common generic humanity." In addition, women must remove all jewelry, including hair ornamentation, for "no one is to take any alien thing down into the water with them." The removal of jewelry symbolizes also the temporary loss of socioeconomic status. Just before their immersion, the initiands are turned to the west, the direction of sunset and darkness, where they renounce Satan and his works. They are then spun 180 degrees to face east, the direction of sunrise and light, where they pledge their fidelity to Christ. After a final exorcism, they are grasped by the head and forced three times under water as the triune name—Father, Son, and Spirit—is invoked. Afterward all are ushered into the waiting community of believers, received into their first Eucharist accompanied by the additional foods of milk and honey to symbolize their infantlike status in the new community, and given their participation in the kiss of peace.

The centerpiece of this elaborate rite is, of course, the baptism itself, where, as Green describes it, "[the initiands] undergo, however briefly, the experience of drowning and asphyxiation,"[43] quite literally a near-death experience that encapsulates a string of humiliating experiences wherein the vulnerability of life and the relative insignificance of social achievements are graphically portrayed. Psychologically such a rite "forced the initiand to confront the unacknowledged vital fears and anxieties that subtly prompt the selfish quest for power or security, and it dramatically rendered irrelevant the frantic quest for wealth or prestige."[44] By mediating death symbolically, baptism became a rite of

43. Green, *Religion and Moral Reason,* 157.
44. Ibid., 159–60.

radical reorientation of one's life and priorities that effectively moved a person away from the natural inclination to self-preservation and placed her in a situation of new social solidarity with others, thus vivifying the moral point of view.

I return finally to the question posed at the beginning of this chapter: how might we approach Finkenwalde in light of Bonhoeffer's journey to martyrdom? If Bonhoeffer's conspiratorial activities in the later years can be understood as a set of personal risks run in service of the moral point of view, then we now have the conceptual means by which to investigate more precisely the relation between those activities and the actual form of life undertaken in this special community of young seminarians. As we have seen, moral risks are difficult to sustain without an awareness of a transmoral realm where God alone judges between good and evil. Plotting one's existence against the transmoral makes it possible both to take moral risks as a matter of rational choice and to do so in freedom, critical matters amid the swarm of voices competing for allegiance in the Germany of the 1930s. But *consciousness* of this realm is difficult to sustain in isolation. Thus separation from the larger social order and induction into an alternative religious community might be said to bring about a set of conditions in which self-sacrifice can be taught and rehearsed and in which the bonds connecting all human beings can be tangibly expressed among a few.

The ethical fruitfulness of life in community does not supplant an ethics based in rationality. Rather, it adds a more humane dimension by opening paths to others trod not obligingly but in love. If we keep these insights close at hand, we can begin to grasp the significance of Finkenwalde as a place of moral training for the extraordinary and excruciatingly difficult ethical dilemmas that Bonhoeffer and his students were facing.

12

Finkenwalde

Training for Martyrdom

It is no small matter to dwell in a religious community, or monastery, to hold thy place there without giving offense, and to continue faithful even unto death. Blessed is he that hath there lived well.

Thomas à Kempis

The primary objective of this final chapter is to venture an interpretation of Bonhoeffer's Finkenwalde period that is both relevant to and consistent with his martyr's death. I bring Ronald Green's model into direct conversation with the aim and practice of the Finkenwalde community, though I do not limit myself only to Green. To see Finkenwalde and Bonhoeffer's martyrdom together is a daunting task, because at first glance his Finkenwalde period appears to be a pacifistic detour in an otherwise politically engaged life. Even when the political dimensions of Finkenwalde are recognized and given their due, it remains possible, in light of its brief and illegal existence, to dismiss its form of life as nonviable in a totalitarian context. In a situation where governmental authority and control extend to every aspect of human life and all opposition is systematically uprooted, what kind of "success" could the framer of an alternative form of life have expected?

Nevertheless, I hope to show that Bonhoeffer's Finkenwalde "experiment" was both political and viable, and that, far from a detour, it can be shown to move along the boulevard of the theological-ethical interests that led him toward martyrdom. Moreover, from the standpoint

227

of Bonhoeffer's personal experience, Finkenwalde was the context in which he honed and crystallized many of his thoughts about death and martyrdom and drew the moral courage to submit himself fully to God by risking himself fully for others. The dialectic of resistance and submission, a key Bonhoefferian concept that, as I earlier observed, aptly fits the martyr's posture of "willing but not too willing," was constitutive of Finkenwalde's life. Thus Finkenwalde seems to enclose within a single frame the problematic portrait of Bonhoeffer's complete personal surrender to Christ and complete devotion to action in the sociopolitical sphere.

The Finkenwalde Form of Life

The growing ideological crisis among state university faculties was the direct occasion for the emergence of five new "preachers' seminaries" in 1934 and 1935 that became, according to Bethge, remarkable "power centers" of theology.[1] Formed against the ideology of state-delivered theological education, these institutions were illegal from the date of their inauguration and thus forced underground. They managed to thrive for two and a half years before being closed by the Gestapo.[2] Clearly these schools were set up as alternatives to the prevailing social order, their very illegality making them, from the state's perspective at least, subversive of that order. From their inception, therefore, these preachers' seminaries were *political* entities struggling against the current of Nazism sweeping the German church.

The Confessing Church put one of these new seminaries under the charge of Dietrich Bonhoeffer and his assistant Wilhelm Rott. Opening in the temporary location of a Zingst youth hostel, the seminary moved to a more stable setting at Finkenwalde after the first term. There Bonhoeffer invited some of the older students to share a monastic-type *vita communis* in what eventually became known as the House of Brethren (Brüderhaus), thus making an immediate move toward Christian practice. Following the Gestapo's shutdown of Finkenwalde in 1937, and with it the Brüderhaus, Bonhoeffer covertly revived the practice of *vita communis* under the guise of "collective pastorates" in remote Pomerania, where, in smaller numbers and under more primitive conditions, students lived together in two vicarages until March 1940, when these too were forced to close. Unfortunately, Bonhoeffer's personal circumstances during this revived attempt made it very difficult for him

1. *DB*, 420.
2. Ibid.

to share as vitally in communal life as he had at Finkenwalde. Though Bonhoeffer's experiment with community came in fits and starts over a five-year period and was scattered geographically, it was nevertheless a single experiment arising from a single vision. The years at Finkenwalde in particular have come to epitomize that vision.

Bonhoeffer planned carefully for the kind of communal life he initiated there. He wrote to his brother Karl Friedrich from London in 1935:

> The restoration of the Church must surely come from a new kind of monasticism, which will have only one thing in common with the old, a life lived without compromise according to the Sermon on the Mount in the following of Jesus. I believe the time has come to gather people together for this.[3]

By framing this "new monasticism" along the lines of Jesus' Sermon on the Mount, the New Testament passage that had so altered his own direction, Bonhoeffer welded the Finkenwalde experiment together with the new turn in his life dating to 1931–1932. Furthermore, since as I emphasized earlier, Bonhoeffer's understanding of Jesus' sermon stresses *active* discipleship, we can safely say also that the phrase "a life lived without compromise according to the Sermon on the Mount" articulates his *moral* intention for Finkenwalde. Later Bonhoeffer would make that moral intention more explicit when he announced that "the goal is not cloistered isolation but the most intense concentration for ministry outside the seminary."[4] Writing from Finkenwalde, Bonhoeffer told Barth:

> Work at the seminary gives me great joy. Academic and practical work are combined splendidly. I find that all along the line the young theologians coming into the seminary raise the very questions that have been troubling me recently, and of course our life together is strongly influenced by this. I am firmly convinced that in view of what the young theologians bring with them from the university and in view of the independent work which will be demanded of them in the parishes—particularly here in the East—they need a completely different kind of training which life together in a seminary like this unquestionably gives. . . . And it is really what everyone is waiting for. Unfortunately I am not up to it, but I remind the brothers of each other, and that seems to me to be the most important thing.[5]

---

3. *GS* III, 25. Translation taken from Mary Bosanquet, *The Life and Death of Dietrich Bonhoeffer* (New York and Evanston: Harper and Row, 1968), 150.

4. *DBWE* 5:120. Ministry on the outside meant, at that moment, "to preach the Word of God toward the goal of commitment and discernment of spirits in the current and coming church struggles, and to be prepared to assume immediately the ministry of preaching in any new crisis that may emerge."

5. *ATTF*, 341.

Wilhelm Rott corroborated Bonhoeffer's emphasis on practice when he relayed details pertaining to their numerous personal conversations during that time. They were once speaking about how different everything would have been were it not for the year 1933, when Dietrich said:

"Well, I might have been called to Giessen (like Harnack), and then perhaps to a larger faculty; but what I am allowed to do now is far better: all the possibilities of direct moulding in a persecuted church!"—"Theory and Practice"—"He who *does* what is true comes to the light" (John iii, 21)—how Bonhoeffer loved those words.[6]

Bonhoeffer designed life at Finkenwalde and its adjoining Brüderhaus for action, both in and out of the community. Because the experiment was prematurely aborted, the political success of Finkenwalde is quite difficult to gauge in any final sense, but there are ample testimonials to its capacity for moral direction. One of those seminarians in Pomerania remarked (of Bonhoeffer's devotion to communal life), "Many owe it to him that they were able to stand up to the Church struggle with a clear conscience."[7] Wolf-Dieter Zimmermann recalls that the students were sent on missions to the people of Lower Pomerania as "a practical application of what we had learned in theory."[8] According to Bethge, these missions became a Finkenwalde institution that grew naturally out of Bonhoeffer's passion for service outside the community, and apparently they were designed to help common laborers, teachers, and farmers to live a life of the cross in the context of Nazi Germany.[9] Albrecht Schönherr adds that Finkenwalde students gradually learned that the daily discipline foisted upon them "was not due to a toying with monkish habits, or to an aestheticizing liturgism . . . but to the innermost concentration on the service for which he prepared us, and for which he lived."[10] Nowhere was the concentration for service more obvious than in Bonhoeffer's preparation for Communion, which, though practiced on the sparse schedule of about once every six weeks, was something the community lived toward for the entire week preceding, and whose primary purpose was not the edification of the individual but the community's nourishment in the church struggle.[11]

6. Wilhelm Rott, "Something Always Occurred to Him," in *IKDB*, 131.
7. Hans-Werner Jensen, "Life Together," in *IKDB*, 153.
8. Wolf-Dieter Zimmermann, "Finkenwalde," in *IKDB*, 111.
9. *DB*, 539.
10. Albrecht Schönherr, "The Single-heartedness of the Provoked," in *IKDB*, 127.
11. A recollection from Albrecht Schönherr during the seminar "Dietrich Bonhoeffer: Christian Community, Discipleship, and Ethics" at Ghost Ranch, New Mexico, 10–17 August 1998.

Paul Busing, reflecting on the experience, judged that it was the community there that gave Bonhoeffer himself the strength he needed,[12] a strength that Bonhoeffer would trace to his participation with the brothers. For example, in one of his 1939 diary entries from America, he wrote this upon learning of Niemöller's arrest: "Again it has been brought home to me how lucky I am always to be in the Community of Brethren. And for the past two years Niemöller has been on his own. Inconceivable."[13] Busing added that Finkenwalde "was meant to forge a bond that would link us for the rest of our days,"[14] which explains Bonhoeffer's devotion to supporting the brothers through circular letters *(Rundbriefe)* after its dissolution.[15]

On 6 September 1935, Bonhoeffer signed his official proposal and rationale for an "Evangelical House of Brethren" to the Council of Brethren of the Old Prussian Union. The rationale, as he explained it, was that preaching could be better sustained by a community than in isolation, that in the current context the question regarding Christian life could be answered only by a concrete experiment in communal life, that by renouncing traditional privileges and comforts members would find the concentration necessary for service outside, and that such a place could serve as a refuge for pastors working without communal support and thus renew their strength for further service. He also explained that the brethren would commit themselves to a daily order of prayer, brotherly exhortation, personal confession, shared theological work, and a very simple lifestyle. In sum, he was proposing a ritual community whose internal order would prove significant for a larger social "order" on the outside. Further, it would be a voluntary community where any could leave as they wished.[16] Amidst criticism, the proposal was reluctantly approved.

Actually, criticism attended the experiment for its duration, most of it aimed at the rigor of Finkenwalde's life. Though no monastic vows were ever taken, it was clearly something like the monastic ideal that Bonhoeffer had in mind.[17] Yet Bonhoeffer instituted only one formal

12. Paul Busing, "Reminiscences of Finkenwalde," *Christian Century* (20 September 1961): 1108–9.

13. *DB*, 581.

14. Busing, "Reminiscences," 1110.

15. On 30 July 1937, Joseph Goebbels, Nazi minister of propaganda, had prohibited circular letters. Thus these letters too were illegal. After Goebbels' prohibition, they were no longer disseminated under the title "Finkenwalde Circular Letter" but were registered as personal letters and signed by hand. See Eberhard Bethge, "One of the Silent Bystanders," in *Friendship and Resistance: Essays on Dietrich Bonhoeffer* (Grand Rapids: Eerdmans, 1995), 65.

16. *DB*, 466.

17. Bonhoeffer instituted the familiar monastic practice of having one of the brothers read aloud during meals. Other aspects of Finkenwalde life such as protracted times of

rule, the well-known "Finkenwaldian Rule": no one could speak about a fellow ordinand in his absence, or, if it should happen, he must inform him afterward.[18] Each day was bracketed by morning and evening services and periods of silence. Services occurred around the dining table.[19] After the morning service came a daily half-hour meditation on a common biblical text set for the whole week. A time of singing, preferably in unison, preceded lunch, and during lunch various readings were done aloud by the candidates.[20]

All in all the students' first impression was that there was too much "must" in the regimen. They complained of an onerous "methodism" and "asceticism" and even mocked it as a cult.[21] The younger students apparently were skeptical of those in the adjoining Brüderhaus, who, though they shared the seminary's timetable, were suspected of fanaticism.[22] Living conditions were described as "primitive," a "makeshift existence." Seeing the library as deficient, Bonhoeffer made his own books available to the candidates. At the seminary proper, it appears that all of the approximately twenty-five Finkenwalde students slept in one large, crowded room, with woefully inadequate bathing facilities.[23] In the Brüderhaus, according to Gerhard Ludwig Müller and Albrecht Schönherr, most of the seminarians slept in the halls.[24] Every student had certain duties to fulfill and had to lend a hand in practical matters. In sum, it was a "hard order of life." But Bonhoeffer insisted upon it.

Finkenwalde life was itself ritual. But a trio of practices instituted by Bonhoeffer became salient elements of its life: personal confession of sin, meditation, and intercessory prayer. These practices, each relevant in its own way to Bonhoeffer's moral aims for the community, were a

---

silence, common sleeping quarters, and the attempt to pray through the Psalter every week were also common monastic practices, as can be seen, for example, in the Rule of St. Benedict.

18. *DB*, 428.

19. Bethge elaborates the order of service as follows: "They invariably began with a Psalm and a hymn specially chosen for the day. There followed a lesson from the Old Testament, a set verse from a hymn (sung daily for several weeks), a New Testament lesson, a period of extempore prayer and the recital of the Lord's Prayer. Each service concluded with another set verse from a hymn. . . . It was only on Saturdays that he also included a sermon, which was usually very direct" (ibid.).

20. *DBWE* 5:123. The majority of "songs and canons were sung from the hymnbook for Protestant youth entitled *Ein neus Lied* (A new song), edited by Otto Riethmüller in 1933."

21. Descriptions of the Finkenwalde time are culled from primarily from personal reflections in *IKDB*.

22. Wolf-Dieter Zimmermann's account in "Finkenwalde," *IKDB*, 107.

23. Ibid.

24. *DBWE* 5:123.

capstone of the Finkenwalde experience, and they made a deep and lasting impression upon the ordinands.

Finkenwalde as Moral Catalyst

Perhaps the most conspicuous of the three was the ritual of personal confession, which preceded Communion and was intended to lead naturally into intercessory prayer. Confession was never forced upon the brethren, for it was "not a law" but rather "an offer of divine help for the sinner." As Bonhoeffer put it, "Confession stands in the realm of the freedom of the Christian."[25] Yet at the same time Bonhoeffer made a strong case for confession by selecting from Luther's *Large Catechism* a saying that was also adopted into *The Book of Concord:* "Therefore when I urge you to go to confession, I am urging you to be a Christian."[26] The ordinands submitted to the guidance of both Bonhoeffer and Luther. Zimmermann tells of the experience:

> So, on this evening we went to see one another and spoke of the many grievances stored up in the last few weeks. It was a great surprise to realize how we had hurt the other person, without intention, by chance, almost *en passant*. Now we knew what it meant to consider other people. . . . At the end [of Communion] Bonhoeffer suggested that we should each choose a brother who would accompany our life in intercession—as an outward sign, as it were, that even in the worst calamity we were not alone.[27]

In *Life Together*, a text in which Bonhoeffer reflected on his communal experiment, he explained more fully the logic of personal confession in the community:

> It is none other than Jesus Christ who openly suffered the shameful death of a sinner in our place, who was not ashamed to be crucified for us as an evildoer. And it is nothing else but our community with Jesus Christ that leads us to the disgraceful dying that comes in confession, so that we may truly share in this cross. The cross of Jesus Christ shatters all pride. We cannot find the cross of Jesus if we are afraid of going to the place where Jesus can be found, to the public death of the sinner. And we refuse to carry the cross when we are ashamed to take upon ourselves the shameful death of the sinner in confession. In confession we break through to the genuine community of the cross of Jesus Christ; in confession we affirm

25. *DBWE* 5:114.
26. Ibid.
27. *IKDB*, 109.

our cross. . . . Confession is following after *[Nachfolge]*. . . . What happened
to us in baptism is given to us anew in confession. . . . Confession is the
renewal of the joy of baptism.[28]

Here confession is described as a living out of the public death died in
baptism.[29] In short, it is a rehearsal of one's death, an acceptance of one's
own cross by breaking through to the cross of Christ. By confessing, an
individual moves more deeply into the mystery of Christian fellowship.
"Those who confess their sins in the presence of another Christian know
that they are no longer alone with themselves."[30] Whereas sin entices
one away from the community, "in confession there takes place a breakthrough to community."[31] For the church is a fellowship of sinners who
live by the grace of God in the cross of Jesus Christ. Here we see not
only Bonhoeffer's belief that confession creates community, but also the
kind of community it creates: a community that lives out concretely the
death of Christ into which its various members have been baptized.

Earlier I made the theological link between baptism and martyrdom
in Bonhoeffer's thought, showing how, as a public rite, baptism signified
actualization of the disciple's breach with the world and placement in
a new fellowship. By the ritual of personal confession, we should note,
Bonhoeffer attempted to elongate temporally the death died at baptism
and weave it tangibly into the structure of daily life as an integral part
of that "direct moulding in a persecuted church" that so enamored and
inspired him.

Like Luther, Bonhoeffer saw that under the devastating conditions of
sin, the self becomes *curvatus in se,* or bent in upon itself, and is thus
rendered incapable of community. In Bonhoeffer's words: "The root of
all sin is pride, *superbia.* I want to be for myself; I have the right to be
myself, a right to my hatred and my desires, my life and my death."[32] Seen
ethically, justification is the liberation of self from self. It makes possible
a life *extra se* in which others move to the center of our focus.

Thus as a return to baptism, or justification, confession is really a
means of liberation for the sake of others. Standing in humility before
the brother, the "old man dies a painful, shameful death" and the new
humanity—an existence for others—arises. The sin that once separated
and isolated the individual from community is now borne by the com-

28. *DBWE* 5:111–12.
29. The link between baptism and confession is found frequently in the church fathers.
30. *DBWE* 5:113.
31. Ibid., 110.
32. Ibid., 111.

munity as a whole, a community of sinners who stand in common need of God's grace.

The ritualized practices of meditation and intercessory prayer were also key in this regard, though the ordinands showed a special frustration with them, not knowing how meditation was supposed to work or what to do during those times. Some admit that they used the time to work on sermons or catch up on sleep. One student complained that it was impossible to meditate without thoughts of others filling the mind, to which Bonhoeffer responded that this was precisely what *should* happen, that in meditation others were to be brought into the text and prayed for.[33]

That Bonhoeffer could consider the "thoughts of others" that crept into personal meditation a means of building solidarity with them was only a natural reflection of the broader value he placed upon intercession. For him, intercessory prayer was absolutely vital to the sustenance of community:

> A Christian fellowship lives and exists by the intercession of its members for one another, or it collapses. I can no longer condemn or hate a brother for whom I pray, no matter how much trouble he causes me. His face . . . is transformed in intercession into the countenance of a brother for whom Christ died, the face of a forgiven sinner. . . . Intercession means no more than to bring our brother into the presence of God, to see him under the cross of Jesus as a poor human being and sinner in the need of grace.[34]

The one who prays for another has his vision of the other transformed in a way that affects behavior. One cannot hate or condemn the one for whom he prays. Just as he did with confession, Bonhoeffer linked this idea directly to the cross. When I pray for another I experience an inflation of his value. Just as I am a poor human being in need of grace, so too is this other *for whom Christ died*. Thus the ritual of intercession brings me into contact with the reality that I share something essential with my brother, and with it I realize that any unpropitious behavior

---

33. A paraphrase of a surviving Finkenwalde student interviewed in *Dietrich Bonhoeffer: Memories and Perspectives*, 90 minutes (produced by Trinity Films, 1983). Bonhoeffer wrote "Anleitung zur täglich Meditation" (Instructions on Daily Meditation), a short instructional essay for the ordinands, which expresses this idea in his own words: "Wenn die Gedanken beim Meditieren zu nahestehenden Menschen oder zu solchen, um die wir in Sorge sind, gehen, dann verveile dort. Da ist der rechte Ort für die Fürbitte" (*GS* 2:480). The following English translation can be found in *Meditating on the Word*, ed. and trans. David McI. Gracie (Boston: Cowley, 1986): "If during meditation our thoughts move to persons who are near to us or to those we are concerned about, then let them linger there. That is a good time to pray for them" (33).

34. *Life Together*, 86.

toward him is to a great extent an injury to myself. When Bonhoeffer later tried to encourage the brethren through his circular letters, he told them numerous times that "above all, we must not neglect the greatest service that is left to us, our faithful daily intercession."[35]

But the scope of intercession went far beyond the confines of the brethren. During the isolated "terrorist incidents" of 1936, "the name of every victim was unfailingly mentioned by Bonhoeffer during prayers, devotions, and meditation." And so it came to pass that "everyone at Finkenwalde was to learn to concern himself like a brother with at least one of these cases."[36] The result was a lively correspondence between the seminary and those persecuted and imprisoned by the state. One of Bonhoeffer's favorite hymns at this time was Gerhardt Tersteegen's "Kommt, Kinder, lasst us gehen," with its lines "Each sets his face with steadfastness toward Jerusalem" and "Where the weaker brother falleth, the stronger grasps his hand."[37]

Looking beyond the immediate community, then, intercession is a mode of prayer wherein others, particularly those who are suffering, are looked upon with compassion and cared for. As D. E. Saliers observed, intercessory prayer is an inherently worldly activity, for it "holds the world in its actuality before God" and its strenuousness "results in a truthful perception of the world's moral ambiguity."[38] Bonhoeffer had more than an inkling of this connection when he reflected on the unity of prayer and work in *Life Together*,[39] but he achieved final clarity on the matter in a set of reflections offered upon the occasion of Dietrich Wilhelm Rüdiger Bethge's baptism. He said:

> Our church, which has been fighting in these years only for its self-pres-ervation, as though that were an end in itself, is incapable of taking the word of reconciliation and redemption to mankind and the world. Our earlier words are therefore bound to lose their force and cease, and our being Christians today will be limited to two things: *prayer and righteous action among men*. All Christian thinking, speaking and organizing must be born anew out of this prayer and action.[40]

Though Bonhoeffer's formula "prayer and righteous action" came later, it was already being practiced at Finkenwalde.

35. *ATTF*, 445.
36. *DB*, 539.
37. *DB*, 540.
38. D. E. Saliers, "Liturgy and Ethics: Some New Beginnings," *Journal of Religious Ethics* 7, no. 2 (1979): 178.
39. *DBWE* 5:74–76.
40. *LPP*, 300. Emphasis added.

Bonhoeffer made an immense personal investment in *vita communis*. He donated large sums of money from his own resources, put his personal possessions at the disposal of all, and by specific acts of humility gave himself to others. As Bethge recalls:

> As early as the second day at Zingst the opportunity arose for him to demonstrate the lesson of this personally to the brethren. A request arrived from the kitchen for help with the washing-up but there were no immediate volunteers. Without saying a word Bonhoeffer rose from the table, disappeared into the kitchen and refused admission to those who wished to follow suit. Later, when he rejoined the students on the beach, he made no comment. And in Finkenwalde many a student was to discover with shame that someone else had made his bed in the big dormitory.[41]

Bonhoeffer did not evade the duty of confession himself. He was known to ask the brethren to hear his confession before Communion. And his own vigilance at prayer, into which "he would put his will, his understanding and his heart,"[42] provided incentive for everyone. Though he never left behind his family's proud, high-class heritage, he chose to pursue a common life with the ordinands, deemphasizing his status. They addressed him not as "Herr Studiendirektor" but simply as "Brother Bonhoeffer." Before his Finkenwalde days, Bonhoeffer's native reserve had permitted him to address only one person (outside his own family) by the intimate pronoun *du*, but as testimony to his personal investment there, that number soon increased.[43]

I submit that Bonhoeffer's plan for a *vita communis* was akin to a laboratory for morality in the midst of a dying church in a dying culture. Though it was "experimental," we should not think of the Finkenwalde laboratory as a place of lesser reality. Somewhere in the course of its ritual "trial runs," Christian life as the "practice of death" gently and quietly became the performance itself. Nearly all the sermons and lectures of this period are preoccupied with the themes of suffering, death, and how to live amidst one's enemies. Nor can we forget that *Discipleship (Nachfolge)*, by which Bonhoeffer laid the challenge of suffering and death upon the ordinands as a matter of Christian discipleship, is the epitomizing work of this period, and its deathlike seriousness to Bonhoeffer hung like a cloud over the work of the seminarians. The prospect of premature death, no doubt, was one of Bonhoeffer's salient reasons for encouraging the ordinands to keep their discipline, for "we should make ourselves ready, through bodily and spiritual discipline,

41. *DB*, 429.
42. Ibid., 465.
43. *IKDB*, 132.

for the day in which we suddenly shall be put to the test."[44] Albrecht Schönherr, a student in Finkenwalde's first term, recollects that Bonhoeffer was continually reminding the ordinands that preliminary drafts of the Augsburg Confession had included suffering and martyrdom as a mark of the church, right alongside the more conspicuous Reformation bulwark of Word and sacrament. Bonhoeffer primarily confined his frequent allusions to Luther to the reformer's early life, when he was continually hounded and harassed. After his return from the Wartburg, says Schönherr, Luther became less interesting to Bonhoeffer, because by that time the ecclesiastical situation had become more stable.[45]

The seriousness, indeed heaviness, of Bonhoeffer's message could be heard as depressing. In the winter of 1935–1936 Bonhoeffer gave the same set of lectures on discipleship at Berlin University, where Hilde Enterlein, at that time Albrecht Schönherr's fiancée, attended. After several happy days, she attended Bonhoeffer's Thursday lecture and wrote these words back to Albrecht:

> Then today was the Bonhoeffer lecture and afterwards I am completely depressed. I still do not know why, but the lecture was so much like either "saying no to everything [*allem absagen*]—or taking leave of Christ," so without joy, just unbearably difficult, that one would most likely want to sit in a corner and cry, and ask why must everything be like this?[46]

It is doubtful that Hilde understood at this point the deeper context of Bonhoeffer's work at Finkenwalde, which, for him, at any rate, was anything but joyless and unbearably difficult. Bonhoeffer might well have responded to Hilde that the unbearable difficulty of following Christ is more than offset by the joy and fellowship found in community. Yet in

44. My translation of the German original, which reads: "Wir sollten uns alle bereit machen, durch liebliche und geistliche Zucht für den Tag, in dem wir einmal auf die Probe gestellt werde." See *GS* 2:486.

45. A conversation between Albrecht Schönherr and me during the seminar "Dietrich Bonhoeffer: Christian Community, Discipleship and Ethics," at Ghost Ranch, New Mexico, 10–17 August 1998. It should be noted that Bonhoeffer is here following Luther. In his treatise *On the Councils and the Church*, Luther added, as a seventh "mark" of the church, "the holy possession of the sacred cross." See *Luther's Works*, vol. 41, *Church and Ministry 3*, ed. Eric W. Gritsch (Philadelphia: Fortress, 1966), 164-65.

46. My translation, taken from a letter from Hilde to Albrecht dated 28 January 1936. See Hilde Enterlein and Albrecht Schönherr, *Lass es uns trotzdem miteinander versuchen: Brautbriefe aus der Zeit des Kirchenkampfes 1935–1936* (Gütersloher: Christian Kaiser Verlaghaus, 1997), 153. The German original reads: "Heut' war dann Bonhoeffer-Kolleg und danach bin ich ganz down; ich weiss noch nicht warum; aber das Kolleg war so nach 'allem absagen – oder sich von Christus lösen,' so ohne Freude, nur unerträglich schwer, dass man sich am liebsten in eine Ecke gesetzt hätte und geheult hätte, und nur fragen möchte: warum."

these lectures Hilde had come to understand well the radical either-or of *Discipleship* that had by now come to epitomize Bonhoeffer's theology, and that for him Christian life was something involving great personal commitment and cost.

As candidates of the Confessing Church, most of the seminarians arrived at Finkenwalde having already been harangued and discriminated against by the *Deutsche Christen*. Some had even been in prison.[47] In the course of time others would be arrested upon, or even before, the completion of their studies. Still others would meet untimely deaths related to the war. The moral seriousness of *Discipleship* and the Finkenwalde routine was not "put on." Rather it was an appropriate deportment of one's self to the realities of the time. Able to read astutely the developments of his age, Bonhoeffer was also able to anticipate the broader social and political hardships that disciples of Jesus would face. And so he made Finkenwalde a laboratory wherein the rigor of active discipleship could be practiced, where the ethic of Jesus' Sermon on the Mount could be made the meter of daily life, and where, ultimately, Christian death itself could be rehearsed and prepared for in the daily sacrifice of one's self to the community.

In the subsequent *Rundbriefe*, Bonhoeffer was able to sustain the brotherhood right into the war period. In these letters he took extraordinary efforts to comfort the brothers who remained, memorialize those who had fallen, and provide encouragement in the struggle that lay ahead.

Naturally, it is also in these *Rundbriefe* that we find some of the powerful thoughts about death and martyrdom I examined earlier, such as the notion of an inner versus outer death. For by this time the brotherhood was struggling to live outside Finkenwalde the life they had prepared for on the inside. As Bonhoeffer had laid his plans for Finkenwalde, he understood the extremity of his time and determined that quite aside from the joy and privilege of participating in community life, which he openly treasured as a gracious byproduct of God's justification, only a community of this kind could prepare people for the kinds of moral risks and difficulties that lay ahead. Bonhoeffer believed that it was possible for a community gathered on the basis of Jesus' Sermon on the Mount to provide the necessary ground for resistance against tyranny. The practices of dying to one's self in confession, meditation, and intercession produced an openness to others and forged the kind of solidarity required for moral risk-taking. In the final analysis, Bonhoeffer's Finkenwalde experiment was anything but a retreat. It was strength training for the moral crucible.

This was something not easily understood from the outside. After Barth read "Anleitung zur täglich Meditation," a small piece Bonhoef-

---

47. *DBWE* 5:122.

fer prepared to aid the ordinands in this "new" practice, he reacted suspiciously to the Finkenwalde program:

> I cannot go with the distinction in principle between theological work and devotional edification which is evident in this piece of writing and which I can also perceive from your letter. Furthermore, an almost indefineable odour of monastic eros and pathos in the former writing disturbs me.[48]

But perhaps Bonhoeffer understood something about Nazism that Barth and others did not. Nazism had imposed a highly ritualized order on the German people as a whole, employing flags, banners, uniforms, parades, films, songs, and strict military discipline, not to mention the eventual ritual killing. Hitler's *Weltanschauung* was not built solely on a political vision. It was religious in the most pernicious sense imaginable. The mythical portrait of a paradisal state characterized by pure Aryan bloodlines, the notion of a "fall" linked most closely with the Jewish race, the idea of genetic reconstruction, and the glorious eschatological culmination of the Third Reich constitute a perverse *Heilsgeschichte* in which Hitler ascends as deified savior of the German people. Perverse though they may be, these ideas make up nothing less than a nature religion built around Hitler's vision of reality as set forth in *Mein Kampf*.[49] It would be too much to say that the ritualized propaganda of the Nazi party was exquisitely constructed to serve Hitler's *Weltanschauung*, but since it was designed to spread Nazi racial ideology, and since Hitler's racial policy was in truth the object of war,[50] the Nazi propaganda was intended to engender a certain kind of behavior.[51]

48. Karl Barth, quoted in Kenneth E. Morris, *Bonhoeffer's Ethic of Discipleship: A Study in Social Psychology, Political Thought, and Religion* (University Park: Pennsylvania State University Press, 1986), 123. This letter of Barth's answers a letter of Bonhoeffer's written from Finkenwalde on 19 September 1936 in which he already anticipates Barth's objections and tries to defend himself. Barth had earlier scolded Bonhoeffer for retreating to London at a time when his church needed his gifts, and presumably Bonhoeffer understood that Barth would be no happier about his new venture. It too would likely be viewed by Barth as a flight from the front lines.

49. I am aware that many historians do not admit that Hitler had anything like a true "ideology" in his worldview. But an excellent discussion of the theological aspects of Hitler's *Mein Kampf* can be found in Michael D. Ryan, "Hitler's Challenge to the Churches: A Theological Political Analysis of *Mein Kampf*," in *The German Church Struggle and the Holocaust*, ed. Franklin H. Littell and Hubert G. Locke (San Francisco: Mellen Research University Press, 1990), 148–64.

50. Sarah Gordon, *Hitler, Germans, and the "Jewish Question"* (Princeton, N.J.: Princeton University Press, 1984), 100. Gordon shows that high-ranking members of the Nazi party also saw World War II as a "racial war."

51. Ibid., 151. Thus Gordon, quoting Hans Buchheim: "To the degree that propaganda is freed from legal or moral restrictions, it will not be content with interpreting events but will attempt to bring about such events as are necessary to its purposes."

Against the disease of that ritual and order that bent the larger *polis* toward behavioral patterns congruent with Nazi mythology, Bonhoeffer responded with the appropriate cure, a cure found within the disease itself. True, compared to the Benedictine and Franciscan rules Finkenwalde's ritual order was anything but severe, but in the context of German Protestantism it was unique. In its illegality it became a kind of ritual-liturgical resistance, or perhaps even liturgical treason. Bonhoeffer understood, I think, that amidst the virtual omnipresence of Nazi rituals and symbols in the larger culture the true church could not sustain itself morally on the sparse diet of the weekly gathering. Its preservation would come by daily immersion in rituals and symbols that deeply inculcated the Christian point of view.

When one considers the origin of Finkenwalde as an alternative institution erected against the increasingly ideological education offered at the universities, the general ritual patternedness of its internal life, its rudimentary nature, the moral significance that Bonhoeffer ascribes to such practices as confession, meditation, and intercession, Bonhoeffer's stated purposes for it, the egalitarian quality of the brotherhood as evidenced above all in the concreteness of Bonhoeffer's own humble service to it, and the fact, perhaps, that seminaries by nature sponsor an existence "betwixt and between" stations of life, there emerges an astonishing degree of affinity with Green's model.

Of course, Bonhoeffer's ministry at the preacher's seminary was not that of instructing catechumens and baptizing. It was an already baptized community that awaited his arrival in 1935. But it *was* undoubtably a ministry of *communitas*, an experiment in the brotherhood of the baptized, purposefully implemented, at a time when the moral threads of the larger society (Germany) and even those of the larger "Christian society" (Christendom) were coming apart. In terms of Green's model, baptism is obviously the pivotal rite culminating the process of separation from one's past. But as *communitas*, and the fresh apprehension of the moral point of view that accompanies it, emerges on the other side of baptism, it must be cultivated and, if lost, reattained.[52] By ritualizing personal confession and couching its meaning in terms of the "disgraceful dying" of the sinner, Bonhoeffer offered a liturgical mechanism by which Finkenwaldians could experience the "moral point of view" so clearly communicated in Christian baptism. Confession was, he said, a "breakthrough to community" precisely because it was a breaking away from the desire to keep one's life and death for one's self. Of course, the

---

52. After the moral collapse of the Confessing Church, Bonhoeffer wrote that "confession of guilt is the re-attainment of the form of Jesus Christ who bore the sin of the world" (*Ethics*, 51).

confession of one's sin meant for him that guilt had now to be borne by all. In this way the community could present itself before God with a common need for grace and experience his forgiveness. Here the objectivity of God's promise to forgive is the necessary corollary of bearing the guilt of others. The bond of *communitas* was also maintained by the practices of meditation and intercession, which accomplished a deepened sense of responsibility for others.

If we hold the general ritual patternedness of Finkenwalde life alongside Grimes's observation that rituals are "trial runs," we might venture that the moral point of view developed there was preparation for some larger moral endeavor. That was true in sundry ways for the seminarians, who would face almost daily the excruciating challenge of subordinating self-interest to the larger interests of the Confessing Church and its congregations, whose needs at the time were nothing shy of overwhelming. But it was also true for Bonhoeffer himself, for whom the notion of *communitas* would transcend the Finkenwalde brethren, and even the Confessing Church, to include the "weakest and most defenseless brothers of Jesus Christ."

Finkenwalde: Station on the Way to Martyrdom

Some recent studies lend credence to Bonhoeffer's strategy. One of these was conducted by P. M. Oliner and S. P. Oliner, who attempted to answer the question "What part did religion play in the rescue decision?" by interviewing some seven hundred individuals involved in the Holocaust.[53] "Character" is cited as a powerful explanation for rescuer behavior. "Clustered around a generalized attribute we call *extensivity* it enabled rescuers to perceive or take advantage of opportunities where others did not or to actively seek opportunities where others did not." Though some interviewees indicated that pleasing external authority, patriotism, or hatred for Nazis was a reason for their involvement, 87 percent said helping Jews had an *ethical* meaning. Of those, 20 percent fell into a category that Oliner and Oliner call an "ethics of equity" (which is said to be exemplified in the Kantian tradition) and the remainder into what they term an "ethic of care" or "the morality of connectedness"

53. Of these, 406 were at the time of the interview certified Yad Vashem "rescuers." A "non-rescuers" control group comprised 126 others, and the remainder were rescued survivors who were used for purposes of statistical comparison. P. M. Oliner and S. P. Oliner, "Rescuers of Jews during the Holocaust: Justice, Care, and Religion," in *Remembering for the Future: Working Papers and Addenda*, vol. 1, *Jews and Christians during and after the Holocaust* (Oxford: Pergamon, 1989), 506–16.

(exemplified in the works of the philosophers Iris Murdoch, Lawrence Blum, and Nel Noddings and the psychologist Carol Gilligan).[54]

After considering numerous religious factors, the Oliners conclude that neither "religious affiliation" nor "religiosity of the home environment" was significant in distinguishing rescuers from nonrescuers. What was significant, however, was the *interpretation* of religious obligations. Rescuers consistently described their ethical obligations *universally*. The following response is illustrative: "My background is Christian Reformed; Israel has a special meaning for me. We have warm feelings for Israel—but that means the whole human race. That is the main principal point."[55]

Though outside the scope of the Oliners' study, one thinks here of the French pastor André Trocmé, who organized nothing short of a "city of refuge" for Jews in the village of Le Chambon. When Trocmé was told about the need to deport the Jews, he replied, "We do not know what a Jew is. We know only men."[56] The frequency of the universal aspect of ethical obligation in the perspectives of rescuers—what Green calls impartiality or omnipartiality—moves the Oliners to conclude that while "religious commitment did not assure a commitment to ethical values," the "ethical content of religious commitments" was a highly significant factor in rescuers' interventions.

Corroborating an earlier study by Pierre Sauvage,[57] the Oliners agree that there was something special about the Christianity of the Christian rescuers. In short, "they were more likely to have internalized ethical standards."[58] In the Oliners' study this internalization is said to have happened most often in the "parental culture" of the rescuer's home. They give this reason for it: "Religion in this context is less an element apart from other conditions of living and relating, but is rather embedded in the whole of living in which trust and mutuality . . . is reenacted in religious expressions."[59]

In other words, the morality of those who aided Jews did not arise ex nihilo. Whether we ascribe rescuers' morality to a good character, as the Oliners do, or to some model of rational decision-making along

---

54. An "ethic of care" is distinguished from an "ethics of equality" in that it "asks that the interest of the actor be abandoned in favor of those of another" (ibid., 507).

55. Ibid., 512.

56. Philip Hallie, *Lest Innocent Blood Be Shed* (New York: Harper and Row, 1979), 103.

57. Pierre Sauvage, "Ten Things I Would Like to Know about Righteous Conduct in Le Chambon and Elsewhere during the Holocaust," *Humboldt Journal of Social Relations* 13, nos. 1–2 (fall/winter and spring/summer 1985–1986): 252–59.

58. Oliner and Oliner, "Rescuers of Jews," 514.

59. Ibid., 515.

the lines of Ronald Green's proposal, the universal thrust of a religion's ethical content is less likely to find an avenue for expression if it is not somehow rehearsed and thereby embedded *wholly* in the lives of its followers.

In another interesting study Douglas Huneke identified nine traits of rescuers: spirit of adventurousness, parental model of moral conduct, religiously inspired nonconformity, empathic imagination, theatrical skill, spirit of hospitality, personal experience with suffering, containment of prejudice, and communal affiliation.[60] Huneke defines empathic imagination as "the ability to place oneself in the actual situation or role of another person and actively visualize the effect and the long-term consequences of the situation or role on that person," a description remarkably close to the "moral point of view." The trait of religious nonconformity was most often rooted in and sustained by the teachings of Jesus, which rescuers understood to constrain them to give food to the hungry, welcome strangers, and share with the needy (Matt. 25:31–46). The admonition to "love your neighbor as yourself" figured prominently, as did the parable of the good Samaritan. Naturally nonconformity is linked to the trait of communal affiliation, which "has tremendous implications for the historical interpretation of the Holocaust." Among other things, free entrance into "a supportive community of coworkers offers the nurturance of a commonly held compassionate vision, affirmation of shared values, a broad base of mutual responsibility," and so forth that can undergird risky moral action.

In a far-reaching study, Herbert C. Kelman and V. Lee Hamilton make a similar proposal.[61] In order to disobey illegitimate orders, that is, to engage in what the authors call a "crime of obedience," a "high value orientation" is essential. The authors contend that rule-oriented individuals tend not to see themselves as having the *capacity* to challenge authority. On the other hand, role-oriented persons are caught up in the authority's definition of the situation and thus they cannot perceive their *right* to challenge the authority, much less will to challenge it. In such situations, avoiding entrapment in the authority's framework requires that the individual's distance from authority be increased.[62] A high value orientation will enable one to engage in an act of civil disobedience,

---

60. Douglas K. Huneke, "Glimpses of Light in a Vast Darkness: A Study of the Moral and Spiritual Development of Nazi Era Rescuers," in *Remembering for the Future: Working Papers and Addenda*, vol. 1, *Jews and Christians during and after the Holocaust* (Oxford: Pergamon, 1989), 490.

61. Herbert C. Kelman and V. Lee Hamilton, *Crimes of Obedience: Towards a Social Psychology of Authority and Responsibility* (New Haven, Conn.: Yale University Press, 1989), 333.

62. Ibid., 322.

and she will be more likely to do so if she is supported by a group that shares and nurtures her values. The authors contend, then, that "collective support makes it possible for individuals to bear the material and psychological costs of acting on their values and increases the likelihood that such action will have an impact on the policy process."

These studies bring to light the enormous importance of community for producing persons of strong moral character. They also reinforce the basic notion of universality or omnipartiality so crucial to risk-laden intervention for others. They must, however, be utilized with caution. Though clearly Finkenwalde was a civilly disobedient entity, it was not organized as an institution of rescue. And it most certainly was not oriented to grand-scale political activities such as tyrannicide or a *Putsch*. So far as I am aware, none of the ordinands, save Bethge, involved themselves in either Jewish rescues or conspiratorial plots. For the ordinands the immediate concerns seem to have been ecclesiastical—the *Kirchenkampf* was all-consuming. Finkenwalde students did not leave the seminary with the impression that a *particular* political action was necessary. It must be remembered that during the period 1935 to 1937 the more horrific crimes against Jews still lay in the future. Furthermore, since no one knew how long the dictatorship would last, the church would possibly have to batten down for the long haul in a totalitarian situation. The task of establishing clear boundaries vis-à-vis the state was thus considered absolutely vital. In hindsight, however, we can lament the preoccupation with confessional boundaries as a deficiency. Speaking also for his colleagues, Bethge expressed his regret: "We resisted by confessing, but we did not confess by resisting."[63] In context, it is understandable that the Finkenwalde community as a whole did not construe its existence politically.

And yet, astonishingly, Finkenwalde's director was in those years making his own transition to confession by resistance. This is what makes the experiment so interesting. We saw how already in 1933 Bonhoeffer had made the link between a "confessing Church" and the plight of the Jews *qua* Jews. Unlike other churchmen, Bonhoeffer had made this a central plank of the church *in status confessionis*. In fact, the resignation of his teaching post following the Christology lectures was due directly to his anger and shame at the racist ideological forces that had captured the universities. Following the London "respite," his reentry into German

63. Eberhard Bethge, "The Confessing Church Then and Now," *Newsletter of the International Bonhoeffer Society—English Language Section* 33 (October 1986): 6. Quoted by J. Patrick Kelly, "The Best of the German Gentiles: Dietrich Bonhoeffer and the Rights of Jews in Hitler's Germany," in *Remembering for the Future: Working Papers and Addenda*, vol. 1, *Jews and Christians during and after the Holocaust* (Oxford: Pergamon, 1989), 89.

politics came, as it were, veiled in the closed circle of the Finkenwalde brethren. The racial disgust so evident in the pre-London writings, chief among then the essay "The Church and the Jewish Question," was still at the forefront of his consciousness when he returned.

In the secondary literature on Bonhoeffer we often find the suggestion that this period of "pacifism" was an experiment only tangentially related to his action as a conspirator. Of course Bonhoeffer himself indicated it was an experiment, but it was an experiment not of "ends" but of "means." Far from a detour, Finkenwalde was a boulevard for Bonhoeffer's ethical interests. Indeed, *at the very roots of his vision for a community there lay a concern for others, particularly Jews.*

Looking back at the early days of the seminary, Bethge saw that Bonhoeffer was introducing the candidates "to the problem of what we today call political resistance."[64] However Finkenwalde's students may have construed the *Kirchenkampf* (church struggle), we must keep in mind that for Bonhoeffer the struggle was not confined to speech against Nazism but included the struggle to speak out on behalf of the victims. Though he worked hard for this himself, and longed for it, such speech was not forthcoming. This matter weighed heavy upon him during the Finkenwalde period. Thus, continuing his reflection, Bethge said, "We were approaching the borderline between confession and resistance; and if we did not cross this border, our confession was going to be no better than cooperation with the criminals."[65]

Bonhoeffer had been marinating this problem while in London, where through contacts with Bishop Bell he had been contemplating association with Mahatma Gandhi and making personal tours through numerous faith communities, among them Presbyterian, Baptist, and Congregational seminaries, the Quakers in Selly Oak near Birmingham,[66] and Anglican monasteries in Kelham, Mirfield, and Oxford.[67] No longer attached to the university, yet not having found his new vocation, Bonhoeffer found London analogous to a liminal experience. While he was in London, it became gradually clearer what in his past was closing off and what was opening up. One of the letters from London portrays this beautifully:

> I no longer have any faith in the university, in fact I have never really had any—much to their annoyance. The whole training of the coming generation of theology students ought to take place in monastery schools [*kirchlich-klösterliche*] in which Christ's true teaching, the Sermon on the

---

64. Eberhard Bethge, *Friendship and Resistance: Essays on Dietrich Bonhoeffer* (Grand Rapids: Eerdmans, 1995), 24.

65. Ibid.

66. *DB*, 412.

67. *IKDB*, 97.

Mount, and the right form of worship are taken seriously. This is not done with regard to any of these three things at the university and it is impossible under existing circumstances. And at long last a stop must be put to that reticence on would-be theological grounds concerning the actions of the state—it is in fact due simply to fear. "Open thy mouth for the dumb." Who in the church today acknowledges that this is the very least of the demands the Bible makes on us in these times?[68]

This letter proves vital to our understanding of Finkenwalde's general orientation. In it three elements are powerfully brought together: the *theological* element of training students in "Christ's true teaching" is rendered as a *political* puissance with an *ethical* intention. "Opening one's mouth for the dumb"—for Jews—is worked into Finkenwalde's very foundation! When Bonhoeffer later insisted that Finkenwalde would not be cut off from life outside,[69] he could not, therefore, have been operating from a cozy vision of Christian piety. He meant, rather, that life in the "cloister" was in fact a way of existing *for the world*.[70] For Finkenwalde's internal structure, Bonhoeffer may have borrowed from the monastic tradition of Catholicism and the several communities he visited in England. In his orientation toward passive resistance, he may have borrowed from Gandhi. But Finkenwalde's worldly orientation—"Open thy mouth for the dumb"—was established much earlier in the Christology lectures. As Christ's existence was for others, so too Christian existence was existence for others.

Postscript

Having probed the case for Bonhoeffer's martyrdom on theological grounds and explored its interpretive possibilities for his own theology,

68. *GS* I, 42. Translation by Eberhard Bethge, "Turning Points in Bonhoeffer's Life and Thought," in *Bonhoeffer in a World Come of Age*, ed. Peter Vorkink II (Philadelphia: Fortress, 1968), 85.

69. The German original reads "Nicht klösterliche Abgeschiedenheit, sondern innerste Konzentration für den Dienst nach aussen das Ziel." Quoted in Sabine Bobert-Stutzel, *Dietrich Bonhoeffers Pastoral Theologie* (Gütersloher: Christian Kaiser/Gütersloher, 1995), 129.

70. Bonhoeffer had no patience with monastic-type communities that practiced piety but failed to understand their worldly responsibility. This is why when the Oxford Movement sent delegates to the House of Brethren they did not meet in Bonhoeffer the ally they anticipated. He would criticize them, together with Nikolaus Ludwig von Zinzendorf, by insisting that Christian communities needed the "pure and genuine air of the Word," not continual self-reflection concerning "change" and matters pertaining to individual "beginnings." For getting the focus off oneself was vital to the extension of oneself toward *others*. See *DB*, 471.

we can see that the popular assessments of him, which consider his martyrdom a *fait accompli,* contain a measure of practical wisdom. True, his death sets before us a series of theological difficulties, most of them having to do with just how a faith founded by Jesus should conduct itself amid powers inimical to God, especially when those powers organize themselves against those who, on the foundation of Jesus' teaching, we are obliged to consider "neighbors." When careful investigation of the historical circumstances surrounding Bonhoeffer's death combines with careful theological reflection, the difficulties and ambiguities pertaining to Bonhoeffer's martyrdom can be overcome. In view of both the early Christian *acta* and recent developmental trends in the phenomenon of martyrdom, these difficulties may even be treated as an intrinsic feature of martyrdom itself, evidence of its participation in the simultaneity of sin and grace and the eschatological conflict of flesh and spirit.

Martyrdom is a circumlocution of sorts for the quite personal and fatal consequence of the ontological collision between the kingdom of God and the kingdoms of this world. As a collision of kingdoms, martyrdom is, and has always been, rife with political overtones. And as contemporary martyrs have shown, seldom is it "neat around the edges." On a clearly reasoned yet sophisticated theological foundation, Bonhoeffer freely brought his faith into the *polis*—brought his confession to action—entering into solidarity with and sacrificing himself for the Jews of the Holocaust, and thus, like Jesus, he laid down his life for others. I conclude, therefore, that Bonhoeffer deserves to be styled a true martyr of the church.

If Bonhoeffer can be established as a martyr on a theological basis, then his martyrdom may become a key for interpreting his own theology. And if Bonhoeffer's martyrdom is moral action, it may also illumine the passageway between his theology and ethics. These two conditional claims appropriately frame my interpretive endeavor as a hypothesis to be tested. I built my interpretation around the supposition that Bonhoeffer, a martyred theologian, is also a theologian of martyrdom. On a scale without historical precedent, death was a pervasive feature of the historical epoch in which he lived. When in 1943 Bonhoeffer said, "We feel that we belong to death already," he was only voicing what everyone around him knew: death had taken possession of whatever life there was left to live. But Bonhoeffer, in a way characteristic of martyrs, managed to transform the inevitability of death into a kind of mastery over it. He refused to allow it to capture him from the outside without having first captured it on the inside.

Calling Bonhoeffer a "theologian of martyrdom" means that each time I proclaim Bonhoeffer as martyr, self-consciously I am doing more than praising his moral sensibilities. I am doing that, of course—how much the world needs to be reminded of such moral conviction and courage! But I am also elevating the claim that his life and theology are fully intelligible, fully revealed to us and received by us, only when we permit them to be understood on the terms of their own omega point. In the manner of his death Bonhoeffer is saying something to us, inviting us to consider, as it were, the life beneath his life, the death beneath his death, and the Logos beneath his logos. As Jesus' death cast a bright light on the kingdom of God, the intensity of which his teaching alone, however brilliant, could not achieve, Bonhoeffer's death as a martyr accomplished something that his theology alone could not. By Jesus Christ and his martyrs, the death that on the meager terms of sin alone is a "collapse" becomes by the riches of God's grace a revelation.

Bonhoeffer's personal piety and theology have a common root burrowed so deeply into the passion of Jesus Christ that in them the trajectory or *telos* of Christ's own life and death is realized. In chapter 7 I issued the caveat that it was not necessary for my interpretive methodology to coincide with Bonhoeffer's own, since, paraphrasing Dilthey, interpreters can be said to stand in a privileged position vis-à-vis their subjects. Yet more than I could have anticipated at that phase in the study, it seems that my interpretation has landed in a Bonhoefferian place after all. As I write these final words, Bonhoeffer the theologian seems clearer to me than ever before. Such clarity is a bit unsettling. Perhaps I have only engaged in an elaborate scheme of self-fulfilling prophecy? I hope my clarity is the result of an engagement with reality itself. I hope too that, at the precipice of a new century and millennium, in some small way I have helped to clear the way for Bonhoeffer's own voice to speak to us more germanely and poignantly. If the trajectory of Christ's life and death can now be spotted more clearly in Bonhoeffer's life and death by the reader, then it is Bonhoeffer, and finally Christ, to whom we owe the debt. For, as Bonhoeffer understood it, a Christian life—and here we must say a Christian death as well!—comprises a small segment of space and time, freely yet actively surrendered, wherein Christ receives the world's being and conforms it to his own.

The words of T. S. Eliot, earlier relegated to a footnote, now seem to merit the status of an apothegm. "A martyrdom," he urged, "is never the design of man; for the true martyr is he who has become the instrument of God." Coming from one of Bonhoeffer's contemporaries, these words seem to draw forth the martyrological importance of Bonhoeffer's ethics of conformation, and along with it what may be Bonhoeffer's lasting contribution to a theology of martyrdom in general. Whereas the early Christian tradition developed martyrdom along the axis of the *imitatio Christi* motif, Bonhoeffer offers us a way to see martyrdom as the conformation of the world to Christ. Bonhoeffer's contribution in no way undermines the *imitatio Christi*. Imitation and conformation are complementary, not competing, concepts. Perhaps imitation conveys martyrdom's transcendent dimensions while conformation highlights its immanent ones. Surely each term faithfully represents God's desire that human life correspond to his Son. Yet in the larger context of Bonhoeffer's ethics, conformation might be said to deepen imitation in that it situates the human being in a vast and complex relationship to the entire created order, making her responsible for preserving and preparing it for the continual reception of Christ even while underscoring the primacy of divine initiative. In the mode of conformation, the martyr's actions are raptured and recast as part of God's own drama. More than a witness to the transcendent Christ, and more than an earthly referent to the divine reality, the martyr's ordeal becomes a concrete instance of God's suffering presence in and to the world.

Select Bibliography

Allchin, A. M. "Martyrdom." *Sobornost* 6, no. 1 (1984): 19–29.

Andersen, Francis I. "Dietrich Bonhoeffer and the Old Testament." *Reformed Theological Review* 34, no. 2 (May-August 1975): 33–45.

Arnold, Hardy. "Conversations with Dietrich Bonhoeffer." *The Plough* 6 (September 1984): 4–6.

Barnett, Victoria. *For the Soul of the People: Protestant Protest against Hitler.* New York: Oxford University Press, 1992.

Barrett, David, ed. *World Christian Encyclopedia: A Comparative Study of Churches and Religions in the Modern World, 1900–2000.* New York: Oxford University Press, 1982.

Barth, Karl. *Letters 1961–1968.* Ed. Geoffrey Bromiley. Grand Rapids: Eerdmans, 1981.

Bauer, Yehuda, ed. *Remembering for the Future: Working Papers and Addenda.* Vol. 1, *Jews and Christians during and after the Holocaust.* Oxford: Pergamon, 1989.

Baum, Markus. *Against the Wind: Eberhard Arnold and the Bruderhof.* Translated by the Bruderhof communities. Farmington, Penn.: Plough, 1998.

Becker, Ernest. *The Denial of Death.* New York: Free Press, 1973.

Bergman, Marvin. "Moral Decision Making in the Light of Kohlberg and Bonhoeffer: A Comparison." *Religious Education* 69, no. 2 (March-April 1974): 227–43.

Bergman, Susan. "Twentieth-Century Martyrs." In *Martyrs: Contemporary Writers on Modern Lives of Faith,* ed. Susan Bergman. San Francisco: Harper and Row, 1996.

Best, S. Payne. *The Venlo Incident.* London: Hutchinson, 1950.

Bethge, Eberhard. "Bonhoeffer and the Jews." In *Ethical Responsibility: Bonhoeffer's Legacy to the Churches,* ed. John D. Godsey and Geffrey B. Kelly, 43–96. Toronto Studies in Theology 6. New York: Edwin Mellen, 1981.

———. "The Challenge of Dietrich Bonhoeffer's Life and Theology." *The Chicago Theological Seminary Register* 51, no. 2 (February 1961): 1–38.

———. *Dietrich Bonhoeffer: A Biography.* Rev. ed. Rev. and ed. Victoria Barnett. Minneapolis: Fortress, 2000.

———. *Friendship and Resistance: Essays on Dietrich Bonhoeffer.* Grand Rapids: Eerdmans, 1995.

———. "The Holocaust and Christian Anti-Semitism: Perspectives of a Christian Survivor." *Union Seminary Quarterly Review* 32, nos. 3–4 (1977): 141–55.

———. "Unfulfilled Tasks?" *Dialog* 34 (winter 1995): 30–31.

Bobert-Stützel, Sabine. *Dietrich Bonhoeffers Pastoral Theologie.* Gütersloh: Kaiser Verlag, 1995.

Bonhoeffer, Dietrich. *Act and Being.* Trans. Bernard Noble. New York: Harper and Row, 1961.

———. *Christ the Center.* Trans. Edwin H. Robertson. San Francisco: Harper and Row, 1978.

———. *The Communion of Saints: A Dogmatic Inquiry into the Sociology of the Church.* New York: Harper and Row, 1963.

_____. *The Cost of Discipleship.* 2d ed. New York: Macmillan, 1963.

_____. *Dietrich Bonhoeffer Werke.* 17 vols. Ed. Eberhard Bethge, Ernst Feil, Christian Gremmels, Wolfgang Huber, Hans Pfiefer, Albrecht Schönherr, and Heinz Eduard Tödt. Munich: Christian Kaiser Verlag, 1986-1999.

_____. *Dietrich Bonhoeffer Works.* Ed. Wayne Whitson Floyd Jr. Minneapolis: Augsburg Fortress, vol. 1: 1998; vol. 2: 1996; vol. 3: 1997; vol. 5: 1996; vol. 4: 2001; vol. 7: 2000; vol. 9: 2003.

_____. *Ethics.* Trans. Neville Horton Smith. New York: Macmillan, 1955.

_____. *Fiction from Prison: Gathering Up the Past.* Trans. Ursula Hoffmann from the German *Fragmente aus Tegel: Drama und Roman* (Munich: Kaiser Verlag, 1978). Philadelphia: Fortress, 1981.

_____. *Gesammelte Schriften.* Ed. Eberhard Bethge. 6 vols. Munich: Christian Kaiser Verlag, vol. 1: 1965; vol. 2: 1965; vol. 3: 1966; vol. 4: 1965; vol. 5: 1972; vol. 6: 1974.

_____. *Letters and Papers from Prison.* Enlg. ed. Ed. Eberhard Bethge. New York: Macmillan, 1972.

_____. *Life Together.* Trans. John W. Doberstein. New York: Harper and Row, 1954.

_____. *Meditating on the Word.* Ed. and trans. David McI. Gracie. Boston: Cowley, 1986.

_____. *No Rusty Swords: Letters, Lectures, and Notes, 1928–1936, from the Collected Works of Dietrich Bonhoeffer,* vol. 1. Ed. Edwin H. Robertson. Trans. Edwin H. Robertson and John Bowden. London: Collins, 1965.

_____. *Spiritual Care.* Trans. Jay C. Rochelle. Philadelphia: Fortress, 1985.

_____. *A Testament to Freedom: The Essential Writings of Dietrich Bonhoeffer.* Ed. Geffrey Kelly and F. Burton Nelson, Rev. ed. New York: HarperCollins, 1995.

_____. *Widerstand und Ergebung: Briefe und Aufzeichnungen aus der Haft.* Munich: Christian Kaiser Verlag, 1956.

Bonner, Gerald. "Martyrdom: Its Place in the Church." *Sobornost* 5, no. 2 (1983): 6–21.

Borg, Marcus. "Death as the Teacher of Wisdom." *Christian Century* (February 26, 1986): 203–6.

Bosanquet, Mary. *The Life and Death of Dietrich Bonhoeffer.* New York: Harper and Row, 1968.

Bowersock, G. W. *Martyrdom and Rome.* Cambridge: Cambridge University Press, 1995.

Brecht, Martin. *Martin Luther.* 3 vols. Trans. James L. Schaaf. Philadelphia: Fortress, 1985–1993.

Buber, Martin. *Tales of the Hasidim: The Later Masters.* Trans. Olga Marx. New York: Schocken, 1961.

Burtness, James H. *Shaping the Future: The Ethics of Dietrich Bonhoeffer.* Philadelphia: Fortress, 1985.

Busing, Paul. "Reminiscences of Finkenwalde." *Christian Century* (September 20, 1961): 1108–11.

Caird, G. B. *New Testament Theology.* Completed and ed. L. D. Hurst. Oxford: Clarendon, 1994.

Canlas, Florentino M. "Darkness or Light? Rahner and Collopy on the Theology of Death." *Bijdragen* 45 (1984): 251–75.

Carr, David. *Time, Narrative, and History.* Studies in Phenomenology and Existential Philosophy Series, ed. James M. Edie. Bloomington: Indiana University Press, 1986.

Carter, Guy. "Confession at Bethel, August 1933—Enduring Witness: The Formation, Revision, and Significance of the First Full Theological Confession of the Evangelical Church Struggle in Nazi Germany." Ph.D. diss., Marquette, 1987.

Chandler, Andrew, ed. *The Terrible Alternative: Christian Martyrdom in the Twentieth Century.* London: Cassell, 1998.

Clements, Keith W. *What Freedom? The Persistent Challenge of Dietrich Bonhoeffer.* Bristol, U.K.: Bristol Baptist College, 1990.

Cochrane, Arthur C. *The Church's Confession under Hitler.* Philadelphia: Westminster, 1962.

Collopy, Bartholomew J. "Theology and the Darkness of Death." *Theological Studies* 39 (March 1978): 22–54.

Copleston, Frederick. *A History of Philosophy.* 6 vols. New York: Doubleday, 1944-1959.

Cox, Harvey. "Using and Misusing Bonhoeffer." *Christianity and Crisis* 24, no. 17 (October 19, 1964): 199–201.

Day, Thomas I. *Dietrich Bonhoeffer on Christian Community and Common Sense.* Toronto Studies in Theology 11, Bonhoeffer Series 2. New York: Edwin Mellen, 1982.

De Gruchy, John W., ed. *Bonhoeffer for a New Day: Theology in a Time of Transition.* Papers Presented at the Seventh Annual International Bonhoeffer Congress, Cape Town, 1996. Grand Rapids: Eerdmans, 1997.

_____, ed. *Dietrich Bonhoeffer: Witness to Jesus Christ.* The Making of Modern Theology, ed. John W. de Gruchy. Minneapolis: Augsburg Fortress, 1991.

Dewar, Diana. *All for Christ: Some Twentieth Century Martyrs.* Oxford: Oxford University Press, 1980.

Dragas, George. "Martyrdom and Orthodoxy in the New Testament Era: The Theme of Μαρτυρία as Witness to the Truth." *Greek Orthodox Theological Review* 30, no. 3 (1985): 287–96.

Drewett, John. "Dietrich Bonhoeffer—Prophet and Martyr." *The Modern Churchman* 11, no. 3 (April 1968): 137–43.

Driver, Tom F. *The Magic of Ritual: Our Need for Liberating Rites That Transform Our Lives and Our Communities.* New York: HarperCollins, 1991.

Droge, Arthur J., and James D. Tabor. *A Noble Death: Suicide and Martyrdom among Christians and Jews in Antiquity.* San Francisco: HarperSanFrancisco, 1992.

Duchrow, Ulrich. *Christenheit und Weltverantwortung: Traditionsgeschichte und systematische Struktur der Zweireichelehre.* Stuttgart: Ernst Klett Verlag, 1970.

_____. *Two Kingdoms: The Use and Misuse of A Lutheran Theological Concept.* Geneva: Lutheran World Federation, 1977.

Dumas, André. *Dietrich Bonhoeffer: Theologian of Reality.* Trans. Robert McAfee Brown. New York: Macmillan, 1971.

Eller, Vernard. "The Course of Discipleship." *Brethren Life and Thought* 26 (winter 1981): 7–13.

Elwell, Walter A., ed. *Evangelical Dictionary of Theology.* Grand Rapids: Baker, 1984.

Enterlein, Hilde, and Albrecht Schönherr. *Lass es uns trotzdem miteinander versuchen: Brautbriefe aus der Zeit des Kirchenkampfes 1935–1936.* Gütersloher: Christian Kaiser Verlaghaus, 1997.

Ericksen, Robert P. *Theologians under Hitler: Gerhard Kittel, Paul Althaus, and Emanuel Hirsch.* New Haven, Conn.: Yale University Press, 1985.

Feil, Ernst. *The Theology of Dietrich Bonhoeffer.* Trans. Martin Rumscheidt. Philadelphia: Fortress, 1985.

Fischel, H. A. "Prophet and Martyr," *Jewish Quarterly Review* 37 (1946–1947): 265–80, 363–86.

Flannery, Edward H. *The Anguish of the Jews: Twenty-three Centuries of Anti-Semitism.* New York: Macmillan, 1965.

Fleischner, Eva. *Judaism in German Christian Theology since 1945.* Metuchen, N.J.: Scarecrow, 1975.

Floyd, Wayne Whitson, Jr. "Bonhoeffer's Many Faces." *Christian Century* (April 26, 1995): 444–45.

_____. *Theology and the Dialectics of Otherness.* New York: University Press of America, 1988.

Floyd, Jr., Wayne Whitson, and Charles Marsh, eds. *Theology and the Practice of Responsibility: Essays on Dietrich Bonhoeffer.* Valley Forge, Penn.: Trinity Press International, 1994.

Forstman, Jack. *Christian Faith in Dark Times: Theological Conflicts in the Shadow of Hitler.* Louisville: Westminster John Knox, 1992.

Frend, W. H. C. *Martyrdom and Persecution in the Early Church: A Study of a Conflict from the Maccabees to Donatus.* Oxford: Basil Blackwell, 1965.

Friedman, Maurice. *The Hidden Human Face.* New York: Delacorte. Rpt. New York: Dell, 1974.

Gelven, Michael. *A Commentary on Heidegger's "Being and Time."* Rev. ed. Dekalb: Northern Illinois University Press, 1989.

Goddard, Donald. *The Last Days of Dietrich Bonhoeffer.* New York: Harper and Row, 1976.

Godsey, John D. "Theologian, Christian, Contemporary." *Interpretation* 25, no. 2 (April 1971): 208–11.

_____. *The Theology of Dietrich Bonhoeffer.* Philadelphia: Westminster Press.

Godsey, John D., and Geffrey B. Kelly. *Ethical Responsibility: Bonhoeffer's Legacy to the Churches.* Toronto Studies in Theology 6. New York: Edwin Mellen, 1981.

Gordon, Sarah. *Hitler, Germans, and the "Jewish Question."* Princeton, N.J.: Princeton University Press, 1984.

Green, Ronald. *Religion and Moral Reason: A New Method for Comparative Study.* New York: Oxford University Press, 1988.

Grimes, Ronald L. "Of Words the Speaker, of Deeds the Doer." *Journal of Religion* 66, no. 1 (January 1986): 1–17.

_____. "Reinventing Ritual." *Soundings* 75, no.1 (spring 1992): 23–41.

Gushee, David P. *The Righteous Gentiles of the Holocaust: A Christian Interpretation.* Minneapolis: Fortress, 1994.

Hakim, Albert B. *Historical Introduction to Philosophy.* 3d ed. Upper Saddle River, N.J.: Prentice-Hall, 1997.

Hall, Douglas John. *Confessing the Faith: Christian Theology in a North American Context.* Minneapolis: Fortress, 1996.

Hallie, Philip. *Lest Innocent Blood Be Shed.* New York: Harper and Row, 1979.

Hauerwas, Stanley, and William H. Willimon. *Resident Aliens: A Provocative Christian Assessment of Culture and Ministry for People Who Know That Something Is Wrong.* Nashville: Abingdon, 1989.

Hefley, James, and Marti Hefley. *By Their Blood: Christian Martyrs of the 20th Century.* Milford, Mich.: Mott Media, 1979.

Hefner, Philip. *The Human Factor: Evolution, Culture, and Religion.* Theology and the Sciences Series, ed. Kevin J. Sharpe. Minneapolis: Augsburg Fortress, 1993.

Heidegger, Martin. *Being and Time.* Trans. John Macquarrie and Edward Robinson. New York: Harper and Row, 1962.

Henry, Marilyn. "Who, Exactly, Is a 'Righteous Gentile?'" *Jerusalem Post* (April 22, 1998).

Hinlicky, Paul R. "What Hope after Holocaust?" *Pro Ecclesia* 7, no. 1 (1999): 12–22.

Hopper, David H. *A Dissent on Bonhoeffer.* Philadelphia: Westminster, 1975.

Horsley, Richard. *Jesus and the Spiral of Violence: Popular Jewish Resistance in Roman Palestine.* San Francisco: Harper and Row, 1987.

Huntemann, Georg. *The Other Bonhoeffer: An Evangelical Reassessment of Dietrich Bonhoeffer.* Trans. Todd Huizinga. Grand Rapids: Eerdmans, 1993.

Jüngel, Eberhard. *Theological Essays.* Ed. and trans. J. B. Webster. Edinburgh: T & T Clark, 1989.

Kallistos of Diokleia. "What Is a Martyr?" *Sobornost* 5, no. 1 (1983): 7–18.

Kelman, Herbert C., and V. Lee Hamilton. *Crimes of Obedience: Toward a Social Psychology of Authority and Responsibility.* New Haven, Conn.: Yale University Press, 1989.

Kemp, Walter. H. "The Polyphonous Christian Community of Dietrich Bonhoeffer." *Lutheran Quarterly* 28, no. 1 (February 1976): 6–20.

Kierkegaard, Søren. *The Concept of Dread.* Trans. Walter Lowrie. Princeton, N.J.: Princeton University Press, 1967.

————. *Thoughts on Crucial Situations in Human Life: Three Discourses on Imagined Occasions.*

Trans. David F. Swenson. Minneapolis: Augsburg, 1941.

King, Norman J., and Barry L. Whitney. "Rahner and Hartshorne on Death and Eternal Life." *Horizons* 15 (fall 1988): 239–61.

Kittel, Gerhard, ed. *Theological Dictionary of the New Testament.* Trans. and ed. Geoffrey W. Bromiley. Grand Rapids: Eerdmans, 1964-1976.

Klassen, A. J., ed. *A Bonhoeffer Legacy: Essays in Understanding.* Grand Rapids: Eerdmans, 1981.

Kuhns, William. *In Pursuit of Dietrich Bonhoeffer.* Garden City, N.Y.: Image, 1969.

Lange, Charles E. "Bonhoeffer: Modern Martyr." *The Episcopalian,* May 1966, 48–49.

Leibholz-Bonhoeffer, Sabine. *The Bonhoeffers: Portrait of a Family.* Chicago: Covenant, 1994.

Littell, Franklin H., and Hubert G. Locke. *The German Church Struggle and the Holocaust.* San Francisco: Mellen Research University Press,1990.

————. *The German Phoenix: Men and Movements in the Church in Germany.* Garden City, N.Y.: Doubleday, 1960.

Magoti, Evaristi. "Aspects of the Theology of Death in Karl Rahner's Thought." *Africa Theological Journal* 19, no. 1 (1990): 3–20.

Manson, T. W. "Martyrs and Martyrdom." *Bulletin of the John Rylands Library* 39 (1957): 463–84.

Marsh, Charles. *Reclaiming Dietrich Bonhoeffer: The Promise of His Theology.* New York: Oxford University Press, 1994.

Marty, Martin E., ed. *The Place of Bonhoeffer: Problems and Possibilities in His Thought.* New York: Association Press, 1962.

Matzko, David Matthew. "Hazarding Theology: Theological Descriptions and Particular Lives." Ph.D. diss., Duke University, 1992.

McClendon, James Wm. *Ethics: Systematic Theology,* vol. 1. Nashville: Abingdon, 1986.

McCord Adams, Marilyn. "Redemptive Suffering." In *Rationality, Religious Belief, and Moral Commitment: New Essays in the Philosophy of Religion,* ed. Robert Audi and William J. Wainwright. Ithaca, N.Y.: Cornell University Press, 1986.

McCormick, Richard A. "Notes on Moral Theology." *Theological Studies* 42 (March 1981): 74–121.

McGrath, Alister E. *Luther's Theology of the Cross: Martin Luther's Theological Breakthrough.* Oxford: Basil Blackwell, 1985.

Mealand, David. "The Text of Bonhoeffer's Last Message." *Modern Churchman* 20 (October 1976–July 1977): 121–22.

Metz, Johannes-Baptist, and Edward Schillebeeckx, eds. *Martyrdom Today.* New York: Seabury, 1983.

Miller, Donald E. "Worship and Moral Reflection: A Phenomenological Analysis." *Anglican Theological Review* 62, no. 4 (October 1980): 307–21.

Mooney, Christopher F. *Man without Tears: Soundings for a Christian Anthropology.* New York: Harper and Row, 1973.

Morris, Kenneth Earl. *Bonhoeffer's Ethic of Discipleship: A Study in Social Psychology, Political Thought, and Religion.* University Park: Pennsylvania State University Press, 1986.

Musurillo, Herbert. *The Acts of the Christian Martyrs.* Oxford Early Christian Texts, ed. Henry Chadwick. Oxford: Clarendon, 1972.

Nelson, F. Burton. "Dietrich Bonhoeffer and the Jews: An Agenda for Exploration and Contemporary Dialogue." In *Ethical Responsibility: Bonhoeffer's Legacy to the Churches,* ed. John Godsey and Geffrey Kelly, 131–42. Toronto Studies in Theology 6. New York: Edwin Mellen, 1981.

Neuhaus, Richard John. "A Martyr." *First Things,* no. 53 (May 1995): 76–77.

Newman, Jay. "The Motivation of Martyrs: A Philosophical Perspective." *Thomist* 35 (October 1971): 581–600.

Niebuhr, Reinhold. "The Death of a Martyr." *Christianity and Crisis* 5, no. 11 (June 25, 1945): 6–7.

Oberman, Heiko A. *Luther: Man between God and the Devil.* Trans. Eileen Walliser-Schwarzbart. New York: Doubleday, 1982.

Okure, Teresa, Jon Sobrino, and Felix Wilfred, eds. *Rethinking Martyrdom.* London: SCM, 2003.

Ott, Heinrich. *Reality and Faith: The Theological Legacy of Dietrich Bonhoeffer.* Trans. Alex A Morrison. Philadelphia: Fortress, 1972.

Pagels, Elaine. *Adam, Eve, and the Serpent.* New York: Random House, 1988.

———. *The Gnostic Gospels.* New York: Random House, 1979.

Paldiel, Mordecai. *Sheltering the Jews: Stories of Holocaust Rescuers.* Minneapolis: Augsburg Fortress, 1996.

Pannenberg, Wolfhart. *Metaphysics and the Idea of God.* Trans. Philip Clayton. Grand Rapids: Eerdmans, 1990.

———. *Systematic Theology.* 3 vols. Trans. Geoffrey W. Bromiley. Grand Rapids: Eerdmans, 1991–1998.

Peck, William J. "From Cain to the Death Camps: An Essay on Bonhoeffer and Judaism." *Union Seminary Quarterly Review* 28, no. 2 (winter 1973): 158–76.

Peck, William J., ed. *New Studies in Bonhoeffer's Ethics.* Toronto Studies in Theology 30, Bonhoeffer Series 3. Lewiston, N.Y.: Edwin Mellen, 1987.

Pfatteicher, Philip H. *Festivals and Commemorations: Handbook to the Calendar in Lutheran Book of Worship.* Minneapolis: Augsburg, 1980.

Phillips, John A. *Christ for Us in the Theology of Dietrich Bonhoeffer.* New York: Harper and Row, 1967.

Quasten, Johannes, and Joseph C. Plumpe, eds. *Ancient Christian Writers.* New York, N.Y.: Newman, 1946- .

Rahner, Hugo. *Church and State in Early Christianity.* Trans. Leo Donald Davis. San Francisco: Ignatius, 1992.

Rahner, Karl. *On The Theology of Death.* New York: Crossroad, 1973.

———. *Theological Investigations,* vol. 7. Trans. David Bourke. New York: Seabury, 1977.

Ramsey, Paul. "Liturgy and Ethics." *Journal of Religious Studies* 7, no. 2 (1979): 139–247.

Rasmussen, Larry. *Dietrich Bonhoeffer: His Significance for North Americans.* Minneapolis: Fortress, 1990.

———. *Dietrich Bonhoeffer: Reality and Resistance.* Studies in Christian Ethics Series. Nashville: Abingdon, 1972.

Roark, Dallas M. *Dietrich Bonhoeffer.* Makers of the Modern Theological Mind Series, ed. Bob E. Patterson. Waco, Tex.: Word, 1972.

Robertson, Edwin. *The Shame and the Sacrifice: The Life and Martyrdom of Dietrich Bonhoeffer.* New York: Macmillan, 1988.

———. "A Study of Dietrich Bonhoeffer and the Jews, January-April 1933." In *Remembering for the Future: Working Papers and Addenda,* vol. 1, *Jews and Christians during and after the Holocaust,* ed. Yehuda Bauer, 121–29. New York: Pergamon, 1989.

Ross, Maggie. *The Fountain and the Furnace: The Way of Tears and Fire.* New York: Paulist, 1987.

Ruether, Rosemary. *Faith and Fratricide: The Theological Roots of Anti-Semitism.* New York: Seabury, 1974.

Sauvage, Pierre. "Ten Things I Would Like to Know about Righteous Conduct in Le Chambon and Elsewhere during the Holocaust." *Humboldt Journal of Social Relations* 13, nos. 1–2 (fall-winter and spring-summer 1985–1986): 252–59.

Schalk, Adolph. "A Second Look at a Modern Martyr." *U.S. Catholic* (July 1972): 19–26.

Sherman, Franklin. "Death of a Modern Martyr." *Expository Times* 76 (April 1965): 204–7.

Smith, Harmon L. *Where Two or Three Are Gathered: Liturgy and the Moral Life.* Cleveland: Pilgrim, 1995.

Smith, Lacey Baldwin. *Fools, Martyrs, Traitors: The Story of Martyrdom in the Western World.* New York: Knopf, 1997.

Smith, William Robertson, James Frazer, S. H. Hooke, and Jane Harrison. *Ritual and Myth,* vol. 5, *Theories of Myth.* Ed. Robert A. Segal. New York: Garland, 1996.

Sponheim, Paul. *Kierkegaard on Christ and Christian Coherence.* New York: Harper and Row, 1968.

Stange, Douglas C. "A Sketch of the Thought of Martin Luther on Martyrdom." *Concordia Theological Monthly* 37, no. 10 (1966): 640–44.

Stark, Rodney. *The Rise of Christianity: A Sociologist Reconsiders History.* Princeton, N.J.: Princeton University Press, 1996.

Stauffer, Ethelbert. "The Anabaptist Theology of Martyrdom." *Mennonite Quarterly Review* 19, no. 3: 179–214.

Taylor, Michael J. *The Mystery of Suffering and Death.* Garden City, N.Y.: Image, 1974.

Thielicke, Helmut. *Living with Death.* Trans. Geoffrey W. Bromiley. Grand Rapids: Eerdmans, 1983.

Tomlin, Graham. "The Theology of the Cross: Subversive Theology for a Postmodern World?" *Themelios* 23: 59–73.

Van Horne, Winston. "St Augustine: Death and Political Resistance." *Journal of Religious Thought* 38 (fall-winter 1981–1982): 34–50.

von Loewenich, Walther. *Luther's Theology of the Cross.* Trans. Herbert J. A. Bouman. Minneapolis: Augsburg, 1976.

Vorkink, Peter, II, ed. *Bonhoeffer in a World Come of Age.* Philadelphia: Fortress, 1968.

Wendebourg, Dorothea. "Das Martyrium in der Alten Kirche als ethisches Problem." *Zeitschrift für Kirchengeschichte* 98, no. 3 (1987): 295–320.

Wilken, Robert L. *The Christians As the Romans Saw Them.* New Haven, Conn: Yale University Press, 1984.

Willis, Robert E. "Bonhoeffer and Barth on Jewish Suffering: Reflections on the Relationship between Theology and Moral Sensibility." *Journal of Ecumenical Studies* 24, no. 4 (fall 1987): 598–615.

———. "The Burden of Auschwitz: Rethinking Morality." *Soundings* 68, no. 2 (summer 1985): 273–93.

Wind, Renate. *Dietrich Bonhoeffer: A Spoke in the Wheel.* Trans. John Bowden. Grand Rapids: Eerdmans, 1991.

Wingren, Gustaf. *Man and the Incarnation: A Study in the Bibilical Theology of Irenaeus.* Trans. Ross MacKenzie. Edinburgh: Oliver and Boyd, 1959.

Wood, Diana, ed. *Martyrs and Martyrologies.* Studies in Church History 30. Papers Read at the Summer 1992 Meeting and the 1993 Winter Meeting of the Ecclesiastical History Society. Cambridge: Basil Blackwell, 1993.

Woodward, Kenneth L. "The Art of Dying Well." *Newsweek,* November 25, 1996, 60–66.

———. *Making Saints: How the Catholic Church Determines Who Becomes a Saint, Who Doesn't, and Why.* New York: Simon and Schuster, 1990.

Yoder, John Howard. *The Politics of Jesus: Vicit Agnus Noster.* 2d ed. Grand Rapids: Eerdmans, 1994.

Young, Robin Darling. *In Procession before the World: Martyrdom as Public Liturgy in Early Christianity.* Père Marquette Lecture in Theology. Milwaukee: Marquette University Press, 2001.

Zerner, Ruth. "Dietrich Bonhoeffer and the Jews: Thoughts and Actions, 1933–1945." *Jewish Social Studies* 37, nos. 3–4 (summer-fall 1975): 235–50.

Zimmermann, Wolf-Dieter, and Ronald Gregor Smith, eds. *I Knew Dietrich Bonhoeffer.* Trans. Käthe Gregor Smith. New York: Harper and Row, 1964.